JOHN FOSTER DULLES

Piety, Pragmatism, and Power in U.S. Foreign Policy

PQZ491265

Richard H. Immerman

Biographies

IN AMERICAN FOREIGN POLICY

Joseph A. Fry, University of Nevada, Las Vegas
Series Editor

The Biographies in American Foreign Policy Series employs the enduring medium of biography to examine the major episodes and themes in the history of U.S. foreign relations. By viewing policy formation and implementation from the perspective of influential participants, the series seeks to humanize and make more accessible those decisions and events that sometimes appear abstract or distant. Particular attention is devoted to those aspects of the subject's background, personality, and intellect that most influenced his or her approach to U.S. foreign policy, and each individual's role is placed in a context that takes into account domestic affairs, national interests and policies, and international and strategic considerations.

The series is directed primarily at undergraduate and graduate courses in U.S. foreign relations, but it is hoped that the genre and format may also prove attractive to the interested general reader. With these objectives in mind, the length of the volumes has been kept manageable, the documentation has been restricted to direct quotes and particularly controversial assertions, and the bibliographic essays have been tailored to provide historiographical assessment without tedium.

Producing books of high scholarly merit to appeal to a wide range of readers is an ambitious undertaking, and an excellent group of authors has agreed to participate. Some have compiled extensive scholarly records while others are just beginning promising careers, but all are distinguished by their comprehensive knowledge of U.S. foreign relations, their cooperative spirit, and their enthusiasm for the project. It has been a distinct pleasure to have been given the opportunity to work with these scholars as well as with Richard Hopper and his staff at Scholarly Resources.

JOHN FOSTER DULLES

Piety, Pragmatism, and Power
in U.S. Foreign Policy

JOHN FOSTER
DULLES

Piety, Pragmatism, and Power
in U.S. Foreign Policy

Richard H. Immerman

A Scholarly Resources Inc. Imprint
Wilmington, Delaware

Scholarly Resources Inc.
104 Greenhill Avenue
Wilmington, DE 19805-1897

Library of Congress Cataloging-in-Publication Data

Immerman, Richard H., 1949–
  John Foster Dulles : piety, pragmatism, and power in U.S.
foreign policy / Richard H. Immerman.
      p.   cm. — (Biographies in American foreign policy)
      ISBN 0-8420-2600-2 (cloth : alk. paper). — ISBN 0-8420-2601-0
(paper : alk. paper)
      1. Dulles, John Foster, 1888–1959. 2. Statesmen—United
States—Biography. 3. United States—Foreign relations—1945–
1953. 4. United States—Foreign relations—1953–1961. I. Title.
II. Series.
E748.D868I46   1998
973.921′092—dc21   98-28869
[B]   CIP

♾ The paper in this publication meets the minimum requirements
of the American National Standard for permanence of paper for
printed library materials, Z39.48, 1984.

For Tyler and Morgan

About the Author

Richard H. Immerman is professor and chair of history at Temple University and director of its Center for the Study of Force and Diplomacy. Among his publications are *The CIA in Guatemala: The Foreign Policy of Intervention* (1981), *John Foster Dulles and the Diplomacy of the Cold War* (1990), and *Waging Peace: How Eisenhower Shaped an Enduring Cold War Strategy for National Security* (1998), coauthored with Robert R. Bowie. His awards include a Social Science Research Council/MacArthur Foundation Fellowship in International Peace and Security, a grant from the National Endowment for the Humanities to write a television documentary on John Foster Dulles, the Society for Historians of American Foreign Relations' Stuart Bernath Book and Lecture Prizes, and the Temple University Paul W. Eberman Faculty Research Award.

Contents

Acknowledgments

Because this study of John Foster Dulles is the product of more than two decades of my writing and research, I cannot possibly acknowledge all the people and institutions from whom I have learned and profited. I must nevertheless single out two special individuals. Fred I. Greenstein has served as my guide and inspiration throughout my academic career. I have been advised and encouraged by Robert R. Bowie almost as much, and for almost as long. I am beholden to both.

I also want to thank two young scholars, Campbell Craig and William I. Hitchcock. By allowing me to read drafts of their books, they challenged me with their arguments and ensured that I was abreast of the most current historiography—and archives. In this regard, I have without question benefited more from my students, my graduate students at Temple University above all, than they have benefited from me. Todd Davis and David Rezelman in particular critiqued the entire manuscript and suggested additional sources for me to consult. It is much better because they did, and they warrant none of the blame for its shortcomings. For these, I alone am responsible.

I am extremely grateful to Andy Fry, general editor of the Biographies in American Foreign Policy Series, for inviting me to contribute this volume and for providing me with insightful comments on the draft. At Scholarly Resources, Richard Hopper and Michelle Slavin were both expert and patient. And without the support of the Temple University Faculty Senate Research and Study Leaves Committee, I would not have had the time to complete this project.

I owe the most to my wife, Marion, and daughters, Tyler and Morgan. They know why but they will never know how much.

Introduction

The Setting

On the eve of the entry of the United States into World War II in 1941, Henry Luce, the legendary publisher of *Time, Life,* and *Fortune* magazines, made famous the phrase "American century." The menace posed by the Axis aggressors to the territorial security, capitalist economy, and democratic institutions of the United States, Luce wrote in a series of editorials that ultimately became a book, was testimony to the vital need to create a new global order that accepted U.S. leadership and embraced its values and ideals. He took it for granted that the United States would soon join in the war, and that, once victory was secured, it would possess the power and will to remake the world in its own image.

No one took Luce's admonition more to heart than John Foster Dulles. Indeed, over the span of five decades, no one struggled longer and harder for, or identified more personally with, the vision of an American century. His life and career embody the best and worst of U.S. foreign policy as it progressed toward international supremacy and, as such, reflect the tension between idealism and realism, between altruism and self-interest, that consistently pervades America's relations with the world. Consequently, as rhetoric about the "enlargement of democracy" circulates throughout the United States at the dawn of the twenty-first century, Dulles's history, for so long held hostage to the passions of the cold war, is one that warrants close scrutiny and reevaluation.

That history begins in 1888, when the United States was at the cusp of global power. It still lagged behind the European empires, especially that of Great Britain, and Germany's unification the previous decade had created an energetic new rival. Moreover, Russia's industrial and territorial expansion that accompanied Czar Alexander II's post–Crimean War reform program signaled its potential potency and ambition as well.

No country's future, however, appeared more promising than that of the United States; its destiny did indeed seem manifest. What emerged from the terrible ordeal of the Civil War and the Reconstruction era was a country more united in purpose than ever before, its spirit of nationalism and ethos of exceptionalism rekindled. What emerged concurrently was the foundation for an unprecedented economic boom that revolutionized state and society. The Jeffersonian ideal of an agrarian-based nation gave way to the steel factories of Andrew Carnegie and oil refineries of John D. Rockefeller. The requisite labor force for these burgeoning industrial giants came cheaply, provided by a continuous stream of displaced farmers and new immigrants. Smalltown America became urban America. The hundreds of thousands of miles of additional railroad track laid to knit together the people and markets of the rapidly growing cities represented the end of frontier society; the ornate railroad terminals symbolized the dawn of the Gilded Age.

This radical transformation was driven by an increased collaboration between business and government. Republicans in particular identified with, and claimed credit for, the economic surge. The Grand Old Party promoted as the core features of its platform a high tariff in order to protect U.S. manufacturers and a tightly controlled supply of money in order to safeguard investors against inflation. With the exception of Grover Cleveland's nonconsecutive two terms in office, the Republicans captured every presidential contest from the end of the Civil War to the election of Woodrow Wilson in 1912.

The Republican elected in 1888 was a zealous nationalist, Benjamin Harrison, great-grandson of a signer of the Declaration of Independence, grandson of former President William Henry "Tippecanoe" Harrison, son of a congressman, and Union general during the Civil War. By the 1880s the expense as well as the rewards of U.S. industrialization and urbanization had become conspicuous. Squalid conditions in overpopulated cities and wages that failed to keep pace with the escalating cost of living bred unionism, strikes, and rioting. Agrarian protesters organized throughout the South and Plains states as farmers were forced to pay higher prices to buy equipment, higher interest rates to borrow money, and higher railroad charges to ship produce. More generally, and most ominously, even as the gross national product grew spectacularly, the United States experienced a severe depression in 1873–78, and then an even more severe one in 1884–85.

Harrison shared the view of most Republicans that programs such as the protective tariff were necessary but insufficient remedies for problems of this magnitude. Despite the huge increase in population, the domestic market alone could not absorb the massive industrial and agricultural production of the United States. In addition, although from 1874 the U.S. balance of trade was regularly favorable, expanding overseas exports could not keep up with productive capacity and output. The consequent glut of goods resulted in high inventories, falling prices, and laid-off workers, all of which threatened continued and progressively deeper economic depression with concomitant social and political turmoil.

The solution was to acquire more overseas markets, and Harrison committed his administration to promoting more aggressively U.S. international interests. To command the respect of the Great Powers and proudly display the U.S. flag to lesser powers, he encouraged the construction of a modern navy. He also advocated building a canal through the Central American isthmus, obtaining bases in the Caribbean to secure U.S. naval power, and acquiring island outposts in the Pacific to project that power toward Asia and its bountiful China market. Harrison's chief priority was to annex the Hawaiian Islands.

Opportunity knocked when the Hawaiian monarch, Queen Liliuokalani, abrogated the constitution in an effort to reassert native authority over a planter class dominated by the descendants of American missionaries. The planters sent a delegation to Washington to seek support for the overthrow of the queen and for the U.S. annexation of Hawaii. The administration's response was indirect but unambiguously favorable. Within months the intervention of U.S. Minister John L. Stevens and Marines from the USS *Boston* proved decisive in the revolution's success in January 1893.

"The Hawaiian pear is now fully ripe, and this is the golden hour for the United States to pluck it," Stevens wrote.* Harrison wholeheartedly agreed, and negotiations for a treaty of annexation fell to John Watson Foster, who in 1892 had succeeded the ailing James G. Blaine as secretary of state. A newspaper editor from Harrison's home state of Indiana, Foster had risen to prominence within the Republican Party. Rewarded for his efforts on behalf of Ulysses S. Grant's 1872 campaign with the post of minister to

*Quoted in Merze Tate, *The United States and the Hawaiian Kingdom: A Political History* (New Haven, 1965), 210.

Mexico, he subsequently served as minister to Russia and to Spain as well. Prior to his appointment as secretary of state, moreover, Foster participated in the negotiations of a number of treaties of reciprocity intended to facilitate greater commerce and to enhance U.S. economic and political influence on a global scale.

Thus, Foster was well prepared for his most important assignment, and in February 1893 he delivered to Harrison a treaty calling for U.S. annexation of Hawaii. Harrison placed it before the Senate with his recommendation for immediate ratification: Not only was Hawaii a valuable stepping-stone to the China market, but also its acquisition by any power other than the United States would endanger U.S. security and world peace. Harrison was a lame duck president, however, and the Democratic majority in the Senate refused to act on a measure that would constitute such a crowning achievement for the Republicans. When the antiannexationist Grover Cleveland resumed the presidency in April, he withdrew the treaty from consideration. From then until Hawaii's ultimate annexation by the United States in the midst of the 1898 Spanish-American War, its disposition generated one of the pivotal debates in U.S. history. Its future became inextricably intertwined with competing visions of the role of the United States in the international system.

John W. Foster never questioned what that role should be. Even as he continued to build up the international law practice he had established in Washington in the 1880s, he remained active in the world of diplomacy. He assisted the State Department during the Cleveland, McKinley, and Theodore Roosevelt administrations, and was one of the founding members of the Carnegie Endowment for Peace. Foster was hired by the Chinese government to provide counsel during the negotiations following the 1894–95 Sino-Japanese War, and ultimately took on as clients numerous other foreign governments and U.S. business concerns with interests overseas.

On February 25, 1888, Foster's daughter, Edith, gave birth to his grandson, John Foster Dulles. Young Dulles's career trajectory would parallel the rise of the United States to global preeminence. In 1953, at the apex of U.S. power, he became secretary of state.

Chronology

1888

    February 25   John Foster Dulles is born in Watertown, New York.

1892

    June 29   John Watson Foster succeeds James G. Blaine as secretary of state to President Benjamin Harrison.

1893

    January 16   The Hawaiian Kingdom's Queen Liliuokalani is overthrown with the assistance of the U.S. minister and Marines.

1898

    April 20   The United States declares war on Spain.

    July 7   Hawaii is annexed by the United States.

    December 10   The United States and Spain sign the Treaty of Paris.

1903

    November 18   The Hay-Bunau-Varilla Treaty is signed, authorizing the United States to build the Panama Canal.

1907

    June 15   The Second Hague Peace Conference convenes.

1915

    June 8   Robert Lansing succeeds William Jennings Bryan as secretary of state to President Woodrow Wilson.

1917

    April 6   The United States declares war on Germany.

    November 15   Red Guards storm Moscow's Kremlin and the Bolsheviks seize power in Russia.

1918

January 8	President Wilson enunciates his Fourteen Points in a speech to the U.S. Congress.
November 18	Germany agrees to an armistice on the basis of the Fourteen Points.

1919

January 12	The Paris Peace Conference convenes.
February 14	Drafting of the Covenant of the League of Nations is completed.
June 28	The Treaty of Versailles is signed.

1920

March 19	For the second and final time the U.S. Senate refuses to ratify the Treaty of Versailles.

1921

August 25	The United States and Germany sign the Berlin Treaty, thereby formally terminating the state of war between the two nations.

1924

April 24	The Dawes Plan, on the payment of German war reparations, is published.

1929

January 15	The U.S. Senate ratifies the Kellogg-Briand Pact, signed the previous August by fifteen nations, outlawing war.

1931

September 30	Japanese destroy part of the South Manchurian railway at Mukden, which Tokyo will use as the excuse to establish the puppet kingdom of Manchukuo in Manchuria.

1933

January 30	Adolf Hitler is appointed chancellor of Germany.
November 16	The United States formally establishes diplomatic relations with the Soviet Union.

1935

March 7	German forces enter the demilitarized Rhineland.
August 31	President Franklin D. Roosevelt signs the first U.S. Neutrality Act.
October 3	Italy invades Abyssinia (Ethiopia).

1937

October 5	In a speech in Chicago, President Roosevelt suggests an international "quarantine" to address the "epidemic of world lawlessness."
November 6	Italy adheres to the Anti-Comintern Pact signed between Germany and Japan the preceding year.

1938

March 13	Austria agrees to join the Third Reich.
September 30	In Munich the British and French agree to cede Czechoslovakia's Sudetenland to Germany.

1939

May 28	Germany and Italy sign the "Pact of Steel."
August 23	The Nazi-Soviet Non-Aggression Pact is signed.
September 1	Germany invades Poland.
December 14	The League of Nations meets for the last time.

1940

June 13	German forces occupy Paris.
July 10	The Vichy regime is established in France.

1941

February 28	Dulles accepts the chairmanship of the Commission to Study the Bases of a Just and Durable Peace, created the previous month by the Federal Council of Churches of Christ in America.
March 11	The U.S. Congress enacts legislation establishing Lend-Lease.
June 22	Germany invades the Soviet Union.
August 12	President Roosevelt and British Prime Minister Winston Churchill agree to the Atlantic Charter.
December 7	Japan attacks Pearl Harbor.
December 11	Germany and Italy declare war on the United States.

1942

November 8	Operation Torch, the Anglo-American invasion of North Africa, begins.

1943

March 26 — Dulles personally presents his "Six Pillars of Peace" to President Roosevelt.

November 28 — The first wartime summit among the Big Three—Roosevelt, Churchill, and the Soviets' Joseph Stalin—convenes in Teheran.

1944

June 6 — The Allies launch Operation Overlord, the cross-Channel invasion of France.

July 1 — The Bretton Woods conference to establish the International Monetary Fund and the International Bank for Reconstruction and Development (World Bank) opens.

August 21 — The Dumbarton Oaks Conference to plan for the establishment of a United Nations convenes.

1945

February 4 — The Big Three meet again at Yalta.

April 12 — Franklin D. Roosevelt dies and Vice President Harry S. Truman succeeds to the U.S. presidency.

April 25 — The San Francisco Conference to establish the United Nations convenes.

May 8 — Germany surrenders.

July 17 — The Potsdam Conference meets to address problems of postwar Europe.

August 6 — The United States drops an atomic bomb on Hiroshima, Japan. Three days later it will drop a second bomb on Nagasaki.

August 14 — Japan surrenders.

September 2 — Ho Chi Minh proclaims the establishment of the Democratic Republic of Vietnam.

September 11 — The Council of Foreign Ministers convenes in London.

December 16 — The Council of Foreign Ministers reconvenes in Moscow.

1946

February 22 — George Kennan sends his "Long Telegram" from Moscow to the State Department.

March 5 — In a speech at Westminster College, Fulton, Missouri, Winston Churchill declares that an "iron curtain" has descended across the

	continent, separating Eastern Europe from the West.
April 25	The Council of Foreign Ministers reconvenes in Paris.
June 3	Dulles publishes "Thoughts on Soviet Foreign Policy" in *Life* magazine. Part 2 of this article will appear the following week.
June 14	Bernard Baruch presents the U.S. plan for the international control of atomic energy to the United Nations.
December 19	The First Indochina War breaks out.

1947

January 21	George C. Marshall succeeds James F. Byrnes as secretary of state.
March 12	President Truman enunciates the Truman Doctrine.
June 4	Secretary of State Marshall proposes a program for the economic recovery of Europe, soon to be called the Marshall Plan.
July 26	The U.S. Congress passes the National Security Act, creating the National Security Agency, the Central Intelligence Agency, and the Department of Defense.

1948

May 14	The United States recognizes the new state of Israel.
March 17	Great Britain, France, the Netherlands, Belgium, and Luxembourg sign the Brussels Pact, a mutual defense alliance for Western Europe.
June 24	The Soviet Union imposes a blockade of Berlin.
June 26	The United States initiates an airlift of supplies to Berlin.
November 2	Truman is elected to a second term as president by defeating Thomas E. Dewey.

1949

January 21	Dean G. Acheson succeeds Marshall as Truman's secretary of state.
April 4	The treaty creating the North Atlantic Treaty Organization (NATO) is signed.
July 21	The U.S. Senate ratifies the NATO treaty.

September 23	Truman announces that the Soviet Union has denonated an atomic device.
December 8	Chiang Kai-shek and the Nationalist Chinese flee to Formosa (Taiwan), leaving mainland China under the control of Mao Tse-tung's Communist regime.
December 19	General Dwight D. Eisenhower is appointed Supreme Allied Commander, Europe.

1950

January 31	Truman announces that he has approved the development of a hydrogen bomb.
April 14	Truman receives the NSC-68 report on U.S. security policy.
June 25	North Korea invades South Korea.
June 30	Truman commits U.S. forces to Korea.
August 3	MAAG, the U.S. Military Assistance and Advisory Group, arrives in southern Indochina.
November 26	Chinese Communist forces cross the Yalu River into Korea.

1951

January 11	Dulles is appointed head of the mission to negotiate the Japanese Peace Treaty.
January 22	Alger Hiss is convicted of perjury after testifying before the House Un-American Activities Committee on charges of espionage.
February 9	In a speech in Wheeling, West Virginia, Senator Joseph McCarthy claims to possess a list of 205 Communists in the U.S. State Department.
April 11	Truman relieves General Douglas MacArthur of his U.S. and UN military commands in Korea.
September 1	Australia, New Zealand, and the United States sign the ANZUS Treaty of mutual security.
September 8	The Japanese Peace Treaty is signed in San Francisco.

1952

May 19	Dulles publishes "A Policy of Boldness" in *Life* magazine.

May 27	The treaty establishing the European Defense Community is signed.
July 11	Eisenhower is nominated as the Republican candidate for president.
November 4	Eisenhower is elected president.
November 20	The position of secretary of state is offered to Dulles by Eisenhower.

1953

January 20	Dwight D. Eisenhower is inaugurated as president.
March 5	Joseph Stalin dies.
April 16	Eisenhower delivers an address on "The Chance for Peace."
June 16	An uprising erupts in East Germany.
July 16	The Solarium Task Forces present their reports to a special meeting of the National Security Council.
July 27	The Korean armistice is signed at Panmunjom.
August 8	The Joint Chiefs of Staff submit a memorandum proposing a "new concept" for U.S. military strategy.
August 20	The CIA's Operation AJAX succeeds in ousting Iran's Prime Minister Muhammad Mossadegh. Two days later, Shah Muhammad Reza Pahlavi will return to Teheran to reassume his throne.
October 30	Eisenhower approves NSC-162/2.

1954

January 12	Dulles publicizes the administration's "New Look" strategy in a speech to the Council on Foreign Relations.
January 25	The Berlin Conference—Dulles and the British, Soviet, and French foreign ministers—convenes.
March 13	The Vietminh attack the French fortress of Dien Bien Phu in Indochina.
March 29	Dulles calls for "United Action" to prevent the Communist conquest of Indochina.
May 7	The French surrender Dien Bien Phu.
May 8	The Indochina phase of the Geneva Conference begins.

June 18	The CIA initiates Operation PBSUCCESS in Guatemala to overthrow the government of Jacobo Arbenz Guzmán.
June 19	Pierre Mendès-France becomes prime minister of France.
July 21	The Geneva Accords are signed dividing Vietnam between North and South and scheduling unification elections for 1956.
August 30	The French National Assembly rejects the European Defense Community treaty.
September 3	The People's Republic of China begins to shell the island of Quemoy.
September 8	The Manila Treaty creating the Southeast Asia Treaty Organization (SEATO) is signed.
October 20	The Paris Conference convenes to confirm the arrangements for West Germany's admission to NATO as agreed upon in London the previous month.
December 2	The United States and the Republic of China sign a mutual defense treaty.

1955

January 29	The U.S. Congress approves the Formosa Resolution granting President Eisenhower discretionary authority to commit U.S. forces to defend Taiwan and "related" territories.
April 23	While attending the Bandung Conference, Chou En-lai announces that the Chinese Communists are willing to halt the shelling of Quemoy and Matsu and negotiate with the United States.
May 9	Officially recognized by the Western Powers as a sovereign state, West Germany is formally admitted to NATO.
May 15	The Austrian State Treaty is signed.
July 21	At the Geneva Summit, Eisenhower proposes "Open Skies," a plan for mutual Soviet-American aerial surveillance.
October 26	Ngo Dinh Diem announces that he is president of an independent Republic of Vietnam.

November 21   The treaty establishing the Middle East Treaty Organization, which evolved from the Baghdad Pact, is signed.

1956

February 25   In a secret speech to the Soviet Communist Party's Twentieth Party Congress, Nikita Khrushchev denounces Stalin and offers greater freedom to the Eastern European satellites.

July 19   Dulles rescinds the U.S. offer to finance the construction of the Aswan Dam in Egypt.

October 29   The British, French, and Israelis launch a joint operation to take over the Suez Canal.

November 3   Dulles undergoes an operation for cancer.

November 4   Armored Soviet forces sweep through Budapest.

November 6   Eisenhower is reelected president.

1957

January 9   Harold Macmillan succeeds Anthony Eden as British prime minister.

March 7   Following the Suez crisis, the U.S. Congress approves the Middle East Resolution, popularly known as the Eisenhower Doctrine, to defend the region against Communist aggression.

March 25   The Treaty of Rome is signed, creating the European Economic Community (Common Market) and European Atomic Energy Community (EURATOM).

August 3   The Soviets conduct the first successful test of an intercontinental ballistic missile (ICBM).

August 13   The Syrian government declares three U.S. diplomats *persona non grata*, alleging that they were participants in a CIA covert operation.

October 4   The Soviets launch the first Sputnik satellite to orbit the Earth.

1958

February 1   Egypt and Syria merge to form the United Arab Republic (UAR).

June 1	Charles de Gaulle forms a new government in France that will lead shortly to the establishment of the Fifth Republic.
July 16	U.S. Marines come ashore in Lebanon in response to its president's request for aid against UAR-inspired strife.
August 23	The People's Republic of China resumes the shelling of Quemoy and Matsu.
November 10	Khrushchev announces the Soviet Union's intention to sign a treaty with East Germany that will supersede the World War II agreements regarding the occupation of Berlin.

1959

March 2	Khrushchev agrees to a meeting of foreign ministers to prepare for a future summit.
May 24	John Foster Dulles dies.
May 27	Dignitaries from throughout the world gather in Washington for Dulles's funeral as the Soviet ultimatum regarding Berlin expires without incident.

1

The Great Enlightenment

As the daughter of a distinguished U.S. diplomat and attorney with a practice that thrived by attracting foreign clients, Edith Foster received what one of her daughters described as an internationalist upbringing. She was but ten when President Ulysses S. Grant appointed her father minister to Mexico, and she subsequently accompanied him to his posts in Russia and Spain. In fact, at the age of seventeen she made her formal debut at a glittering ball in St. Petersburg.

And it was in Paris that Edith met the Reverend Allen Macy Dulles, whose religious preparation was leavened by an internationalist perspective only slightly less impressive than his future wife's. Originally from Ireland, the Dulles family emigrated to South Carolina and fought in the war for America's independence. The Reverend Dulles's father, John Wesley Dulles, had served as a missionary to Madras, India, before settling in Philadelphia, where Allen Macy was born. Although of modest means, John Wesley Dulles ensured that his son received an education befitting his keen mind and gift for languages. Allen Macy graduated from Princeton University and went on to study further in Leipzig and Göttingen. He was returning from a trip to the Middle East when he encountered Edith Foster in Paris.

John Foster Dulles, therefore, was the product of the union of powerful religious and secular influences, with a heavy internationalist orientation overlaying both. Because the Dulleses were in the process of moving from Detroit to Watertown, New York, Foster, as he was always called, was born in Washington, DC, where his maternal grandfather, after whom he was named, lived. This was most appropriate; John Watson Foster acted as his eldest grandson's mentor throughout his childhood, instilling in him the cosmopolitan worldview of America's turn-of-the-century elite, whose definition of U.S. interests and faith in its exceptionalism and mission drove them to proselytize internationalist policies that propelled the country toward world power.

A factory town located in rural upstate New York, Watertown was not cosmopolitan. There Dulles grew up, along with his brother, Allen, who would gain almost as much notoriety as Foster himself as director of the Central Intelligence Agency in the 1950s and early 1960s. Foster had three sisters, one of whom, Eleanor, would teach economics at Bryn Mawr and Harvard and, after serving with the Allied Control Commission in Austria following World War II, would become special assistant to the State Department's director of the Office of German Affairs.

The Reverend Mr. Dulles was the pastor of Watertown's First Presbyterian Church, and religion pervaded the lives of all his children. Weekdays began with cold baths and mother Edith playing hymns on the piano. Prior to school the children would sit on hard wooden benches, reading together the day's Bible selection, singing the chosen hymn, listening to their father's brief lecture, and then kneeling to pray collectively. On Sundays, Bibles in hand, the entire family walked to the Reverend Mr. Dulles's church on Washington Street, where the children attended Sunday School, followed by three services. They were required to take notes on the sermon because their father would question them about it at dinner. He also expected each child to recite a hymn and passage of Scripture memorized since the previous Sunday.

The popular 1950s stereotype of Foster Dulles as an inflexible Calvinist dogmatically wedded to the orthodox doctrines of an unforgiving Presbyterian Church is nevertheless a misleading caricature. His public demeanor was invariably stern and taciturn. Still, there was little fire and brimstone in the religion he learned. By the late nineteenth century most Presbyterians had repudiated the Calvinist concept of predestination. More significant, confronted with the intellectual challenge posed by Charles Darwin's theory of evolution, Protestantism was dividing into two rival factions. The conservatives, who would become known as fundamentalists after World War I, maintained that the Bible was "inerrant" in all of its parts and thus was to be interpreted literally. Liberals, however, drew on archaeology to analyze critically the earliest Biblical texts. Impressed by findings that provided robust evidence that the texts were written by ordinary people, they came to accept Darwinist explanations for human development and reject the Bible's inerrancy.

Liberal Protestants accordingly acknowledged that a concept such as God creating a "kingdom on Earth" was intended as a metaphor for establishing a good and spiritual society. It was out of this nineteenth-century theological liberalism that the twentieth-century social gospel tradition evolved that saw in the convictions of Christianity the antidote to national and international pathologies.

The Reverend Mr. Dulles was a theological liberal, which appealed to his son. Foster's own son Avery, who converted to Roman Catholicism and became a celebrated theologian, has repeatedly stressed that his father never showed any "particular signs of piety" and was convinced that the Bible consisted primarily of myths. As a young attorney in the 1920s, Foster Dulles clashed with the fundamentalist William Jennings Bryan, thrice a candidate for president and Woodrow Wilson's first secretary of state. Dulles defended in the ecclesiastical courts several clergymen whose licenses to preach were challenged in the Presbyterian Church's General Assembly because they questioned the Virgin Birth.[1]

In line with the evolving social gospel, Foster Dulles came to believe that faith depended primarily on practical needs. At its best, religion "could create a sense of obligation to promote universal harmony." No doubt this stress on the secular utility of spiritualism, which became for Dulles a mantra by the 1930s and allowed him readily to reconcile idealism and pragmatism, reflected the influence of the Foster as much as the Dulles side of the family.[2]

Although six hundred difficult miles separated Watertown from Washington, John Watson Foster frequently invited his grandson for prolonged visits to his four-story mansion, where he mingled with senators, ambassadors, and State Department officials. In addition, the former secretary of state helped the Reverend Mr. Dulles build a lodge and several guest cottages on Lake Ontario in Henderson, New York. The Dulles family spent their summers there, and among their guests who came to sail and fish were William Howard Taft, John W. Davis, Andrew Carnegie, and Bernard Baruch. Another visitor to Henderson Harbor was Watertown attorney Robert Lansing. Appointed Woodrow Wilson's secretary of state following Bryan's resignation in 1915, Lansing married Dulles's mother's sister, Eleanor Foster. After he became secretary of state, Foster Dulles hung portraits of both his grandfather and "Uncle Bert" in his office.

The Dulleses also traveled to Europe to expand the children's horizons, and Foster attended private school to ensure that he received more intellectual stimulation than Watertown's public system could provide. He graduated from high school when only fifteen: too young to go to college, according to his parents. So they took him and the rest of the family on a vacation to France, and arranged for Foster to go on to Switzerland to live with a family for several months.

In 1904, Foster Dulles entered Princeton University, the alma mater of his father and several uncles. He was still too young; at age sixteen, he was the youngest member of his class. Socially this was a problem. Dulles was quiet, reserved, and, notwithstanding his travels and pedigree, by some Princetonians' standards, unsophisticated. He was a member of the chess team but not of any of the select eating clubs that defined the rungs on Princeton's social ladder.

Intellectually, however, Dulles shone. He won the Junior Oratorical Contest and was named valedictorian after graduating second in his class, magna cum laude. Reflecting his father's influence, he majored in philosophy, receiving the Chancellor Green Mental Science Fellowship for his essay on "The Theory of Judgment" and his performance on a special examination that tested his knowledge of great philosophers, theoretical ethics, metaphysics, psychology, and inductive logic. Reflecting his grandfather's influence, he studied history and political science almost as extensively. Among the classes that Dulles took was Woodrow Wilson's famous course on constitutional government, which he later claimed stimulated his interest in public affairs.

Wilson's influence on Dulles was indeed profound, yet he owed his interest in public affairs more to his grandfather. John W. Foster introduced Dulles to the rarified atmosphere of global diplomacy. In 1907 the Chinese government appointed Foster its representative to the Second Hague Peace Conference. He invited his grandson to accompany him as the secretary-clerk for the delegation. The nineteen-year-old Princeton junior enthusiastically accepted, and the university excused him for the spring semester. He found the experience exhilarating and fulfilling.

Despite this hiatus, Dulles graduated with his class in 1908. His $600 Chancellor Green Fellowship enabled him to spend the next year in Paris, where he studied at the Sorbonne with the Nobel prize-winning philosopher Henri Bergson. He was particularly impressed with Bergson's notion that reality was in a constant state of flux, and thus change was integral to the human condition. Dulles would borrow liberally from Bergson when formulating his own theory that because the global system was inexorably evolving, international peace depended on the accommodation of national "dynamism."

Ironically, Dulles's postgraduate education in Paris reinforced his predisposition to follow in his grandfather's, not his father's, footsteps. His work in philosophy with Bergson further confirmed his view that religion could be highly superstitious and "intelligence is for the sake of life." At the Sorbonne, moreover, he took his first courses in international law. Dulles toured Germany and Spain before returning to the United States, and by the time he arrived home he had decided international law was the field for him. His parents were disappointed but hardly surprised.[3]

In 1909, Dulles enrolled in George Washington University Law School. It was not challenging for a student of his ability. Dulles graduated in only two years but still earned the highest grades in the school's history. He selected George Washington so that he could live with the Fosters. He worked part-time for his grandfather's international law practice and traveled within the capital city's highest social circles. Yet, in affairs of the heart, Dulles remained rooted in upstate New York. On the day that he passed the bar in the summer of 1911 he proposed to Janet Avery from Auburn, where his father now held the Chair of Theism and Apologetics at the Theological Seminary. They were married the next year.

John W. Foster not only inspired his grandson's choice of career, but he also was directly responsible for launching it. What mattered most to the partners at the prestigious law firms to which the recent graduate applied for a position was that George Washington was neither Harvard nor Yale. Despite everything that the young Dulles had seen and done, he was rejected by all. Foster interceded. He arranged for his grandson to be hired by the Wall Street firm of Sullivan & Cromwell.

It was a perfect match. Although on several occasions he would take extended leaves of absence, Dulles remained with Sullivan & Cromwell until 1950. It was not just that it was one of the most eminent firms in the United States, but Sullivan & Cromwell had become so prominent because it promoted the interests of its elite financial clientele by cultivating relations with the most powerful public officials, both nationally and internationally. Its representation of the New Panama Canal Company between 1896 and 1903 is illustrative. Founding partner William Nelson Cromwell's personal contacts in Washington, ranging from Presidents William McKinley and Theodore Roosevelt to Senators John Spooner (R-WI) and Mark Hanna (R-OH), resulted in Congress's altering the route of the projected Central American canal so that it ran through Panama and not Nicaragua. In short, Sullivan & Cromwell prospered because it was guided by the premise that economics, politics, and diplomacy were inextricably intertwined.

This premise also guided the rise to power of the United States in the twentieth century, and Dulles rose along with it. As he did, he became progressively more involved in global affairs. Beginning as a junior clerk with a monthly salary of $50, he was soon providing legal counsel to a distinguished international clientele. Following the outbreak of the Great War, he moved to Washington at the behest of his Uncle Bert Lansing, who was counselor to the Department of State before becoming secretary in 1915. At first, Lansing asked his nephew merely to furnish information about foreign governments that he could learn through his many Sullivan & Cromwell clients. But in 1917 he asked Dulles to provide more formal service.

Lansing was concerned with a potential threat to the integrity of the Panama Canal, which Sullivan & Cromwell had been so instrumental in building. The German government's announcement on February 1 that it was resuming unrestricted submarine warfare, followed almost immediately by the disclosure of the Zimmermann telegram that proposed an anti-American alliance with Mexico, indicated that U.S. entry into World War I was imminent. Consequently, Lansing sent Dulles on a secret mission to Panama, Nicaragua, and Costa Rica to bring them "into alignment with us against Germany . . . so that we can effectively protect the Panama Canal without infringing any neutral rights." Dulles's skillful negotiations assured the Central American governments' cooperation. His initiation into matters of security and geopolitics was a success.[4]

The United States declared war on Germany in April 1917. Ineligible for military service because of his poor eyesight, Dulles spent most of the war as the assistant to Vance McCormick, chairman of the War Trade Board. The board was responsible for supervising U.S. commerce so that it conformed with the "trading with the enemy" acts, and negotiating with neutral states to enhance the effectiveness of the Allied blockade. Dulles thus developed an even greater understanding of the intricacies of international law and finance at the same time that he sharpened his negotiating skills.

He also gained his first direct exposure to Russia. Dulles's mother had frequently spoken fondly of her experiences there while John Watson Foster was the U.S. minister, and the Wilson administration had reacted positively to the March 1917 revolution that overthrew Czar Nicholas II. But the U.S. attitude soured rapidly after the Bolsheviks seized power in November 1917. McCormick was particularly concerned; he wanted to ensure that Russia (later the Union of Soviet Socialist Republics) continued both to enforce the blockade of Germany and to respect foreign investments, of which his relative, the agricultural industry magnate Cyrus McCormick, had many. In May 1918, Vance McCormick appointed a committee to oversee Soviet-American economic relations. Dulles was one of its three members. In October the committee recommended that President Woodrow Wilson establish the Russian Bureau Inc., wholly owned by the U.S. government, to provide assistance for the Czech forces and their sympathizers who were fighting the Bolsheviks in Siberia. Wilson agreed, and John Foster Dulles became the Russian Bureau's secretary-treasurer.

Dulles's involvement in this initial anti-Bolshevik campaign was more an omen for the future than anything else. By the time Wilson decided to intervene militarily against the Soviet regime, Dulles was serving the president in another capacity, one that would leave an indelible mark on his memory. In January 1919, Wilson appointed Bernard Baruch, the fabulously wealthy stock market speculator, to head the U.S. representation on the Commission on the Reparation of Damage, the body established at the Paris (Versailles) Peace Conference to assess what financial penalty Germany should pay for its role in World War I. Baruch had known Dulles since their summers together at Henderson Harbor. Their relationship had grown after Dulles joined Sullivan & Cromwell, and deepened further during the war. Baruch chaired the War Industries Board, which worked closely with the War Trade Board. For his new assignment, Baruch chose Dulles as his legal advisor.

Over the next eight months Dulles became the primary spokesman and draftsman for the U.S. delegation on the Reparations Commission. As such, he was intimately involved in one of the most heated and fateful debates throughout the contentious treaty-writing process. In Dulles's opinion, reparations "proved, perhaps, the most troublesome single problem of the Peace Conference."[5]

Dulles's judgment was valid. Led by Britain and France, the Allies, with whom the United States had been "associated" from 1917 to 1918, demanded that Germany reimburse them for the entire cost of the war. This reimbursement entailed compensation for all expenses incurred for arms, munitions, and supplies, and the replacement of whatever public or private property had been lost or damaged during the fighting. Americans were horrified. The assessment that the Allies sought to levy on Germany was in the neighborhood of $300 billion (in contemporary dollars). The Wilson administration calculated that to impose on Germany a financial burden greater than $25 to $30 billion would cripple its economy and generate uncontainable resentment and chaos. The result would be European-wide poverty and instability, creating conditions incompatible with a healthy U.S. economy and global peace. The Wilson administration was right. As America's inability to avoid the contagion of World War II proved, in an interdependent world the United States would pay the price in both dollars and blood. The U.S. national interest demanded the rehabilitation of Europe, and Germany had to be the cornerstone.

Mainly because of Dulles's legalistic reasoning and diplomatic acumen, the Americans chipped away at the Allies' position. On the legal front, Dulles argued that neither the principles nor precedents of international law supported the demand that Germany reimburse the Allied governments for all their wartime expenses. Furthermore, to require Germany to compensate the victors for damaged public property would violate the Pre-Armistice Agreement, which both the United States and Allies had signed with Germany in November 1918. Dulles likened the agreement to a contract, and pointed out that it specifically committed Germany to pay reparations only on civilian property.

Dulles supplemented his legal case with a diplomatic gambit that was absolutely Machiavellian. He explained to the continental states that had fought the Germans, France in particular, that their expenditures for the actual conduct of the war were far less than that of Britain and, for that matter, of the United States. Conversely, they had suffered far greater damage to the civilian population and property. He therefore convinced the French that they would receive a substantially lower percentage of the total reparations figure if the German obligation included war costs in addition to civilian costs. As a consequence, Dulles succeeded in driving a wedge between France and Britain.

Having placed the Allies on the defensive, Dulles then seized the initiative, a strategy that would become his hallmark. At the end of February 1919 he preempted both the French and British by drafting clauses concerning German reparations. Thus, when discussions began on the precise wording of the treaty, the starting point would be a proposal from the United States, as opposed to a more extreme one submitted by an ally.

Moreover, to guarantee that the Allies would agree to use his proposal as the initial basis for discussions, Dulles's draft accommodated their general position, albeit only partway. The German government would "make reparation for the entire cost of the war to the governments with which Germany has been at war and the indirect damage flowing therefrom," Dulles wrote. Juxtaposed with this sentence, however, was one that read, "[T]he ability of the German Government and nation to make such reparation is limited to such an extent as will render the making of such complete reparation impractical." Dulles had accepted *in theory* Germany's liability for both civilian damages and war costs but emphasized that *in practice* there had to be a limit on its liability commensurate with its resources.[6]

Dulles was therefore instrumental in weaning the Allies from their most draconian objectives. After weeks of additional haggling, they approved, on practical grounds, his disclaimer of total restitution. The U.S. victory, however, proved to be Pyrrhic. The price of winning agreement on the pragmatic necessity of limiting German reparations was acquiescence to the Allied insistence that Germany be forced to acknowledge its exclusive moral responsibility for the outbreak of war and the destruction it had caused. As a consequence, Dulles also ended up participating in designing the infamous "war guilt" clause that opened the door to the eventual imposition on Germany of a reparations bill that far exceeded the reasonable limits that he thought he had established. In this context the modifier "eventual" is critical, and for this Dulles was largely responsible as well.

When negotiations broke down over the fixed amount of German reparations to be stipulated in the final treaty, Dulles suggested that a decision be postponed pending the creation of a committee to evaluate the sum total of claims against Germany. This suggestion became the blueprint for creating the Reparations Commission as provided for in the Treaty of Versailles. By the time the Commission completed its work in 1921, however, it lacked U.S. representation. The Senate had refused to ratify the treaty in 1919. Without the moderating voice of the Americans, the Commission, factoring veteran pensions, a "separation allowance," and the like into the "civilian" costs of the war, saddled Germany with a reparations bill of $33 billion, with France claiming more than 50 percent. Although modest by initial Allied standards, the amount was exorbitant by American standards, particularly because the scheduled biannual payments had to be made in gold. Within three years, German inflation had skyrocketed to unprecedented levels, its government had suspended reparations payments, Adolf Hitler had led an unsuccessful coup d'état, and France had deployed its forces to occupy Germany's industrial Ruhr Valley.

Dulles was barely thirty when he went to Versailles, and his official position was but a subordinate one. His contribution was significant nonetheless, and he took personally the defeat of his, and the Wilson administration's, effort to fashion a just and durable peace. As is generally the case with searing experiences during one's youth, the lessons that Dulles learned at Versailles stayed with him for the remainder of his life, and they transcended matters of international law and economics. One lesson was that the effectiveness of a secretary of state was contingent upon his retaining the confidence of the president. Uncle Bert's failure to do so had led to his isolation and eventual firing.

Another lesson that Dulles learned was more substantive: the long-term interests of victors dictated seeking reconciliation with, not taking vengeance on, defeated enemies. "I had some part in the Paris conference which created the treaty of Versailles," he said when discussing German reunification with the Soviets in 1954. He then reviewed the Carthaginian terms that Germany was forced to accept and linked them to the outbreak of World War II. Efforts to bankrupt and humiliate a nation, he concluded, "merely incite a people of vigor and of courage to break the bonds imposed upon them. . . . Prohibitions thus incite the very acts that are prohibited."[7]

It would be more than a quarter-century before Dulles had another opportunity to put into practice what he had learned at Versailles. In 1919 he returned to the United States, and, like many disappointed and disillusioned Wilsonians, he turned his energies from making the world safe for democracy to making money. But making money with a firm such as Sullivan & Cromwell meant remaining intimately involved in the elite circles of global politics and finance.

Dulles traveled in the highest of these circles, and he made lots of money. He took leave from Sullivan & Cromwell in 1917 as a junior member of the firm. When he returned in 1919 it was as a full partner; by 1926 he had been named managing partner. In 1931, *Fortune* magazine profiled Dulles as one of the young lions of U.S. corporate law. Sullivan & Cromwell's clientele was comprised of a who's who of national and international banking and business concerns including J. P. Morgan & Company; Dillon, Read & Company; Brown Brothers & Harriman; Goldman, Sachs; the New York Life Insurance Company; the American and Foreign Power Company; the International Nickel Company; the Overseas Securities Corporation; United Railways of Central America; and the United Fruit Company. As the firm's managing partner, Dulles became accustomed to orchestrating multimillion-dollar deals worldwide. Rumored to be the highest paid lawyer on Wall Street, he moved from East 91st Street in New York City to Cold Spring Harbor on Long Island and also built a cabin on Lake Ontario's Duck Island, not far from Henderson Harbor. The Dulles family, which now included two sons and a daughter, lived well.

In the most fundamental sense, Dulles's life and outlook during the 1920s and 1930s mirrored that of the United States. In contrast to the immediate aftermath of World War I, this was a time of unbridled optimism and prosperity. World War I transformed the United States from a debtor to creditor nation, and New York replaced London as the financial capital of the world. The business of America's government, President Calvin Coolidge declared, was business.

In this regard, Coolidge's foreign policy, and that of Warren G. Harding and Herbert Hoover, the other Republican presidents of the 1920s, was anything but isolationist, as the conventional wisdom had once held. It could not afford to be. Undeniably, the bitter residue left by World War I, the Versailles negotiations, and the struggle over U.S. membership in the League of Nations militated against political entanglements with foreign powers. But Republican-led Washington actively sought and received the cooperation of the private sector to promote U.S. ideas and interests abroad. Historians have characterized this foreign policy as "independent internationalism." Its goal, as Warren Cohen has cogently written, was an "Empire without Tears."[8]

Dulles did his part to achieve this goal by ably assisting his many banking and corporate clients whose fortunes depended on acquiring global markets and foreign subsidiaries and securing investments throughout the world. Moreover, when the consequences of the Versailles Treaty threatened Europe with financial ruin, political instability, and perhaps even military hostilities, Dulles enthusiastically lent a hand to efforts to provide a solution. After Germany's suspension of reparations payments precipitated France's occupation of the Ruhr, he helped to implement the American-sponsored Dawes Plan in 1924. This plan scaled down German payments for the future, established a committee to resolve the difficult problem of currency transfer, and arranged for Germany to receive an international loan. Dulles also collaborated with Jean Monnet, his friend since Versailles, in devising the Polish Stabilization Plan, and assisted the developers of the Young Plan, the Dawes Plan's 1929 successor.

The Great Depression and collapse of the Versailles system in the 1930s, however, proved that such economic diplomacy was insufficient. Europe's continuing financial woes could not be separated from its pervasive political anxieties, which were exacerbated by the U.S. refusal to exercise leadership and make commitments. Dulles followed the deterioration of conditions worldwide with unmitigated horror, but he was not surprised.

Even as he and his clients profited from the global economy of the 1920s, Dulles remained concerned over the potential fallout from the World War I settlement and, perhaps even more important, the implications of the U.S. refusal to join the League of Nations and otherwise subscribe to the Wilsonian precepts of international interdependence. In 1921 like-minded Americans from the worlds of banking, law, commerce, journalism, and scholarship founded the Council on Foreign Relations in an effort to study global events and, through its journal *Foreign Affairs*, encourage public interest in world affairs and counter isolationist sentiment. Unlike the many peace organizations that evolved concurrently, the Council supported the maintenance and, if necessary, the use of U.S. power.

Despite Dulles's heavy schedule at Sullivan & Cromwell, he regularly participated in the Council's meetings and study groups. In the inaugural issue of *Foreign Affairs* in 1922, he published the first of what would become many articles in the distinguished organ of the Eastern Establishment. Its title was, appropriately, "The Allied Debt." Dulles continued to write extensively about international affairs throughout the 1920s. In addition, he attended meetings of, and frequently addressed, a host of other organizations that shared his activist global outlook. Among the most significant were the Carnegie Endowment for International Peace (of which John Watson Foster was a founding member), the American Society for International Law, the National Economic League, the International Chamber of Commerce, and the Foreign Policy Association, all of which rivaled the Council on Foreign Relations for Dulles's time and allegiance.

The demands of Dulles's Sullivan & Cromwell clients increased with the disintegration of the global economy and the concomitant unleashing of the pent-up aggressions of countries whose national memories remained fixated on their perceived mistreatment at Versailles. The most blatant manifestation, of course, was the ascendancy of Adolf Hitler and his Nazi party to power in Germany. Hitler threatened not only peace and security but also the prosperity of the many banks and corporations with interests in Germany that Dulles, the attorney, had been retained to protect. Hitler's intensely nationalistic economic policies frequently discriminated against U.S. imports and suspended Reichsbank payments to U.S. creditors. Predictably, even as these travails of his clients required Dulles to draw extensively from his vast knowledge of international law and finance, his thoughts focused increasingly on war and peace, on force and diplomacy.

After German rearmament and occupation of the Rhineland, the Italian attack on Ethiopia, foreign intervention in the Spanish Civil War, and the outbreak of the Sino-Japanese War, in 1937 President Franklin D. Roosevelt declared an "epidemic of world lawlessness." Dulles fully agreed and turned his attention to prescribing the antidote. But first he had to diagnose the cause.[9]

For Dulles, the dissatisfaction and resentment produced by the Treaty of Versailles reflected and in fact exacerbated pathologies that had infected the global environment long before the outbreak of World War I. Indeed, the starting point for his diagnosis was the philosophical notion of reality's fluidity, a concept that he had learned while studying with Henri Bergson at the Sorbonne, and one that Dulles believed was equally central to the political philosophy of Woodrow Wilson. The most fundamental reason for the rapid disintegration of the international order, Dulles deduced, could be traced to the failure of national leaders, most pronounced in Britain and France, to accept that their wealth and power was inherently contingent. "The true explanation of the imminence of war lies in the inevitability of change and the fact that peace efforts have been misdirected toward the prevention of change," Dulles wrote for the *Atlantic Monthly* as early as 1935. "Thereby forces which are in the long run irresistible are temporarily dammed up. When they finally break through, they do so with violence."[10]

Over the next few years, as Dulles sharpened his diagnosis of the world's ills, he simultaneously developed his prescription for curing them. The turning point, as it was with President Roosevelt, came in 1937. In the summer of that year, Dulles was invited to Paris to preside over a session at the Institute of Intellectual Cooperation's International Studies Conference sponsored by the League of Nations. He left disappointed and depressed. The delegates from different countries could not agree on any basic principles concerning peaceful change, the session's topic. Dulles attributed the problem to their refusal to examine the issue from a perspective that transcended each delegate's particular national interest.

From this conference Dulles went on to attend another held at Oxford University on "Church, Community, and State" under the auspices of the Universal Christian Council for Life and Work, one of the organizations that would later evolve into the World Council of Churches. Dulles categorized himself as a "nominal Christian" during the years since his return to Sullivan & Cromwell in 1919. Initially, he regularly took his family to Sunday services at the Park Avenue Presbyterian Church, where he was an elder. He even imitated some of his father's practices by having his children sing hymns and summarize the sermon. But religion became progressively less relevant to his life as an international lawyer. Once the Dulleses moved to Long Island, they rarely attended church.[11]

Because of his stature and frequent writings on international affairs, and the Reverend Mr. Dulles's reputation as a distinguished Protestant intellectual, Dulles was asked by Dr. Joseph Oldham, a British layman who was the Oxford conference's organizing secretary, to address the meeting and chair a subcommittee that would examine Christianity's potential for mitigating international animosity. Dulles was pleased with the reception accorded his address, "The Problem of Peace in a Dynamic World," which built on the Bergsonian themes that he first espoused publicly in his *Atlantic Monthly* article. He was more pleased by the tenor of his subcommittee's discussions and by the sessions that he attended. In contrast to the Paris meeting's "distrustful atmosphere of national competition," at Oxford he found an impressive spirit of mutual understanding and cooperation.[12]

Dulles described the experience as his "great enlightenment." His interest in theology was no deeper than it had been previously. Yet at Oxford, he later told the Watertown congregation of his youth, he "began to understand the profound significance of the spiritual values that my mother and father had taught." He concluded that the church, or more precisely, its principles, could be applied pragmatically to resolve global problems that appeared so intractable because national behavior was parochial, materialistic, and selfish. But Christianity, at least as Dulles understood it and the Oxford conference seemed to attest, stood for universalist ideals of brotherhood and equality.[13]

Dulles underwent something of a spiritual revival after 1937; religious convictions henceforth suffused his writings and speeches on international affairs. As the global system broke apart with the onset of World War II and then the cold war, he repeatedly argued that, united with Bergson's theory on the inevitability of change and Wilson's progressive ideas about interdependence, the concepts of Christianity had the potential "for creating an international ethos which would be essential as a foundation for any lasting political structure." Further, Dulles became exponentially more active in church organizations at both the national and international levels, and he used these activities as stepping-stones to political influence and, ultimately, to power. Doubtless his father and grandfather each would have been proud.[14]

Notes

1. Avery Dulles, S.J., "John Foster Dulles: His Religious and Political Heritage," Flora Levy Lecture in the Humanities, University of Southwestern Louisiana, 1994 (available through the University of Southwestern Louisiana), 4.

2. Ibid., 8.

3. Ibid., 6.

4. Quoted in Ronald W. Pruessen, *John Foster Dulles: The Road to Power* (New York, 1982), 22.

5. Quoted in ibid., 32.

6. Quoted in Philip Burnett, *Reparations at the Paris Peace Conference: From the Standpoint of the American Delegation*, 2 vols. (New York, 1940), 1:600–604.

7. The U.S. Delegation at the Berlin Conference to the Department of State, January 26, 1954, *Foreign Relations of the United States, 1952–54*, 7:829 (hereafter cited as *FR*, followed by appropriate year).

8. Warren I. Cohen, *Empire without Tears: America's Foreign Relations, 1921–1933* (New York, 1987), 17.

9. Quoted in Robert Dallek, *Franklin D. Roosevelt and American Foreign Policy, 1932–1945* (New York, 1981), 148.

10. John Foster Dulles, "The Road to Peace," *Atlantic Monthly* 156 (October 1935): 492–99.

11. Avery Dulles, "John Foster Dulles," 10.

12. Quoted in Mark G. Toulouse, *The Transformation of John Foster Dulles: From Prophet of Realism to Priest of Nationalism* (Macon, GA, 1985), 52.

13. Quoted in ibid., 52, 54.

14. Avery Dulles, "John Foster Dulles," 17.

2

The Cold War Consensus

Dulles firmly believed that the most effective way to clarify his thoughts was to articulate them. He went nowhere without a pencil and yellow legal pad of paper, and by 1953 he had written two books, close to one hundred articles; and, more than sixty position papers. Excluding press conferences, congressional testimony, and interviews, he also had delivered almost two hundred speeches; and, despite the hectic pace of his tenure as secretary of state, he continued to draft them himself. Not surprisingly, therefore, in that summer of 1937, Dulles began to commit to paper his revised ideas about the causes of the unrest and aggression that were enveloping the world and the remedies for them. Indeed, writing in longhand on a deck chair of the ocean liner that brought him back from Europe, Dulles all but composed a first draft of *War, Peace, and Change*.

Dulles wrote in the preface to his book, which was published in 1939 (as fate would have it, the same year that war broke out in Europe), that his "thoughts" were "the result of much thinking and study since the Paris Conference of 1919." The more proximate inspiration for *War, Peace, and Change*, nevertheless, was the Oxford conference. Since the mid-1930s Dulles had been advocating political solutions to what he called the global "cycle of recurrent violence." What he witnessed at Oxford, especially when contrasted with his experience at the previous meeting in Paris, persuaded him that the efficacy of political solutions required their correlation with religious and ethical concepts. Still, he remained convinced that the reverse was no less true. Dulles had arrived at a lifelong conviction: in international relations, "realism" and "idealism" were not only mutually reinforcing, they were also wholly interdependent.[1]

Although at the most rudimentary level Dulles's overarching perspective reflected the political culture in which he matured intellectually and prospered financially, his explanation for the endemic conflict among nations was an idiosyncratic amalgam of Protestantism, Bergsonianism, and Wilsonianism. The premise of *War, Peace, and Change* was that selfishness "is a basic human instinct," and "the fact that human beings, all selfish, are in contact with each other inevitably brings dissatisfaction." This premise led to a second: the "conflict of selfish desires assumes, in its simple form, a struggle between those who primarily are satisfied and wish to retain that which they have and those who are dissatisfied and wish to acquire at the expense of others."[2]

Dulles characterized the two opposing tendencies as the "static" and the "dynamic" and argued that because "the dynamic prevails over the static," peoples and societies have progressed. Yet when applied to relations among peoples and societies—when applied to international relations—this phenomenon had produced war. Historically, Dulles averred, diplomacy has not been "designed to provide a status of reasonable flux between the static and dynamic forces of the world." As a consequence, the global order "merely reflects the fact that, at the moment, there is a preponderance of power in a certain nation or group of nations." Accordingly, changes to that order could come about only by other nations or groups wresting that power, which required the use of force. Diplomats needed to appreciate that peace and stability required "elasticity," not "rigidity."[3]

That President Wilson did appreciate this principle, Dulles made clear. He made equally clear that in the wake of the disappointing results of Wilson's valiant efforts at Versailles, the renewal of international conflict was all but inevitable. Dulles argued that having by and large achieved their fundamental objectives following World War I, France (and to a lesser extent Britain) not only resisted any modification of the Treaty of Versailles in order to address its adverse consequences, but also that they conceived of the League of Nations as "an alliance to perpetuate rigidly the post war status." In fact, France and Britain grotesquely corrupted the concept of collective security by their attempts to apply the "economic and military power of other League members" against "those seeking change," whom they "branded as potential 'aggressors.'"[4]

By the time Dulles was writing *War, Peace, and Change,* "potential" was no longer an appropriate adjective for these "aggressors," primarily the Germans, Italians, and Japanese. Dulles now labeled them the "three great despotisms." Even more revealing was his explanation for how and why they had become so. On the one hand, all three (even Japan and Italy, "victors" but nonetheless treated with contempt by their erstwhile allies) were subjected to an "intentionally repressive" treaty that "embodied many injustices." On the other hand, they were "dynamic" powers, composed of peoples of "great energy," "industry," "discipline," and a "willingness to sacrifice." Dulles maintained that, confronted by an international order "too rigid in its structure and thinking" to accommodate these attributes, they logically turned toward violent measures to effect change. Thus, the sequence of acts of global aggression during the 1930s, "which we can trace in the case of Japan, Italy, and Germany, is precisely that which we ought to have expected and been able to foresee."[5]

Critics later charged that Dulles was too tolerant of, and even sympathetic toward, the Axis. Such criticism is unjust. "The foregoing recitals are not by way of defense," he wrote after his explanation of each aggressor nation's conduct. "What has happened to China and Ethiopia and to many Austrians and Czechs is repugnant to civilized mankind." Yet without question he highlighted the culpability of those countries that had behaved so vengefully at Versailles and so shortsightedly afterward. Dulles directly connected their insistence on treating the Peace of Paris as "sacred" and hence not subject to change (which Dulles likened to the fundamentalist interpretation of the Bible), their efforts to repress capable and energetic peoples, and their identification of their national interests with universal virtue, to the rise of Hitler, Mussolini, and Tojo.[6]

Heading his recommended list of reforms was a revived and revitalized international organization that recognized that sovereignty was not inviolate. It had to be empowered to revise existing treaties and even readjust territorial boundaries as a means to accommodate legitimate national aspirations (including those of colonial peoples). It also had to be committed to promoting liberal trade and travel as means to facilitate the exchange of values as well as of goods, thereby fostering empathy and a spirit of community as well as prosperity.

Dulles did not specify how this organization would be structured or operate (he dismissed the idea of a world government as "obviously impracticable"). But he was specific as to the prerequisite for its effectiveness. State leaders, like the religious leaders who had gathered at Oxford, must be guided by moral law, not national chauvinism. In addition to political reform the world needed spiritual renewal in order to "alter and broaden the concept of what is worthy of devotion and sacrifice" and to mitigate conflicts of selfish desires.[7]

The German invasion of Poland shortly after the publication of *War, Peace, and Change* rendered moot much of Dulles's analysis, at least for the immediate future. His arguments, however, explain why he did not share the enthusiasm of many U.S. internationalists for providing assistance to the Axis' opponents. If "the world is bound into a cycle of recurrent violence," he repeated his mantra when writing to former chairman of the Senate Foreign Relations Committee William Borah (R-Idaho), "then I should like to see the United States avoid this involvement."[8]

Dulles continued, "if any program could be evolved which would break the cycle and give some promise of reestablishing a real era of peace rather than mere armistices, then we should play a part." In *War, Peace, and Change* Dulles had prescribed such a program. Indeed, even as he was counseling U.S. restraint given the circumstances of the spreading war, he began to participate in efforts to plan for the peace that would follow its conclusion. This participation occurred within the context of his own religious revival. Dulles did not represent a political constituency in 1939. But he recognized that he could represent a religious constituency, and he believed that the teachings of the Bible placed Christians in a unique position to understand the moral law upon which enduring global political structures must be built. He seized the opportunity presented by Christian organizations to provide him with a platform.[9]

At the International Conference of Lay Experts and Ecumenical Leaders convened in Geneva by the World Council of Churches in 1939, the delegates proposed that church groups throughout the world undertake a study of the problem of war. Toward this end, the next year the Department of International Justice and Goodwill of the Federal Council of Churches of Christ in America sponsored a National Study Conference on the Churches and the International Situation in Philadelphia, Pennsylvania. Dulles delivered the keynote address and was asked afterward to chair a Commission on the American Churches and the Peace and War Problem. By the end of the year he had emerged as the Federal

Council's principal lay spokesperson. When its Executive Committee established a 100-member Commission to Study the Bases of a Just and Durable Peace, it invited Dulles to serve as the chair.

Dulles did not want to supervise merely another study group. He accepted the position in February 1941 only after receiving the Federal Council's assurance that the commission's ultimate objective was to influence public policy. His reservations allayed, Dulles tackled his assignment with the missionary zeal and seemingly inexhaustible energy for which he would later become internationally renowned, and frequently lampooned. He drove himself and his associates relentlessly, calling meeting after meeting to discuss issue after issue. Within two years the commission had produced an impressive list of publications: articles, pamphlets, and statements of "guiding principles." On his omnipresent yellow legal pad, Dulles wrote the initial drafts of practically every one.

During the year following the Japanese attack on Pearl Harbor in December 1941 and the German and Italian declarations of war against the United States, the commission's primary purpose, its directive stipulated, was to educate Christians about the "moral, political, and economic foundations of an enduring peace" and prepare them "for assuming their appropriate responsibility for the establishment of such a peace." In addition to writing regular reports in the *Federal Council Bulletin*, the commission disseminated its publications to churches throughout the world and convened conferences of Protestant leaders to discuss both substantive issues and the churches's role in addressing them. "Intellectually," said one Methodist Bishop about a meeting held at Ohio Wesleyan University in March 1942, it was "the most distinguished American church gathering I have seen in 50 years."[10]

Dulles sought a wider audience, and his objective was more ambitious than achieving intellectual distinction. In the aftermath of the Allied invasion of North Africa, Roosevelt's meeting with British Prime Minister Winston Churchill at Casablanca, and the Soviet defeat of the Germans at Stalingrad, he turned his attention to policymakers. At Dulles's initiative and under his guidance, in early 1943 the commission (read Dulles) formulated a "Statement of Political Propositions" derived from its previous articulation of "ethical principles upon which world order must be based." Dulles sent it to the Executive Council of the Federal Council with a cover letter that explained, "In the statement we describe six 'pillars of peace' that are needed to support a just and durable world order and to the establishment of which this nation ought now to be committed." Henceforth the statement would be known as the "Six Pillars of Peace." The Executive Committee adopted it on March 16.[11]

Intended to stimulate "thinking and action along realistic lines," the "Six Pillars" was a synthesis of theology and political philosophy. As such, it reflected Dulles's personal ideology and conviction that "Christians should, as citizens, seek to translate their beliefs into realities." The document's underlying premise was that "disregard for moral law brings affliction," and "we must find a way to bring into ordered harmony the interdependent life of the nations." Its underlying purpose was to outline "six areas within which national interdependence is demonstrated, and where, accordingly, international collaboration needs to be organized." These areas, the "pillars" necessary to support a just and durable peace, encapsulated the essence of Dulles's *War, Peace, and Change.*[12]

To prevent future wars, the "Six Pillars" began, the Grand Alliance must not only endure following the Axis powers defeat, but it also must rapidly be expanded to envelop both neutrals and enemies and be institutionalized by establishing a world organization. This organization would promote and, to the extent possible, supervise the remaining pillars. These included multilateral economic agreements based on liberal trade principles; flexible treaty structures that could accommodate changing conditions; guarantees for self-determination of subject peoples; provisions for controlling arms and military establishments; and recognition of the right of all people to religious and intellectual freedom.

The parallels between the "Six Pillars" and the Fourteen Points are obvious, and, like Wilson, Dulles viewed the establishment of a world organization as the linchpin. It would provide the political mechanism for galvanizing and implementing international cooperation. The United States had a special responsibility to lead, because it had refused membership in the League of Nations and because it was a Christian nation. Notwithstanding the Federal Council's wide distribution of the "Six Pillars," and the favorable press it received in the United States and abroad, Dulles arranged for an audience with President Roosevelt. Ignoring his doctor's orders that he remain in bed for a severe attack of phlebitis, he drove from New York to Washington. "Splendid," was Roosevelt's assessment of the document, adding that he wanted "to make some public reference" to it "at some near future date." For the time being, however, the president preferred that the conversation remain private.[13]

No doubt, Roosevelt wanted to avoid Wilson's mistake by carefully cultivating public and congressional opinion before going on record as favoring U.S. sponsorship of another international organization. Further, he did not want to commit himself to any postwar design that might complicate his forthcoming meeting at Teheran with Churchill and, for the first time, Soviet premier Joseph Stalin. Still, Dulles had hoped for an immediate presidential endorsement of the "Six Pillars" and interpreted Roosevelt's caution as a failure of leadership. "It is perfectly clear to me that the present Administration," he fumed, "does not possess the competence to deal with the problem of bringing this war to an acceptable end and making quick and orderly transition to some better post-war order. . . . There is complete chaos and confusion, conflict of authority and lack of decision."[14]

Dulles was prone to hyperbole, and at Teheran Roosevelt did champion the establishment of a postwar organization of united nations. Dulles remained dissatisfied nonetheless. Roosevelt preferred the structure of the new organization to reflect the primary authority of "Four Policemen," which to Dulles suggested too much emphasis on traditional power politics and too little appreciation of the need for a new internationalism. By the time concrete planning for the United Nations began at Dumbarton Oaks in August 1944, Dulles was deeply engaged in campaigning for a different president.

Despite his grandfather's prominent position in the Republican Party, politics had never been a high priority for Dulles. What is more, because of his Wilsonian convictions he had not been adverse to voting Democratic. But Dulles became more partisan as the 1944 election approached. He wanted a president who would share his beliefs and who would welcome his advice. Thomas E. Dewey met both criteria.

In 1937, following Dewey's success as special prosecutor during the investigation of organized crime in New York, Dulles had invited Dewey to become head of Sullivan & Cromwell's litigation department. Dewey instead ran for the office of New York governor. He lost, but was convinced by his strong showing that he had a bright future in national politics. He assembled a corps of "elder statesmen" to provide him with direction. Dulles, although just turned fifty, was among them. Experienced only in local politics,

Dewey adopted Dulles's internationalist views. In return, he paved the way for Dulles's rise to political influence.

Dewey's triumph in New York's 1942 gubernatorial race catapulted him to the forefront of Republicans vying to be the party's standard-bearer in 1944. Dulles perceived the advice he gave Dewey and speeches he wrote for him as integral to promoting the "Six Pillars of Peace." It soon became apparent, however, that the GOP would never unify around such an internationalist platform. In opposition to Dewey's prospective candidacy, Midwestern nationalists and unrepentant isolationists rallied behind Ohio Senator Robert A. Taft. In early 1944 the party leaders asked Senator Arthur Vandenberg of Michigan to draft a statement on foreign policy acceptable to both wings. Dewey, by then the clear front-runner, suggested that Vandenberg solicit Dulles's counsel.

Thus began for Dulles a political relationship that at the time was second in importance only to that with Dewey. Together, he and Vandenberg fashioned a Republican position that on the one hand affirmed U.S. global "responsibility" and pledged GOP support for a "postwar cooperative government," but on the other hand emphasized that the party remain committed to "sovereign rights" and "self-government." When necessary to achieve his objectives, Dulles diluted his principles. He could live with this compromise. So could most Republicans. At the Chicago convention in June, the party approved the statement. Dewey secured the nomination on the first ballot.[15]

With Dulles supplying the ammunition, Dewey, his professed devotion to suppressing partisan sniping in the face of an alien predator notwithstanding, fired away at Roosevelt's foreign policy. He blamed the incumbent president for tragedies from Pearl Harbor to the Warsaw uprising, but he reserved his most pointed—and responsible—criticisms for what Dulles considered the most fundamental issues. Dewey unequivocally promoted the principle of a new League of Nations. He charged, however, that when representatives of Britain, France, and China joined with those from the United States at Dumbarton Oaks to plan its structure, they perverted the concept of cooperative internationalism. Dewey indicted Roosevelt for fostering the "rankest form of imperialism" by seeking to "subject the nations of the world, great and small, permanently to the coercive power of the four nations holding the conference." He also attacked Roosevelt's (the Morgenthau) plan to deindustrialize Germany. Germany must "forever be forbidden to make military weapons for use," he explained, but it must not be motivated to take "vengeance on the world twenty-five years from now."[16]

Few Americans in 1944 thought that Roosevelt's global vision was so seriously flawed. Besides, probably nothing Dewey might have said could have convinced the American people to vote a popular president out of office while a war remained to be run—and won. From the campaign's start Dewey had been realistic about his chances, and, albeit disappointed, he was encouraged by the margin of his defeat. He lost by only some 2,500,000 votes, making the election far closer than Roosevelt's three previous ones. Dewey considered his prospects for 1948 good. He intended to win the second time around, and appoint Dulles as his secretary of state.

Dulles no longer had to rely exclusively on Dewey for his political stature. He emerged from the 1944 election with a prestige within the Republican Party that he could add to his considerable base within the Protestant church. Both of these constituencies made him an attractive candidate for the Roosevelt administration's effort to co-opt GOP opposition to its internationalist initiatives by ensuring bipartisan representation. After Vandenberg lobbied vigorously for his selection, Dulles was appointed an advisor to the U.S. delegation to the April 1945 conference convened in San Francisco to write the charter of the United Nations. Dulles soon came to personify bipartisan foreign policy or, put another way, the cold war consensus. For this reason he proved indispensable to Roosevelt's successor, Harry S. Truman. During the Truman administration, Dulles served as special advisor to the secretary of state and ambassador-at-large, and he attended on behalf of the United States some ten conferences of foreign ministers and United Nations General Assemblies.

To Dulles none of these meetings held greater implications for the future than the 1945 San Francisco conference. He had repeatedly expressed his concern that the discussions at Dumbarton Oaks in 1944 suggested a misplaced nostalgia for an atavistic global order predicated on a static balance of power. Dulles hoped that something different would be born in San Francisco. For the United Nations to succeed where the League of Nations had failed, its architects had to appreciate what he had written in *War, Peace, and Change* and proselytized in the "Six Pillars of Peace."

Dulles was disappointed. The negotiations in San Francisco, whether between the lesser and greater powers or among the great powers themselves, were characterized by intense acrimony. The bifurcation of the organization between a General Assembly and a

Security Council left no doubt about the locus of authority, and the veto power vested in the Security Council's permanent members and the priority accorded regional alliances signaled that the national interests of each would remain paramount. The establishment of an Economic and Social Council and a Trusteeship Council did manifest the attention paid to domestic sources of unrest and "dynamic" urges for self-determination. Still, the system of empires remained intact.

Dulles was more than disappointed; he was frustrated. If anything, he had been in a position of less influence at San Francisco than he had been at Versailles. He would henceforth work assiduously to increase his leverage with both Republicans and Democrats. This explains in part why Dulles subsequently muted the universalist, idealist points of view associated with his writings and church activities. His increasingly more strident nationalism was calculated to appeal to a U.S. political culture inherently resistant to his earlier admonition that state leaders refrain from indicting others as morally inferior.

This admonition indicates the other part of the explanation for Dulles's shift to a more nationalist stance after the San Francisco conference. His abstract professions to the contrary, Dulles was immersed in America's political culture. Like Wilson, he never considered his prescriptions for a more "just" global system to be discordant with the most effective possible defense and promotion of U.S. interests. What is more, he personally attributed others' rejection of these prescriptions to their moral inferiority. Only the United States could save the world from itself. The behavior of the British and French after 1939 signified that they remained unchastened. The behavior of the Soviet Union after 1945 signified that it never could be.

Since serving as the Russian Bureau's secretary-treasurer in 1918, Dulles had displayed remarkably little interest in the Soviet Union until its sudden emergence as America's wartime ally. Once it did, he was favorably impressed. "The war and Russia's performance in it," Dulles commented shortly after the Battle of Stalingrad, "have somewhat allayed the very strong anti-Soviet feeling which existed up until 1940." By the time the "Big Three" finally convened at Teheran, his perspective had become even more positive. "Russia's success against Germany has demonstrated in a way that none could question that there must have been very solid accomplishment under the U.S.S.R.," he wrote.[17]

Consequently, Americans have "come to a new understanding of Russia," Dulles advised Dewey during the 1944 campaign. The "devoted and sacrificial and immensely successful effort of the Russian people shows values to which we had been blind." This is not to say that Dulles regarded Bolshevik values as any less repugnant than he did when Lenin seized power in 1917. He identified the Soviet government with "tyranny, ruthlessness, atheism, denial of individual freedoms, etc.," but he located a silver lining in the Kremlin's pursuit of global power and influence. Echoing his favorite theme, Dulles explained that the Soviet Union was ruled by "dynamic" leaders who possessed "the cardinal virtue of being creative." The challenge they posed to "Anglo-Saxons" could "be a stimulating thing for the whole world. It could lift us up out of the apathy into which we have fallen in recent years and restore our sense of mission in the world."[18]

Dulles's encounters with the Soviets rapidly eroded his wartime optimism. He was particularly chagrined when Foreign Minister V. M. Molotov at first appeared disinclined to attend the San Francisco conference personally, and after he decided to participate, vigorously argued that the United Nations (UN) Charter should extend to permanent members of the Security Council the authority to veto subjects for discussion as well as decisions. Dulles interpreted this demeanor, which immediately followed Stalin's rejection of Western appeals to broaden the composition of the Polish government, as indicating not only Soviet disinterest in an effective international organization but, more ominously, its determination to ride herd over a bloc of nations and cordon them off from the rest of the world.

As his hopes for Moscow's international cooperation fell, Dulles's official standing and responsibilities rose. The Truman administration's conviction that the deteriorating world environment demanded U.S. global activism drove it to seek greater bipartisan support for its foreign policies. Dulles was well suited for this purpose. He represented the views of Dewey and Vandenberg while retaining the confidence of Taft. He had the respect of the Council on Foreign Relations and the Federal Council of Churches. Accordingly, after San Francisco, Dulles for the first time in his life represented the United States at an international conference in more than an advisory capacity. In January 1946, when the United Nations General Assembly held its initial formal session in London, Dulles was a member of the U.S. delegation. When Secretary of

State James Byrnes attended the Council of Foreign Ministers meetings in London in the fall of 1945 and in Paris in the spring of 1946, he took Dulles with him. These firsthand experiences with the Soviets reinforced Dulles's increasingly severe estimate of the threat they posed to peace and security.

Dulles remained, however, less alarmist than many Americans at this time. Certainly, Soviet behavior confirmed that Bolshevism was anathema to both the political and religious principles on which he believed world order must be built. This more than offset any salutary consequences that might arise from their "dynamism." Yet Dulles saw no need to overreact. After 1945 he began to study Soviet dynamics with the same intensity that he had studied global dynamics after World War I. He pored over *Pravda* and read and reread what he called the Kremlin's "bible," Stalin's *Problems of Leninism*. (As secretary of state he would keep a copy alongside the Bible on his desk.) From what he learned and from what he inferred after meeting with the Soviets and observing their conduct in Eastern Europe and elsewhere, Dulles was confident that he understood "why the Russian bear ticks the way he does."[19]

As had become his standard practice, Dulles clarified his thinking by putting it into words. He returned from the Paris conference of the Council of Foreign Ministers in February 1946. In June, *Life* magazine published his "Thoughts on Soviet Foreign Policy and What to Do About it" as a two-part series. The Kremlin's hostility to the West, Dulles began, was ideologically motivated. Its leaders perceived freedom as a threat to communism, and thus were guided by the axiom that the security of the Soviet state required "eradicating the non-Soviet type of society which now dangerously divides the one world into incompatible halves." This could only lead to conflict between the halves. History and geography would determine the conflict's flashpoints and character, but it would be without boundaries.

Thus "it would be foolish to rest our hope of peace on any genuine reconciliation of our faith with that now held by the Soviet leadership," Dulles cautioned. It would be even more foolish to assume that war was inevitable and act on that assumption. In fact, while Dulles described in great detail the nature and extent of the threat emanating from Moscow, he devoted equal effort to highlighting the Soviet Union's weaknesses. Its concentrated bureaucracy, obsessive secrecy, and bankrupt message would frustrate the Kremlin's implementation of programs designed to extend its influence beyond easy reach. Its success in much of the world (which

Dulles categorized as the "Outer Zone") would be intrinsically limited and could be circumscribed further by prudent Western countermeasures.

According to Dulles's geopolitical framework, there was also an "Inner Zone" (already under Moscow's direct jurisdiction) and a "Middle Zone" (territory in Eastern Europe and Asia "not yet ripe for incorporation into the U.S.S.R." but susceptible to coercion). The Soviets' dominion over even these areas was not without problems. Their need to rely on repressive instruments of control would inexorably breed discontent, disloyalty, and resistance.

Dulles predicted that such vulnerabilities would deter Soviet adventurism. Clear signs of the West's "spiritual" unity and resolute commitment to defend freedom against aggression would be an even more effective deterrent. Dulles maintained that just as the Kremlin's insecurity drove its expansionist policies, it would also curtail them. While the Soviets saw the world through the lens of Bolshevism, Dulles wrote, Stalin and his "lackeys" were "shrewd and realistic politicians" who "are not as fanatical as were their predecessors." Hence, it was logical to "expect that they will, as a matter of expediency, desist from methods which cannot succeed and which probably will provoke disaster." In Dulles's estimation, Stalin would seek to exploit any opportunity to expand Soviet influence, but he would carefully calibrate the risks and retreat whenever he encountered opposition. He was too cunning to recklessly jeopardize his World War II gains. "Self-interest" remained the "dominant human motive."[20]

There was a striking similarity between Dulles's outlook in 1946 and that of George Kennan, whose "Long Telegram" that year to the State Department and "Mr. X" article the following year in *Foreign Affairs* would contribute substantially to the evolving U.S. strategy of containment. And over the subsequent years, whether by representing the United States at international conferences and the UN, testifying to Congress, or writing for the public, Dulles supported and helped to implement the Truman administration's foreign policies and programs. He enthusiastically embraced the principles of collective security and Atlantic community, suppressing his personal belief that America's European allies were insufficiently dynamic. Dulles was especially instrumental in deflecting Republican opposition to the European Recovery (Marshall) Plan and the North Alantic Treaty Organization (NATO).

Even when Dulles resumed his role as Dewey's chief advisor on international affairs and arbiter between the Republican factions for the 1948 presidential campaign, he remained loyal, to the extent politically practicable, to Truman's initiatives. Dewey was the heavy favorite (to many pundits he was a shoo-in as late as election day), and Truman's upset victory resulted in part from the GOP foreign policy platform of "Me Tooism" that Dulles helped to craft (although the return of U.S. prosperity was also critical). As in 1944, moreover, Dulles and Dewey had to tread lightly on Truman's diplomatic record. The more specific the positions on global issues they took, the more likely would be defections from the Republican ranks.

Because Dewey lost he could not appoint Dulles secretary of state. But because Dewey was still the governor of New York, he could appoint Dulles to the state's vacancy in the U.S. Senate created by longtime incumbent Robert Wagner's resignation in 1949. It was traditional in the upper chamber that junior senators not be heard from at least for the first year, and Dulles served for less time than that. He nevertheless gained national notoriety for his impassioned speech in favor of ratifying the treaty establishing NATO, with the United States as a charter member. He received a note of gratitude as well as congratulations from Truman's newly appointed secretary of state, Dean Acheson. In early 1950, shortly after Dulles's efforts to win election to the Senate in his own right failed (and he finally resigned from Sullivan & Cromwell), Acheson designated him his special advisor with primary responsibility for negotiating an end to the occupation of Japan. By the time the Japanese Peace Treaty was signed and ratified in 1951, Dulles was officially a U.S. ambassador-at-large.

Dulles provided such unstinting support for Truman's foreign policies and programs because he believed them absolutely necessary. He became progressively more doubtful, however, that they would prove sufficient. At issue was whether he, and the administration, had not grossly underestimated the severity of the Soviet threat. Dulles revised his initial assessment of the Kremlin in the aftermath of the civil war in Greece in 1947 and the Communist coup in Czechoslovakia and blockade of Berlin in 1948. Whereas his 1946 *Life* magazine article described the Soviet leaders as "not as fanatical as were their predecessors," he now portrayed them as "fanatical people who feel sure they are right and who are prepared to go to any lengths to make the rest of the world agree with them." Moreover, because Bolsheviks lacked "moral restraints of the kind which tend to inhibit us," once they acquired atomic capabilities they could be expected to become more aggressive and more dangerous.[21]

In late 1949 the Soviets acquired an atomic capability, and in Dulles's estimate they became more dangerous. In June 1950, after many months of hesitation, Stalin consented to North Korea's invasion of the South. The assault "may mark a new phase of Bolshevik Communist aggression," Dulles warned, indicating whom he held responsible. "It may invalidate the assumption that the Soviet Union would not risk general war." To "sit by while Korea is overrun by unprovoked armed attack," he advised Truman, would encourage Soviet risk taking and could precipitate a "disastrous chain of events leading most probably to world war." In order to "paralyze the slimy, octopus-like tentacles that reach out from Moscow to suck our blood," he recommended the deployment of U.S. forces to Korea and applauded Truman's decision to do so. But he publicly criticized Truman for having allowed Stalin to think that he could get away with aggression in the first place.[22]

By 1950, Dulles was publicly criticizing much of Truman's foreign policy. His second book, *War or Peace*, published just prior to the outbreak of the Korean War (*Life* magazine ran a condensed version), was a polemic on "the inadequacy of present policies" regarding the "global whole." Dulles remained supportive of the security architecture that he had helped to erect in Europe. He argued, nevertheless, that the success of initiatives such as NATO and the Marshall Plan had bred complacency and shortsightedness. Citing the Communist victory in China and progress in Indochina as prominent examples, Dulles asserted that Stalin, his ambitions frustrated in Europe, had turned his attention to the Third World, to Asia above all. He coveted its teeming population, wealth of vital resources, and industrial potential. Stalin's shift in tactics had caught the Truman administration woefully unprepared. As a result, "there has been a very definite shift in the balance in the world, and that shift has been in favor of Soviet Communism."

The problem, as Dulles saw it, transcended Truman's limited geopolitical vision. It was rooted in his limited strategic vision—in the concept of "containment." By definition containment reflected a commitment to defending the status quo. Hence, by definition it violated Dulles's dictum that the dynamic triumph over the static. For peoples whose priority was recovery and security, in other words for Europeans, such a violation was acceptable as a pragmatic expedient. But it was not acceptable, even temporarily, to the peoples of Asia and elsewhere in the developing world, to those for whom the status quo meant colonial subjugation. Containment offered nothing dynamic, positive, or "spiritual" to satisfy the nationalist aspirations and economic grievances of subjugated peoples. This allowed the Soviets to masquerade as champions of freedom and progress to "the discontented and the idealists who want to change radically the existing order." The Kremlin perceived, in Dulles's estimate accurately, that the West's identification with the "existing order" was its "Achilles' heel—the point through which a mortal blow could be struck."[23]

In short, Dulles attributed the extraordinary success of the Communists in expanding their influence outside of Europe and the extraordinary threat they posed to the non-Communist world not to military or economic might, but to their deceptive appropriation of the rhetoric of freedom, equality, and fraternity. "United States foreign policies today represent the core of potential [anti-Soviet] unity and that core is rotten unless it is a core of moral principle," Dulles wrote Kennan in response to the latter's publication of his treatise on the need for realism in U.S. foreign policy, *American Diplomacy*. "The so-called 'containment' policy," however, "is a current example of non-moral diplomacy." As had the European democracies after World War I, the United States appeared concerned only with stability and the balance of power—with self-preservation. Also as had the European democracies after World War I, the United States appeared unconcerned with universal good and moral law.[24]

To Dulles, containment was an affront to U.S. history and its Christian heritage. The "past dynamism of our nation has genuinely stemmed from a profound popular faith in such concepts as justice and righteousness and from the sense that our nation had a mission to promote these ideals," he thundered. The future of civilization depended on the United States recapturing that dynamism and renewing that mission. It had to launch a "spiritual offensive."[25]

There can be no question that Dulles's criticisms of Truman's foreign policy represented genuine convictions born of decades of experience and reflection. But there also can be no question of their political motivation. By resurrecting the Dulles who had written *War, Peace, and Change* and the "Six Pillars of Peace," he was distancing himself from the Dulles who personified bipartisanship. Dulles was sixty-four years old in 1952. He was politically influential and publicly visible. Yet he lacked the requisite power to put his theories into practice and to satisfy his personal ambition.

Dewey's defeats in 1944 and 1948 had denied Dulles the opportunity to become secretary of state. He saw the approach of the 1952 election as his last chance, and he intended to make the most of it.

Notes

1. John Foster Dulles, *War, Peace, and Change* (New York, 1939), ix. Dulles used the phrase "cycle of recurrent violence" repeatedly in his publications and correspondence.

2. Ibid., 6–7.

3. Ibid., 112–18, 41–42, 50–51.

4. Ibid., 82–85.

5. Ibid., ix, 81–82, 144–51.

6. Ibid., 148–49.

7. Ibid., 135, 150–51, 118.

8. Dulles to William E. Borah, April 3, 1939, "Borah, William E.—1939," John Foster Dulles Papers, Princeton University, Princeton, New Jersey (hereafter cited as DP-Princeton in order to distinguish this collection from the Dulles Papers on deposit at the Dwight D. Eisenhower Library in Abilene, Kansas).

9. Ibid.

10. Quoted in Mark G. Toulouse, *The Transformation of John Foster Dulles: From Prophet of Realism to Priest of Nationalism* (Macon, GA, 1985), 58; quoted in Ronald W. Pruessen, *John Foster Dulles: The Road to Power* (New York, 1982), 195.

11. Quoted in Toulouse, *Transformation of John Foster Dulles*, 66–67.

12. Quoted in ibid., 67–68; "A Christian Message on World Order from the International Round Table of Christian Leaders," July 1943, "Church Activities—1943," DP-Princeton.

13. Memorandum of conference with the president, March 26, 1943, "Federal Council of the Churches of Christ in America—Commission to Study the Bases of a Just and Durable Peace—1943," DP-Princeton.

14. Quoted in Pruessen, *John Foster Dulles*, 227.

15. Quoted in ibid., 224–26.

16. Quoted in ibid., 227–28, 233.

17. Dulles to the Right Honorable Viscount Astor, February 18, 1943, "Astor, Waldorf—1943," DP-Princeton; Dulles to Arthur Hays Sulzberger, October 21, 1943, "Sulzberger, Arthur Hays—1943," ibid.

18. Quoted in Pruessen, *John Foster Dulles*, 270; Dulles to Henry P. Van Dusen, November 17, 1941, "Van Dusen, Henry P.—1941," DP-Princeton; Dulles to Sulzberger, October 21, 1943; Dulles to Edward C. Carter, January 22, 1947, "Nehru, Jawaharlal—1947," ibid.

19. Dulles, "What I've Learned about the Russians," *Colliers*, March 12, 1949, 25, 57; Dulles to the Right Honorable Hector McNeil, M.P., May 3, 1948, "Soviet Union and the Communist Party—1948," DP-Princeton.

20. Dulles, "Thoughts on Soviet Foreign Policy," *Life*, June 3, 1946, 112–26; and June 10, 1946, 118ff.

21. Dulles, "What I've Learned about the Russians," 25, 57; Minutes of Council of Foreign Ministers Meeting, June 6, 1947, "Council of Foreign Ministers Meetings—1947," DP-Princeton.

22. Quoted in Harry S. Truman, *Memoirs: Years of Trial and Hope* (Garden City, NY, 1956), 336; quoted in Pruessen, *John Foster Dulles*, 454; Department of State Press Release, May 29, 1951, "Soviet Union and the Communist Party—1951," DP-Princeton.

23. Dulles, *War or Peace* (New York, 1950), 2, 162–63, 74–78.

24. Dulles to Kennan, October 2, 1952, "Kennan, George F.—1952," DP-Princeton.

25. Ibid.; Dulles, "For a Spiritual Offensive: An Appeal for a Dynamic Foreign Policy under the Moral Law," *Princeton Alumni Weekly*, March 7, 1952, 11–12.

3

A Policy of Boldness

Dulles directed his broadsides against a deeply scarred president and mortally wounded presidency. In the national interest, Republicans had refrained from assailing Truman's foreign policy during the 1948 election. In the party's interest they were determined not to repeat the mistake. When the Soviets broke the U.S. atomic monopoly and the Chinese Communists breached the line of containment at the end of 1949, Republicans seized the opportunity to stake out their turf. Vituperative partisan attacks on Truman's security programs resonated through the halls of Congress. After former State Department official (and New Dealer) Alger Hiss's conviction for perjury in January 1950, the attacks resonated throughout the nation. "I have here in my hand," declared Wisconsin's Senator Joseph McCarthy the next month to the Ohio County Women's Republican Club in Wheeling, West Virginia, "a list of [205] names [of members of the Communist Party] known to the Secretary of State and who nevertheless are still working and shaping the policy of the State Department."[1]

It did not matter that McCarthy had no such list. Nor did it matter that he changed his numbers of known Communists to eighty-one, then fifty-seven, and ended up by saying simply that there were a lot of them. What mattered was that McCarthy fueled Americans' anxiety that Truman could not be entrusted with safeguarding the nation's security, and in fact, that under his stewardship the United States was losing the cold war.

The Democratic leadership immediately launched a Senate investigation aimed at discrediting McCarthy, and Truman publicly called him "the greatest asset that the Kremlin has." This counterattack did nothing to mitigate McCarthy's reckless crusade, but it did galvanize Republican support for it—and him. Moreover, by sanctioning development of the hydrogen bomb and instructing his chief advisors to reassess defense policy from top to bottom, the president all but conceded that his previous programs were inadequate. Estimating that the United States and its allies were at grave risk, NSC 68, the new statement of national security policy, concluded that "It is imperative that [the] present trend be reversed. . . . This will be costly."[2]

NSC 68 presented fiscally conservative Republicans with another inviting target. What is more, even before Truman approved it in September 1950, the "present trend" had taken a marked turn for the worse. The outbreak of the Korean War in June at Communist North Korea's initiative but with Stalin's (albeit reluctant) approval and complicity seemed to confirm NSC 68's most ominous predictions—and those of Republican critics. Truman's decisive response was welcomed. When the president rapidly committed U.S. forces under General Douglas MacArthur, most Americans cheered. After MacArthur's amphibious landing at Inchon decimated the North Korean invaders, their cheers grew louder, drowning out Republican complaints that Truman had usurped congressional authority to declare war in deploying U.S. troops as part of a UN "police action." Truman then secured UN permission for MacArthur to press north of the 38th parallel and expel the North Koreans from the country. By rolling back communism to the China border, the president would prove his determination to go beyond containment.

To an extent Truman's militancy offset McCarthy's mischief. In the November 1950 elections Republican gains were smaller than usual for the opposition party in an off year. But a few weeks later hundreds of thousands of Communist Chinese "volunteers" stormed across the Yalu River into North Korea, sending MacArthur's forces—and the administration—into a free-fall retreat. Even as Truman rejected the demands of Republicans that he dismiss Secretary of State Acheson, he poured salt on their wounds by announcing his intention to contribute U.S. troops to NATO's embryonic defense force. The president was again sacrificing Asia to Europe, Republicans raged. He also was again running roughshod over the U.S. Constitution and jeopardizing the U.S. economy to do it.

Unlike the previous year, Truman's political fortunes in 1951 did not improve with the tide of battle. As the tenor of partisan sniping degenerated to historically low levels, MacArthur's forces fought their way back up to the 38th parallel. With America's European allies expressing concern over both the war's potential to escalate and their vulnerability to Soviet aggression, Truman took steps to negotiate a truce as soon as the front stabilized. By doing so he exacerbated the frustration of an American public accustomed to achieving nothing less than a total victory, and he infuriated Douglas MacArthur. MacArthur proposed expanding the war into China even if it meant using atomic weapons. "[W]e must win," he wrote Republican House leader Joseph Martin. "There is no substitute for victory." When Martin made public this letter in April, Truman fired MacArthur for undermining his authority as commander in chief.[3]

On his return to the United States, MacArthur received a welcome more befitting a conquering hero than a cashiered general. "Our only choice is to impeach President Truman," railed McCarthy's ally, Indiana Senator William Jenner. Ultimately the GOP leadership, recognizing that Truman's action was indisputably constitutional and probably justified, dropped the idea. They orchestrated a Senate investigation of Truman's management of the war, however. The hearings failed to turn up any "smoking guns" for the Republicans to exploit. But they dragged on, as did the stalemated war and armistice talks.[4]

While war raged in Korea and on the American homefront, Dulles supervised completion of the Japanese Peace Treaty. It was a masterful feat. Full independence was restored to Japan, but on U.S. terms. Tokyo guaranteed the United States military bases on both Japan and Okinawa for ten years (renewable thereafter). It also agreed not to trade with Communist China despite Prime Minister Shigeru Yoshida's protests that Japan's geography and economy dictated that it do so. Dulles's most remarkable accomplishment was to exclude the Soviets from playing any role in Japan's future while at the same time winning support for the treaty from its World War II victims.

The time and effort Dulles put into the negotiations did not prevent him from attentively following political developments in the United States. Although he would not wish a war or a McCarthy on any president, he was acutely aware that in combination they posed a deadly threat to Truman's chances for reelection. The question was whom the Republicans would run against him and whether their choice would embrace Dulles and his internationalist agenda. Dulles wanted to be secretary of state in any GOP administration and believed he had earned that right. But his "insurance," Thomas Dewey, had taken himself out of the race. Dulles had a warm and long-standing relationship with the front-runner, Ohio Senator Robert A. Taft. "Mr. Republican's" constituency, however, was the isolationist/unilateralist wing of the party. More specifically, Taft's hostility toward collective security arrangements with Europe, including NATO and the Marshall Plan, put him at odds with Dulles's positions.

The wild card, for Dulles and the party leadership, was General Dwight D. Eisenhower. With his irresistible grin and down-home demeanor, the World War II hero was phenomenally popular throughout the United States, and as the initial commander of NATO's armed forces, he was perceived by Republican internationalists as the perfect alternative to Taft. Yet Eisenhower had squashed efforts to draft him to run for president in 1948, and it was uncertain that he would change his mind. Complicating matters further, although always a Republican, Eisenhower had conscientiously avoided identification with either party and hence was an enticing prospective candidate for both.

Intending to settle the issue prior to taking up his NATO command, Eisenhower was prepared in January 1951 to announce that "my name may not be used by anyone as a candidate for President—and if any do I will repudiate such efforts." But first he wanted assurance that, if elected, Taft would not withdraw U.S. security guarantees from Europe. He drafted a statement to this effect for Taft to sign at a private meeting at the Pentagon. Taft's refusal "aroused my fears that isolationism was stronger in the Congress than I had previously suspected," Eisenhower wrote. He scrapped the statement and his planned announcement.[5]

In the following months, Eisenhower devoted his time to organizing NATO's forces. Republican internationalists, led by Dewey and Massachusetts Senator Henry Cabot Lodge, Jr., devoted theirs to persuading Eisenhower to seek the Republican nomination. They argued that with Truman's approval rating hovering at around 23 percent (below that of any sitting president before—or since), only Eisenhower stood in the way of Taft's election and the danger his administration posed for the security of the United States and the free world. Eisenhower's resistance decreased as Taft's momentum increased. In January 1952 he allowed his name to be entered in the New Hampshire primary. He defeated Taft handily. At the end of March, Truman declared that he would not stand for reelection. His compunction about running against his commander in chief now removed, Eisenhower returned to the United States to campaign for the presidency.

Concurrently, Dulles resigned his State Department position in order to participate in the election. He was inclined to support Eisenhower but wary of committing himself. If he did so prematurely and Taft secured the nomination, Dulles would all but have eliminated himself from consideration for secretary of state. He was reluctant to entrust his future irrevocably to Eisenhower because at the time they were only what could charitably be called casual acquaintances. Eisenhower was scheduled to arrive back in the United States in June. To get a better sense of where he stood with the general, Dulles arranged a May meeting in Paris.

In advance of the meeting, Dulles sent Eisenhower a lengthy memorandum on foreign policy. The memorandum was in fact an early draft of what would become one of the most notorious of Dulles's extensive writings. Published in May by *Life* magazine under the title "A Policy of Boldness," the article represented the Republican party's challenge to Truman's policy of containment. When sent to Eisenhower in April, however, it represented Dulles's challenge. Hoping to emerge from their impending meeting as the candidate's clear choice for secretary of state, Dulles wanted to determine the extent to which Eisenhower shared his views and, if there were areas of disagreement, have ample opportunity for revision.

Fundamentally, Dulles remained true to the concepts he had espoused in *War or Peace,* but he layered on top of them notions that he had developed since the outbreak of the Korean War. The perilous situation confronting the United States, Dulles wrote, underscored that Truman's programs, as useful as many were, had proven inadequate. Because they were reactive, in Dulles's word "negative," they generated anxiety among America's allies and the nonaligned nations, who feared that the United States would come to their defense only after an emergency had arisen, by which time it might be too late. For this same reason, Truman's cautious posture also increased the likelihood that the Soviets might calculate that the United States would not respond to an emergency at all.

Exacerbating these problems, Dulles continued, was the costliness of Truman's scattershot approach. The maintenance of conventional forces at the level needed to put out all the brushfires that the containment policy would surely encourage the Communists to ignite would produce severe budget deficits and inflation, jeopardizing the U.S. economy. The government would be left with no choice but to impose wage and price controls and otherwise regiment society, thereby undermining the very freedoms that the United States was waging the cold war to preserve.

Dulles proposed an alternative strategy that, he confidently predicted, would be more effective, cost efficient, and coherent. The first step was to stop allowing the Soviets to set the parameters of the military confrontation. The U.S. and allied forces were overextended and invariably on the defensive because Moscow chose when, where, and how to do battle. In addition, by relying on proxies to do their fighting for them, the Soviets could husband their resources while remaining out of harm's way. The antidote, Dulles wrote, was to exploit more fully that element of U.S. military strength that the Kremlin feared most: nuclear supremacy. "There is one solution and only one: that is for the free world to develop the will and organize the means to retaliate instantly against open aggression by Red Armies, so that, if it occurred anywhere, we would strike back where it hurts, by means of our choosing." The best way to combat aggression was to deter it from beginning. In Dulles's view, a doctrine of instant retaliation, or what later became known as massive retaliation, was the ultimate deterrent.

If making better use of America's nuclear superiority was vital to effective containment, U.S. intellectual and spiritual superiority was vital to moving beyond this ineffective strategy. As he had stressed frequently in his writings, Dulles argued that containment was a static concept that violated the laws of nature and was alien to the U.S. experience. The United States had grown from its feeble origins to its present greatness because it had confidently and vigorously pursued its destiny and mission. Dulles attributed the Communist successes primarily to the Kremlin's disingenous claims to a "higher" destiny and mission.

Therefore, the United States had to reaffirm its moral ascendency. It had to recapture the spirit of the American Revolution and project worldwide its political, social, and economic ideals. Specifically, the United States should replace containment with the pledge to bring about "genuine independence in the nations of Europe and Asia now dominated by Moscow." Like Wilson's principle of self-determination, Dulles intended this concept of "liberation" to appeal to humanity's yearning for freedom. Its positive message would energize "captive peoples" and prove "more explosive than dynamite." Forced to address the resultant unrest and instability, the Soviets would be put on the defensive far beyond what would be possible by military means alone. Because the dynamic always triumphed over the static, their efforts would be futile.[6]

Eisenhower responded to Dulles's memorandum by writing that he was "deeply impressed" with "the directness and simplicity of your approach to such complex problems." He suggested, however, that the approach was a bit too simplistic. Eisenhower needed more time to digest the implications of the liberation concept, especially how it could be implemented without running an unacceptably high risk of provoking a Soviet military response. But the five-star general replied that after years of "pondering" he, too, had concluded that the United States should rely more heavily on its nuclear capability to deter Communist aggression. Nevertheless, Eisenhower fretted that because Taft also advocated greater reliance on nuclear weapons, the U.S. public and its allies might interpret the doctrine of "massive retaliation" as a code word for the unilateral or even "Fortress America" strategy, identified with the Republican right wing, in which the United States would retreat behind a nuclear shield. Eisenhower also expressed severe reservations about the usefulness of the doctrine to defend against minor incursions or internal subversion in remote areas. "What should we do," he asked Dulles, against "Soviet *political* aggression." As opposed to, for example, a Soviet attack on Berlin, Eisenhower commented, in a case such as Czechoslovakia (where a Communist coup occurred in 1948) "the theory of 'retaliation' falls down."[7]

"You put your finger on a weak point in my presentation," Dulles wrote back, promising to "cover it in a revision." But he did so only to the extent of adding that all "free nations should have the ability to resist attack from within," and declaring that developing the capability and will to retaliate instantly "does not mean that old ways of defending the peace should be abandoned." For the time being Dulles did not think more revision was necessary or advisable. As was apparent from their correspondence and reinforced when when they met in Paris on May 3, Eisenhower in principle sympathized with Dulles's ideas. Dulles did not want to burn any bridges between himself and Taft should the senator win the nomination. In addition, should Eisenhower win, which was more likely and Dulles's preference, his election required Taft's support.[8]

Dulles put off publicly announcing his preference for either candidate after returning to the United States. He told both that just as he had previously personified bipartisanship, he now sought to personify Republican unity. In turn, the candidates agreed to

assign Dulles the responsibility of crafting a foreign policy platform on which either could run.

Dulles (who of course was familiar with this role) had anticipated the assignment when writing "A Policy of Boldness," and
the platform he presented to the GOP leadership borrowed liber-
ally from it. The Democrats' "negative, futile, and immoral" policy
of containment "abandons countless human beings to a despotic
and godless terrorism," the platform charged. In order to "set up
strains and stresses within the captive world which will make the
rulers impotent to continue in their monstrous ways and mark the
beginning of the end," a Republican administration would "revive
the contagious, liberating influences which are inherent in freedom." Toward this end it would "repudiate all commitments contained in secret understandings such as those of Yalta which aid
Communist enslavement." The "twenty-year record of Democratic
stewardship" was a history of "tragic blunders."[9]

The platform included planks on collective security and
America's leadership of the free world, but it soft-pedaled U.S. responsibilities to NATO, the UN, and Europe's recovery. At
Eisenhower's insistence Dulles deleted the words "retaliatory striking power" from his initial draft. What remained was clear enough.
"[D]efense against sudden attack requires the quickest possible
development of appropriate and completely-adequate air power
and the simultaneous readiness of coordinated air, land, and sea
forces, with all necessary installations, bases, supplies and munitions, including atomic energy weapons in abundance." Eisenhower
later expressed his discomfort with what he called the platform's
bellicose, "'prosecuting-attorney' style." At the time he recognized
its political utility, and after winning the nomination on the first
ballot, ran using the Dulles creation. "I know something of the solemn responsibility of leading a crusade," Eisenhower told the delegates who attended the acrimonious GOP convention. "I accept
your summons. I will lead this crusade."[10]

Leading the crusade, however, presented Eisenhower with a
complex dilemma. The platform Dulles cobbled together merely
papered over the profound differences that distinguished Eisenhower and Dulles's views on foreign and defense policy from those
of Taft and his acolytes. The challenge for Eisenhower throughout
the campaign, therefore, was to generate and maintain the allegiance of the Taft wing of his party without repudiating the fundamental tenets of internationalism and collective security that he
and Dulles had helped to develop and execute and still advocated.

Eisenhower's "hidden-hand" political strategy, as a consequence, foreshadowed that of his presidency. He chose foreign policy as the subject of the speech that formally launched his candidacy on September 4, but he left it to others to make the most strident attacks on his opponent, Adlai E. Stevenson, and on the Democratic record. It was Eisenhower's running mate, Richard M. Nixon, who saddled Stevenson, an avid cold warrior, with the label "Adlai the Appeaser" and described the wealthy and witty governor of Illinois as a graduate of "Dean Acheson's Cowardly College of Communist Containment." It was McCarthy who indicted George Marshall, who had served in Truman's cabinet first as secretary of state and then as secretary of defense, for participating in "a conspiracy so immense and an infamy so black as to dwarf any previous venture in the history of man." To Dulles (who rarely traveled with Eisenhower) fell primary responsibility for expounding on the theme of liberation. Dulles shouldered this responsibility with such ardor that Eisenhower censured his truculence. Following one Dulles press conference, Eisenhower reprimanded the Republican foreign policy spokesman for omitting from his diatribe advocating liberation the qualifier, "by all peaceful means."[11]

Eisenhower's admonishment of Dulles was the exception. As a rule he tolerated such inflammatory rhetoric as the price required to woo "captive" ethnic minorities and the Republican Old Guard. What is more, Nixon, McCarthy, and above all Dulles became lightning rods for the domestic and international criticism this rhetoric engendered. Eisenhower was thus able to take the political high road.

In his speeches Eisenhower delicately sidestepped issues that could disrupt the fragile harmony among the Republican factions. For example, by allowing his record as Supreme Commander, Allied Forces in Europe (SACEUR) to speak for itself, he successfully skirted the GOP's internecine feud over America's contribution to NATO. He also refrained from attacking the premises of the containment policy, with which he essentially concurred, and instead concentrated his criticisms on how it had been managed. He did not denounce decisions made during the Korean War but the bungling that led to it. The fundamental problem with America's defense posture, he asserted, was that the cost produced by incoherent and erratic planning far exceeded what a sound economy could bear. Eisenhower divulged little of his own thinking about nuclear weapons, but he promised to better integrate strategy and advances in U.S. technology and capabilities and take a "long haul" approach to policymaking. He would "plan for the future on something more solid than yesterday's headlines."[12]

In short, Eisenhower personally did not pledge to replace containment with liberation or to threaten the Soviets with massive retaliation. His pledge was less dramatic but probably more effective: to safeguard U.S. security by applying the same leadership skills and management techniques that had proven so successful in his World War II and NATO commands. To navigate the perilous international waters, "we must have a firm hand at the tiller to sail the ship along a consistent course," he said. "If the experience of 40 years in the military service of my country can help bring security with solvency to my fellow citizens, I am yours to command."[13]

An anxious U.S. electorate fervently responded to the offer. After one of the few presidential campaigns in U.S. history dominated by foreign policy, on November 4, 1952, Eisenhower defeated Stevenson by some six and one-half million votes. He even carried some states in the previously solid Democratic South. The overwhelming margin of victory, however, reflected Eisenhower's popularity and the public's confidence in him, not Dulles's biting criticisms of containment. As pollster Louis Harris noted, voters saw in Eisenhower "a safety valve for [their] emotions." Furthermore, Eisenhower distanced himself from the Republican platform that Dulles wrote nearly as much as he distanced himself from the Democratic platform, and his coattails were commensurately short. The Republicans retained majorities in both houses of Congress, but by razor-thin margins in each. (They owed their majority in the Senate to the decision of Oregon's Wayne Morse, elected as an independent, to line up with the GOP for the purpose of organizing the upper chamber's committees and chairs.) Because he was assured of resistance from the Republican Old Guard, Eisenhower required cooperation from the other side of the aisle to pursue his internationalist agenda.[14]

Eisenhower's need for Democratic support almost cost Dulles his appointment as secretary of state. The president-elect had the highest regard for Dulles's intellect and experience, but he worried about his propensity for hyperbole and oversimplification. Eisenhower noted in his private diary that Dulles "seems to have a curious lack of understanding as to how his words and manner may affect another personality." That effect, the campaign demonstrated, was often negative. Many Europeans came to see Dulles as a fire-and-brimstone anti-Communist fanatic who would risk the nuclear annihilation of the continent in an effort to blow a hole in the Iron Curtain. British Foreign Minister Anthony Eden went so far as to explicitly express his hope to Eisenhower that he would not appoint Dulles. Eisenhower was sure that he could allay the concerns of allied leaders by building on his long-established relationship with them. He was not certain that he could assuage the Democrats' resentment over what they considered Dulles's traitorous disavowal of his previous bipartisanship. If they took revenge by responding in kind to Eisenhower's overtures, his foreign policies would be dead in the water.[15]

In the end, after discussing the matter with his political advisors, Eisenhower determined that the assets Dulles would bring to the administration outweighed the liabilities. Summoning Dulles on November 20 to his transition headquarters at New York City's Hotel Commodore, Eisenhower offered him the post of secretary of state. Dulles was overjoyed; before leaving the room he drafted in longhand his letter of acceptance. The president-elect's "desire for our nation is a just and durable peace," wrote Dulles, explicitly connecting his future to his past. "I shall gladly serve in that cause."[16]

Dulles's service began immediately. In the late stages of the campaign Eisenhower had electrified the public by announcing that he would "go to Korea." Realistically, he doubted that by doing so he would gain better information or insight. But opportunistically, he saw the trip as an occasion to instill an ethic of teamwork among his advisors and jumpstart their discussion of the paramount issues his administration would confront. Within weeks of his election he made his top-level cabinet appointments. Chief among them were George Humphrey (Treasury), Joseph Dodge (Budget), Charles Wilson (Defense), and, of course, John Foster Dulles (State).

Eisenhower arrived in South Korea on December 2. For three days he received detailed briefings and toured the countryside. Dulles and the others flew to Wake Island, where they joined Eisenhower for a return voyage aboard the cruiser *Helena*. Initial discussions concentrated on budgetary questions and the State of the Union address. Eisenhower shifted the focus to matters of national security after Joint Chiefs of Staff (JCS) Chairman General Omar Bradley and Admiral Arthur Radford, who would soon succeed Bradley, joined the party.

Dulles strongly believed that Truman had ceded too much responsibility for the conduct of U.S. international affairs to the

Pentagon. As secretary of state, he should be the president's un-challenged chief foreign policy advisor. It immediately became apparent this was Eisenhower's expectation as well. He allowed Dulles to frame the problems for future debate and decision through domination of the *Helena* talks from beginning to end.

Dulles did not mince words. The Soviet aim, he emphasized, was to "extend our resources & our patience and divide us inter-nally by mounting a series of local actions around the world at times and places of their choosing." The Truman admininstration had responded "like a boxer who abides by the Marquis of Queensberry rules." The Eisenhower administration must take off the gloves. "The way to stop him [the Soviets] is to be ready and able to beat him at his own game." Dulles acknowledged that his recommen-dation entailed "increased risks" but predicted that if the United States refused to accept them and persisted along its present course "disaster is almost a *certainty*."[17]

Eisenhower knew that it was premature to debate policy, and he listened quietly as Dulles fulminated. His intention was to sat-isfy himself that Dulles's rage was genuine, not politically moti-vated. He was convinced. No less important, judging from the reaction of his other advisors, Eisenhower was also satisfied that they would not be intimidated by the secretary of state-designate's forceful personality. Eisenhower entrusted Dulles with great power to influence. He always, however, reserved final decisions for him-self. To inform those decisions he wanted from his advisors the "fre-est and fullest kind of discussion and argumentation, even in those cases where they found it impossible to reach an agreement." Dulles's presentation and the free-for-all that followed bolstered Eisenhower's confidence he had chosen his advisors well.[18]

Until his death in May 1959, Dulles's role as Eisenhower's pre-eminent foreign policy advisor was never in question. As presi-dent and secretary of state, they cultivated a relationship based on mutual respect and trust that may well be unparalleled in twenti-eth century and perhaps in all U.S. history. In part because he un-derstood that his power rested on the president's confidence in him, but in much greater part because he had so much confidence in the president, Dulles never tried to bypass or in any other way tres-pass on Eisenhower's authority. Eisenhower always made the decisions—but always after consulting Dulles. They conferred fre-quently, in person or over the phone, and regularly exchanged tele-grams when the peripatetic Dulles was away from Washington, which was more often than any previous or subsequent U.S. secretary of state. To the extent that their busy schedules permitted, they ended the day by meeting in the Oval Office, mostly alone but sometimes joined by Central Intelligence Agency (CIA) director Allen Dulles, or one or two others. In this relaxed setting they talked about policies, plans, and developments.

Dulles provided his formal advice, however, at the weekly meetings of the National Security Council (NSC). Congress had established the NSC in 1947 to improve coordination among the departments and agencies with responsibilities for foreign and defense policy. Eisenhower attributed what he considered to be Truman's mismanagement of both to his having allowed the NSC to atrophy. As a candidate he promised to revitalize it. As president-elect he initiated a process to reform it.

The advisors Eisenhower took with him on *Helena* and the discussions he encouraged them to hold suggested the direction of his intended reforms of the NSC. He appointed Robert Cutler as his agent. Cutler, a Boston banker who had served in the Pentagon and on Truman's NSC senior staff, carried the title of White House special assistant for national security affairs, but he was not to be Dulles's competitor. Cutler's role was custodial, not advisory. He oversaw the NSC's reorganization and then managed its operations.

Cutler set to work even before the inauguration, and in March 1953 Eisenhower approved his recommendations. In keeping with the administration's "Great Equation"—the balance between requisite military strength and economic vitality—the secretary of the treasury and budget bureau director were mandated, along with the NSC's statutory members (the president, vice president, secretaries of state and defense, and director of the Mutual Security Agency—renamed the Foreign Operations Agency in August 1953), to attend meetings regularly. So, too, were the CIA director, who would begin each meeting with a briefing on the most recently available intelligence, and the chairman of the JCS. Other officials, such as the chiefs of staff, service secretaries, chairman of the Atomic Energy Commission, and secretary of commerce were asked to attend depending on the agenda.

The objective of expanding attendance at NSC meetings was to improve the level of expertise, coordination, and "esprit de corps." To promote the informed and vigorous discussions that Eisenhower demanded, Cutler established an NSC Planning Board. Each Board member was the senior planning official for his department or agency. Thus, he was guaranteed an open door to his chief and the entire bureaucracy. Like the NSC itself, the Planning Board also had access to the most current national intelligence estimates and other data. It met twice or more a week to analyze trends, identify problems, consider proposed solutions, and confront—explicitly— questions of means and ends. From these deliberations it produced drafts of policy statements. These drafts (which included an appended budget) incorporated disputes between the members (and by extension the departments or agencies they represented) that could not be resolved. These "splits" were set in columns side by side and worded as sharply and precisely as possible. Cutler then scheduled the drafts for discussion at the NSC meeting and circulated them beforehand.

The drafts structured and informed the NSC debates. The members had in advance of the meeting a document that identified the core questions attendant to any particular policy, an estimated price tag, the preferences of each department, and their differences. Members were therefore prepared to debate, and they did so, often heatedly and over the course of several weeks. During the interim the Planning Board incrementally revised the papers to reflect the ongoing deliberations. Eisenhower never approved a policy statement at a Council meeting. He did so only afterward, following informal discussions with Dulles, the secretary of defense, and a few other officials directly concerned with the issue. Rarely was everyone satisfied. Nevertheless, the process by which policy statements were drafted, debated, and redrafted prior to Eisenower's approving them ensured that each NSC member (and his key subordinates) was intimately familiar with the substance and rationale and had the chance to argue his case.

Dulles attentively, even jealously, guarded his preeminence among Eisenhower's security advisors. He nonetheless enthusiastically embraced the NSC system. Befitting his position, at each meeting he sat, doodling incessantly and appearing deeply contemplative, by Eisenhower's right side at a table just large enough to hold the regular NSC members and special attendees. After Dulles's brother Allen briefed the Council on current intelligence, Cutler ticked off the items on the agenda. Typically, the president asked Dulles to make the first comment. He held forth, arguing with the skill and tenacity of a trained lawyer and experienced propagandist. Dulles was not a dynamic orator, but he was an intense one. He thrived on counterarguments, seizing on them as opportunities to sharpen his own. Many more times than not, Dulles carried the day.

Dulles did not rely solely on the power of his convictions and the force of his personality, nor for that matter on preexisting beliefs derived from his decades of experience and study. Certainly, as had long been evident, Dulles had great confidence in his expertise and judgments. By the time he became secretary of state he had formed many opinions and was highly resistant to changing them. Yet the popular perception in the 1950s that Dulles behaved like the Lone Ranger and "carried the State Department in his hat" was a misperception. Dulles was so convincing at NSC meetings in large part because he was so well prepared. He was well prepared not only because he had meticulously examined the issues and draft policy statements, but also because he had assiduously solicited advice and information from his subordinates.

Prior to every NSC meeting Dulles received a memorandum explaining the items on the agenda from his representative on the NSC Planning Board, the equally argumentative Harvard Law School professor Robert Bowie for most of Dulles's tenure, who also directed the State Department's Policy Planning Staff. Then, along with the relevant assistant secretaries and department experts, they met to dissect the papers scheduled for NSC discussion. Dulles encouraged ideas that differed from his own, and his epic debates with Bowie became legendary inside the State Department, although unknown outside of it. He also canvassed the views of a wide range of department officials at meetings virtually every morning, and not infrequently summoned some of them to his house on weekends.

As a consequence, while the NSC debates forced Dulles to think on his feet, he never had to speak off the top of his head. He was able to anticipate most of the resistance he encountered and effectively rebut it. Dulles's most powerful trump card, however, and the primary source of his power, was the support of Eisenhower. Their fundamental agreement became apparent even before the NSC system was fully functioning.

Before formulating his own cold war strategy, Eisenhower planned to reassess current estimates of the Communist threat; the soundness of existing policies, programs, and plans; and the current allocation of U.S. human, financial, and material resources. In the best of all possible worlds, he would have directed his NSC apparatus to analyze, discuss, and provide advice on these intimately related questions simultaneously. The U.S. political system, however, is not the best of all possible worlds. It required the new president to present his alternative to the fiscal year 1954 budget that had already been submitted by Truman before the start of the new fiscal year on July 1, 1953.

This timeline confronted Eisenhower with a formidable challenge. Truman had nearly quadrupled the defense budget since the outbreak of the Korean War. The estimate he submitted in January 1953 for fiscal year 1954 anticipated spending more than $45 billion on the military and over $41 billion in new obligational authority. In addition, according to a top-level reexamination of security programs completed just as Truman was leaving office (NSC 141), these figures were dangerously low. Eisenhower strenuously disagreed. He was convinced that defense spending could be decreased *and* that security could be increased.

The pressure of the budgetary process necessitated that the administration decide how to reduce Truman's estimates before it had the opportunity to review systematically existing foreign policy and strategy. Eisenhower directed that work begin less than a month after his inauguration, prior to the institutionalization of Cutler's reforms for the NSC. The lines of battle were rapidly drawn. On the one side, the president's military experts, the JCS in particular, refused to budge from their position that current levels of defense spending were inadequate. Regardless of how and how soon peace was restored in Korea, the growth of Soviet power and the threat it posed to the United States and its allies demanded "continuous and progressive improvements in our military forces," both conventional and nuclear. As JCS chairman General Omar Bradley put it, the "build-up of the military strength of the United States is the keystone and, indeed, the very life blood" of the free world's strategy "to frustrate the Kremlin design of a world dominated by its will."[19]

On the other side, Secretary of the Treasury George Humphrey and Budget Director Joseph Dodge were equally rigid. Their foremost priority was to balance the general budget by the next fiscal year. Because raising taxes was out of the question, they proposed to establish a ceiling on overall spending. The military would have to make do with "what it could buy" from its predetermined share. If the Pentagon wanted more funding for nuclear weapons and delivery systems, for example, it would have to request less for conventional forces. Citing Dulles's "massive retaliation" concept as justification, they maintained that this was an acceptable price to pay for solvency.[20]

Dulles, however, did not endorse their recommendation. In fact, in the context of the war of words and memoranda waged between the extremist positions, the secretary of state emerged as the voice of reason and moderation. The administration could not formulate policy and strategy, he argued, until it had "brought together and looked at together" the interdependent "pieces of the puzzle"— military, political, and financial. Before doing so, to impose a ceiling on defense spending would be recklessly premature. At a minimum, radical cuts must be accompanied by careful diplomacy lest they be perceived overseas as portending a U.S. return to isolationism. It was equally premature for the JCS summarily to reject the possibility of meaningful reductions in the military budget. Dulles believed that greater reliance on nuclear weapons could produce significant savings, and that more could be achieved simply by cutting down on overhead and waste and by purchasing expensive material in gradual increments.[21]

Dulles's remarks, which extended over several meetings of the NSC, made sense to the majority of the members. Most important, they made sense to Eisenhower. Time and again the president's and the secretary of state's comments were mutually reinforcing, until by the beginning of April the correspondence of their outlooks was evident to everyone. The Planning Board, now operational, produced a policy statement (NSC 149/2) that reflected that correspondence. It calculated that even without a settlement of the Korean War, several billion dollars could be pared immediately from Truman's estimated defense budget through the measures recommended by Eisenhower and Dulles. Moreover, procurement expenses could be stretched out by planning for a "floating D-Day" rather than an imminent year of "maximum danger." Military spending could thereby be progressively decreased and the budget balanced, but not so abruptly as to endanger U.S. security or shake other nations' confidence in U.S. commitments.

To the severe disappointment of the JCS, Eisenhower's initial budget was consistent with this policy, and although submitted prior to the review of strategy, it anticipated key elements of what what would mature as his "New Look." Dulles saw this as a personal victory, not only because his ideas had prevailed but also (and more important) because their congruity with Eisenhower's ideas was so evident. The budget battle strongly suggested that the president both trusted and agreed with his secretary of state. Dulles understood that the effective exercise of a secretary of state's power, nationally and internationally, required this harmony.

The Eisenhower-Dulles relationship was still in its infancy, and Dulles worried that it could quickly sour, as had his Uncle Bert

Lansing's relationship with Woodrow Wilson. He knew from the campaign that the president had reservations about some of his notions. Moreover, Eisenhower did not receive all the advice Dulles offered during their initial months in office with equal enthusiasm. Even as the administration struggled to make the deadline for submitting its first budget, it was interrupted by a development with the potential to reconfigure the global environment. On March 5, 1953, Joseph Stalin suddenly died. Since the 1930s Stalin had been perceived as the embodiment of the Soviet state. Was the Kremlin more or less dangerous without his leadership, or should the United States expect little fundamental change? In short, Stalin's death complicated efforts to assess Soviet intentions, develop an appropriate response, and determine the most cost-effective way to execute it.

Lacking intelligence estimates on the implications of Stalin's passing, let alone the time to prepare and debate policy statements, the administration proceeded in a much less systematic manner than Eisenhower or Dulles preferred. Discussion took place primarily among ad hoc meetings of officials trying to draft an appropriate speech for the president to deliver rather than within the NSC. This was because Charles ("C. D.") Jackson, Eisenhower's psychological warfare expert and longtime cohort of Henry Luce at Time-Life, preemptorily took control of the agenda.

Arguing that Stalin's death provided the United States with a prime opportunity to launch an aggressive propaganda campaign to seize the initiative from the Communists, Jackson drafted a "dramatic" address that he proposed that Eisenhower deliver and have broadcast throughout the world—in the East as well as in the West. Its "strategic purpose" would be to confront Stalin's successor or successors with difficult choices sure to generate conflict, to inspire the Eastern bloc and neutral peoples to identify their aspirations with America's, and to rally the U.S. and the free world publics behind Eisenhower's leadership and programs. Toward this end, what Jackson called the "guts" of his draft was an invitation to the Soviets to resuscitate the Council of Foreign Ministers, which had laid dormant since 1949. The council would consider U.S. proposals to settle the Korean War, reunify Germany, end the occupation of Austria, and control the arms race. To win the secretary of state's support, Jackson wrote Dulles a lengthy memorandum filled with Dullesian concepts and phraseology. The specifics of the speech, he emphasized, were not as important as its "dynamic quality." By projecting a "unifying sense of purpose and destiny" it would signal the "fundamental change" in U.S. foreign policy that "you your-self have wished."[22]

For Dulles, the devil was in the details. While he emotionally and philosophically sympathized with Jackson's ends, he had prag-matic objections to the means. His concern focused on the poten-tial effect of Jackson's plan for negotiations on what he deemed the administration's most pressing task: the enhancement of the strength and cohesion of the Western coalition. Both history and his own experience "proved that the Soviets would resort to all their devices for delay and obstruction." At a Council of Foreign Ministers meeting the Soviets would undoubtedly say anything they thought would exacerbate allied differences by giving "new heart" to "neutralists." For example, Dulles warned, the Soviets would exploit any arms control initiative in order to undermine U.S. efforts to bolster its nuclear deterrent while it still enjoyed atomic supremacy. Of more immediate danger, they would seize any proposal to reunify Germany as a means to intensify French resistance to ratification of the U.S.-supported treaty to rearm West Germany and integrate its forces within a European Defense Com-munity (EDC).[23]

President Eisenhower did not disagree with any of his secre-tary of state's arguments, and he was equally opposed to propos-ing negotiations with a specific agenda. Nevertheless, he was confident that by concentrating on general themes he could give a speech that avoided the pitfalls that Dulles enumerated yet was more substantive than Jackson's "double talk" and "slick propa-ganda." Eisenhower proposed to emphasize the deleterious impact on worldwide living standards of the unconscionable sums being spent on armaments. He could also, without risk of entrapment, simply "delineate, at least in outline, the steps or measures that we believe necessary to bring about satisfactory relationships with re-sultant elimination or lowering of tensions throughout the world." He would then conclude by declaring that he was "ready and will-ing to meet with anyone anywhere from the Soviet Union provided the basis for the meeting was honest and practical." In Eisenhower's opinion, such a speech could "rally the peoples of the world around some idea, some hope, of a better future." At a mimimum, the ad-ministration could judge by Moscow's reaction to the address whether, now that Stalin was dead, the Kremlin leopard had to any significant extent changed its spots.[24]

Notwithstanding Dulles's reservations, Eisenhower decided to give a speech, which he entitled "A Chance for Peace." But neither

Jackson nor any of his other speechwriters could provide the president with a draft he liked. The more they struggled, the more adamantly Dulles protested. No matter how the speech was worded, he complained, it would encourage Western wishful thinking and be used by the Kremlin to derail progress toward free world unity and collective security. "I just don't see [a] solid purpose in this," he concluded, advising Eisenhower to drop the idea altogether.[25]

As Dulles's opposition grew, so did the president's irritation. "We are in an armaments race. Where will it lead us?" Eisenhower said, pacing around the Oval Office in a wide arc. "You come up to these terrible issues, you know what is in almost everyone's heart is peace." Finally, Eisenhower exploded. "[I] want so much to do something," and if all Dulles could do was list the reasons not to, "I am in the wrong pew."[26]

From then on, Eisenhower personally supervised the drafting process. On April 16, fighting through the agony of a severe intestinal disorder, he delivered the speech that he wanted. He challenged the new Soviet leadership to seize the "precious opportunity" afforded by Stalin's death to "turn the tide of history." Even a few "clear and specific acts . . . would be impressive signs of sincere intent," and he surveyed the global hotspots and "unnatural divisions" through which the Kremlin could prove by "deeds" it would not remain captive to Stalin's legacy. Eisenhower plainly stated the differences in ideology and values that separated the East and West. But he concentrated on their common interest in decreasing the possibility of general war and increasing the general welfare.[27]

Moscow's reaction was lukewarm, and Eisenhower's speech soon became yet another cold war artifact. For this the Soviets bear most of the responsibility; nevertheless, Eisenhower and Dulles share some responsibility. The president insisted on delivering the speech because, as he explained, he felt compelled "to do something" to determine if Stalin's death might present even a remote "Chance for Peace," or at least a chance for mitigating some of the causes for international tension. He was not optimistic, however, and wanted to leave no doubt in the minds of either friend or foe that "we are going to go RIGHT AHEAD rearming until it's clear we no longer have to." Dulles was well suited for this assignment, and two days after Eisenhower gave his speech, he had his secretary of state give a very different one.[28]

"We are not dancing to any Russian tune," Dulles began, establishing an abrasive tone from the start. The United States sought peace in Korea, but "we will not play the role of supplicants" in order to achieve it. Nor would the administration slacken in the slightest its efforts to build up the West's military strength in Europe to "deter attack from without." Dulles went on to recycle what by now was his familiar discourse. Stalin's death did not change the fundamental fact that "vast power is possessed by men who accept no guidance from the moral law." For this reason, the prospects for peace were and "must always remain obscure." The United States could not shirk from its responsibility to defend civilization and uphold the moral law. A people with "the tradition and power of the United States," Dulles intoned, "must act boldly and strongly for what they believe to be right."[29]

To a degree, Eisenhower's doubts about the new Soviet regime's receptivity to his speech became a self-fulfilling prophecy once he gave Dulles license to give his speech. There was, as Eisenhower suspected, never much likelihood of the Kremlin responding positively to what the president described as his "serious bid for peace." After Dulles's polemic, there was no likelihood at all. In the Soviets' view, as indeed in the view of much of the world, it was the secretary of state, not the president, who was the true architect of, and spokesman for, U.S. foreign policy.[30]

Dulles knew better. He also knew that although Eisenhower correctly conceived of the two speeches as complementary, as the proverbial two sides of the same coin, the contrasting attitudes and priorities between him and the president had surfaced strikingly. Dulles did not know what this meant for their future relationship and the future of U.S. foreign policy. That uncertainty made him very uneasy.

Notes

1. Quoted in David M. Oshinksy, *A Conspiracy So Immense: The World of Joe McCarthy* (New York, 1983), 108–109.

2. Quoted in Gary W. Reichard, *Politics as Usual: The Age of Truman and Eisenhower* (New York, 1988), 59; NSC 68, "U.S. Objectives and Programs for National Security," April 14, 1950, in Ernest R. May, ed., *American Cold War Strategy: Interpreting NSC 68* (Boston, 1993), 79–80.

3. Quoted in Burton I. Kaufman, *The Korean War: Challenges in Crisis, Credibility, and Command* (New York, 1986), 161.

4. Quoted in Reichard, *Politics as Usual*, 68.

5. Eisenhower, *At Ease: Stories I Tell to Friends* (Garden City, NY, 1967), 371–72; Interview with Dwight D. Eisenhower, Columbia Oral History Collection, Columbia University, New York, NY.

6. Dulles, "Foreign Policy Memorandum," April 11, 1952, "Dulles, John Foster, 1952," Allen W. Dulles Papers, Princeton University, Princeton, NJ.

7. Eisenhower to Dulles, April 15, 1952, *Papers of Dwight David Eisenhower* (Baltimore, 1970–) 13:1179.

8. Dulles to Eisenhower, April 25, 1952, "Dulles, John Foster," Dwight D. Eisenhower Pre-Presidential Papers, Dwight D. Eisenhower Library, Abilene, KS; Dulles, "Policy of Boldness," *Life,* May 19, 1952, 152.

9. "1952 Republican Platform", *National Party Platforms, 1840–1956,* comp. Kirk H. Porter and Donald Bruce Johnson (Urbana, IL, 1956), 497–99.

10. C. L. Sulzberger, *A Long Row of Candles: Memoirs and Diaries, 1934–1954* (New York, 1969), 770; "1952 Republican Platform", 497–99; Eisenhower, *Mandate for Change* (Garden City, NY, 1963), 41; quoted in Herbert S. Parmet, *Eisenhower and the American Crusades* (New York, 1972), 101.

11. Fred I. Greenstein, *The Hidden-Hand Presidency: Eisenhower as Leader* (New York, 1982); quoted in Oshinsky, *Conspiracy So Immense,* 197; quoted in Parmet, *Eisenhower,* 124–25.

12. Eisenhower Address at Baltimore, Maryland, September 25, 1952, "Sept. 15, 1952—Sept. 25, 1952," Speech Series, Eisenhower Papers as President (Whitman File), Eisenhower Library, Abilene, KS (hereafter cited as Whitman File).

13. Eisenhower Address at San Francisco, CA, October 8, 1952, "September 26, 1952," Speech Series, Whitman File.

14. Quoted in Reichard, *Politics as Usual,* 82.

15. Entry for May 14, 1953, Robert H. Ferrell, ed., *The Eisenhower Diaries* (New York, 1981), 237.

16. Quoted in Louis L. Gerson, *John Foster Dulles* (New York, 1967), 97.

17. Summary of J. F. D. remarks at meeting with Eisenhower, Wilson, Brownell, Bradley, and Radford, Kaneohe, Hawaii, December 11, 1952, Subject Series, "S.S. *Helena* Notes," Dulles Papers, Eisenhower Library, Abilene, KS. Emphasis in original. (hereafter cited as DP-Eisenhower)

18. Notes, December 4, 1953, "Bermuda—President's Notes December 1953 (1)," International Series, Whitman File.

19. JSPC 851/76, Report by the Joint Strategic Plans Committee, January 31, 1953, CCS 381 U.S. (1-31-50) sec. 23, RG 218, U.S. National Archives II, College Park, MD; JSPC 851/81, February 16, 1953, CCS 370 (8-19-45) sec. 39, ibid.; General Omar N. Bradley memorandum for the Secretary of Defense, "Effect of Approaching a Balanced Budget in FY 1954 and Achieving a Balanced Budget in FY 1955," March 19, 1953, CD 111 (1954) 1953, RG330, ibid.

20. Memorandum of special NSC meeting, March 31, 1953, *FR, 1952–54* 2:264–81.

21. Memorandum of NSC meeting on February 18, 1953, February 19, 1953, "132nd Meeting of the NSC," NSC Series, Whitman File.

22. Jackson to Dulles, March 10, 1953, "Time Inc. File—Stalin's Death: Speech Text and Comments—Full Evolution," C. D. Jackson Papers, Eisenhower Library, Abilene, KS.

23. Memorandum of NSC meeting, March 11, 1953, *FR, 1952–54* 8:1117–25.

24. Quoted in Emmet H. Hughes, *The Ordeal of Power: A Political Memoir of the Eisenhower Years* (New York, 1975), 103–104; Memorandum of NSC meeting, March 11, 1953, 1117–25.

25. Entry for March 13, 1953, "Diary Notes 1953," Emmet J. Hughes Papers, Princeton University, Princeton, NJ (hereafter cited as Hughes Papers).

26. Quoted in Hughes, *Ordeal of Power*, 103–105.

27. Eisenhower, "The Chance for Peace," April 16, 1953, *FR, 1952–54* 8:1147–55.

28. Entry for April 8, 1953, "Diary Notes 1953," Hughes Papers.

29. Dulles, "The Eisenhower Foreign Policy: A World-Wide Peace Offensive," April 18, 1953," reproduced in Walt W. Rostow, *Europe After Stalin: Eisenhower's Three Decisions of March 11, 1953* (Austin, 1982), appendix E, 122–31.

30. Quoted in Hughes, *Ordeal of Power*, 105.

4

The New Look

The Eisenhower administration's early debates left Dulles both frustrated and apprehensive. The positions he took during the discussions of the defense budget and the response to Stalin's death revealed unmistakably his belief that an effective policy and strategy toward the Communists required a foundation of strength, and that Washington should forego any diplomatic overtures or gestures aimed at reducing tension until the West's strength was substantially more robust. From his perspective, Eisenhower's general desire to create a more stable global environment and his specific desire to mitigate the arms race was too risky. Dulles was sure that Eisenhower shared his views on the requisites for building military strength, but he was deeply concerned that the president insufficiently appreciated the reluctance of America's allies to contribute their fair share.

The most fundamental difference between Eisenhower and Dulles lay in their assessments of the free world partnership. Eisenhower based his on his World War II experience. Despite all the difficulties he encountered as Supreme Commander, especially his disputes with the British and the French, he never doubted their courage, vitality, and resolve. Now that they were engaged in a cold war, he was confident that they would again act in concert with the United States to achieve victory.

Dulles, however, had formed his image of Britain and France during the Versailles conference and subsequent interwar years. In his view, they still lacked the dynamic spirit and willingness to make the sacrifices for the collective good essential for vigorously pursuing his ambitious agenda. As a consequence, NATO force goals remained unfulfilled even as the EDC treaty remained unratified. Moreover, while the Europeans sought economy under the protection of the U.S. nuclear umbrella, they publicly manifested so much anxiety over the possible use of these weapons as to undermine the credibility of the threat of massive retaliation, and thus of the nuclear deterrent.

Dulles had opposed Eisenhower's "Chance for Peace" address because he feared that the Soviets could exploit it to manipulate the Europeans' shortsightedness and timidity. His fears were not realized. Still, the episode further convinced the secretary of state that U.S. policy, his policy of boldness, must not be left hostage to the wishful thinking and static complacency of its allies.

The administration initiated its formal reexamination of the Truman legacy immediately after Eisenhower's and Dulles's speeches and the completion of the initial Eisenhower defense budget. Dulles could wait no longer. For the first time he told the president how profoundly distressed he was about the current state of international affairs and the prospects for free world collective security. "It is difficult to conclude that time is working in our favor," Dulles began a late afternoon meeting in early May with the president and a few select other advisors in the White House solarium. "In the world chess game, the Reds today have the better position. . . . Practically everywhere one looks, there is no strong holding point and danger everywhere of Communist penetration." Unless the administration rapidly took dramatic and forceful steps to respond to this erosion, he insisted, "we will lose bit by bit the free world, and break ourselves financially."

Dulles had said much the same thing before, publicly and privately. But he had blamed the peril primarily on Truman's policies. He now charged America's allies with much of the responsibility. His critique of their attitudes and behavior paralleled that of his pre-World War II writings, but was, if anything, more biting. Dulles described Europe's leaders as "shattered 'old people'" who lacked "the strength, the dynamic" required to meet a threat more severe than that of Hitler's Third Reich. They "want to spend their remaining days in peace and repose." Hence, they were "willing and glad to gamble" that the "Soviets, like Ghenghes [*sic*] Khan, will get on their little Tartar ponies and ride back whence they came."

How, then, "can Western civilization survive?" Dulles asked, reaching the climax of his presentation. The only answer was for the administration "to take leadership at a fast and vigorous pace," even if this meant that allies would resist following. Putting the Communists on notice that further expansion would not be tolerated was a first minimum step. A way to do so, Dulles proposed, would be to "draw a line and tell the Soviets that if one more country on our side of the line should succumb to Communism by overt or covert aggression," the United States would hold Moscow accountable and, accepting the risk of "global war," respond accordingly by force.

Dulles was far from through, however. He had repeatedly stressed that, although necessary, containment, no matter how aggressively pursued, could never be sufficient. Because the "Communists have won victory after victory in the post-war years," a "success for the free peoples is badly needed" in order to restore the West's prestige and morale. Dulles defined success only as "winning in one or more areas," and he left unmentioned the methods by which these unspecified areas could be won. That he was promoting a policy of liberation, nevertheless, was clear. The United States must force the Kremlin to "think more of holding what it has" and "less of gaining additional territory and peoples." The result would turn the tide of the cold war. Fainthearted allies and fence-sitting neutrals would then fall in line behind U.S. leadership and rally in support of its dynamism. A progressively enfeebled Kremlin would be helpless against a free world stronger and more united than ever before. The Soviet empire would self-destruct; the regime would disintegrate.

Eisenhower waited patiently for Dulles to finish. His response was measured and to the point. He did not believe that time was on the side of the Soviets. While concurring that "the present policy was leading to disaster," he reminded Dulles and the others in the room that he had agreed to run for president to preserve the U.S. commitment to collective security. The goal for the administration must be to strengthen the cohesion of the alliance, not to give up on it and act unilaterally. "We cannot live alone. We need allies." Rather than alienate them by drawing lines that risked general war, Eisenhower said, we must convince "our friends of the rightness" of U.S. policies. Further, by focusing exclusively on who controlled what territory, Dulles was forgetting what he had preached for so long: the cold war was a battle over ideals and principles. At this point Dulles could constrain himself no longer. If the last several years proved anything, he blurted out, it was "that talk about 'liberty' doesn't stop people from becoming Communist." That just affirms my point, Eisenhower retorted. "It's men's minds and hearts that must be won." Winning them "will take time, but it must be done or we will lose in the end."

As Eisenhower was taking him to task, Dulles was probably second-guessing his decision to speak his mind so candidly, and undoubtedly wondering whether he had much of a future as secretary of state. The president, however, had something very different in mind. He did not see his disagreement with Dulles as a reason to dismiss him. To the contrary, he wanted from his advisors just this kind of honesty. What is more, the stark contrast between their views gave Eisenhower an idea. Instead of closing the debate, he could organize it.

Eisenhower concluded his remarks by proposing that the administration "set up some teams of bright young fellows" to analyze competing national strategies for dealing with the Communist threat. Each team would "take an alternative" strategy, Eisenhower explained, and "tackle" it "with a real belief in it just the way a good advocate tackles a law case—and then when the teams are prepared, each should put on in some White House room, with maps, charts, all the basic supporting figures and estimates, just what each alternative would mean in terms of goal, risk, cost in money and men and world relations." There, in the presence of the entire NSC, each team would lay out the "facts . . . cold and hard."[1]

By this process the Dulles monologue that precipitated the Dulles-Eisenhower dialogue became the catalyst for an exercise unique in the history of U.S. national security policymaking. It was named Project Solarium after the room of its origin, and by the end of May the teams—Task Forces A, B, and C—had been assembled from experts drawn from the public and private sectors. A special panel provided *each* team with "precise and detailed terms of reference."[2]

Task Force A was to propose programs that continued the policy Eisenhower inherited from Truman. Its components included maintaining armed forces for as long as necessary to defend the United States and its vital interests; providing economic and military assistance to U.S. allies; and without "materially increasing the risk of general war," taking "political, economic, and psychological measures" directed at "the vulnerabilities of the Soviets and their satellites." The assignment of Task Force B was to develop Dulles's suggestion that the United States unilaterally place a no-trespassing sign along the current boundary of the Soviet orbit. The administration would "make clear to the Soviet rulers" in an "appropriate and unmistakable way" that it reserved complete "freedom of action, in the event of indigenous Communist seizure of power in countries on our side of the line, to take all measures necessary to reestablish a situation compatible with the security interests of the U.S. and its allies."[3]

This left defending a liberation policy to Task Force C. The overall objective of liberation was "to force the Soviets to shift their efforts to holding what they already have rather than concentrating on gaining control of additional territories and peoples and at the same time to produce a climate of victory encouraging to the free world." In pursuit of these interdependent goals, the United States would seek "(1) To increase efforts to disturb and weaken the Soviet bloc and to accelerate the consolidation and strengthening of the free world"; and "(2) To create the maximum disruption and popular resistance throughout the Soviet Bloc." Task Force C was instructed not to design a policy intended to "provoke a war with the Soviet Union" but to recognize that a program aimed at liberation "involves a substantial risk of general war."[4]

The Solarium task forces set to work in early June, cloistered in the National War College. Over the ensuing six weeks, each drafted a detailed written "brief" in support of the assigned policy alternative on which their oral arguments to the NSC were to be based. Even as the task forces prepared additional grist for the policy-making mill, however, the rapid pace of world developments required Eisenhower to make policy decisions—decisions that, with regard to Dulles's promotion of liberation, were fraught with implications.

On June 16, 1953, several hundred construction laborers in East Berlin, responding to oppressive work conditions and severe food shortages, called for a general strike and staged a political demonstration against the regime headed by hard-line Communist Walter Ulbricht. By the next day, the demonstration had escalated into spontaneous mass rioting throughout the German Democratic Republic (GDR). Ultimately, encouraged by the U.S. radio station in Berlin (Radio in the American Sector—RIAS), more than 500,000 East Germans in more than 500 GDR towns took part.

The East German uprising caught the Eisenhower administration completely by surprise. It was well aware of the widespread discontent with Ulbricht's policy; more than 10,000 East Germans were fleeing to the West each month. Yet in Washington's estimate, the new Kremlin leadership was no less committed to maintaining the GDR as its client than Stalin had been. Indeed, the CIA thought that Moscow might have instigated the riots in order to justify removing the unpopular Ulbricht or, worse, moving USSR military forces into East Berlin from where they could threaten, and even capture, the entire city. In addition, there was concern that the Kremlin was scheming to use the rioting to recycle the 1952 "Stalin Note" that sought to undermine the prospects for EDC ratification and support for West German chancellor Konrad Adenauer by disingenuously raising the specter of a neutral reunited Germany. It seemed prudent, therefore, to monitor developments closely but exercise restraint in responding to them.

There were good reasons, nevertheless, to respond more aggressively. Inaction could prove politically costly. Liberation had been integral to Republican campaign rhetoric and was a cherished ideal among the GOP right wing. Were Eisenhower to do nothing to assist the East German protesters, what little party unity there was could evaporate. To Dulles the uprising presented the opportunity to substitute boldness for prudence, and thereby score the victory that the free world so desperately needed. In his judgment failure to take advantage of this manifest discontent would leave the free world even worse off than before.

Dulles could not suggest a way to turn the uprising into a Western victory. When the NSC convened on June 18 to discuss the potential options, it became evident that no one else had any suggestions either. Ironically, the Soviets' behavior resolved the administration's indecision. Shortly after the NSC meeting adjourned, Soviet tanks rolled into East Berlin to suppress the riots. The USSR subsequently declared martial law over the GDR. The uprising came to an abrupt and bloody end. So, too, did whatever opportunity Dulles thought the uprising presented to roll back communism.

Moscow's brutal suppression of the protest did provide Eisenhower ammunition with which to wage his battle for the world's hearts and minds. Graphic accounts of the events dominated Radio Free Europe's broadcasts. More significant, on July 1, Eisenhower approved a large-scale program to distribute food to the East Germans by means of thirty-five centers located in the Western sector of Berlin (travel between East and West Berlin was still permitted in 1953). In making food available free of charge to undernourished East Germans, the United States projected an image of humanitarian concern while at the same time advertising the bounties of capitalism. No less important, as Washington had predicted, efforts by the Ulbricht regime to discredit and restrict the food relief program aggravated its relations with the general populace.

Dulles would have preferred that the United States take an initiative more dynamic and dramatic than the distribution of food. He was satisfied, nevertheless, that in light of time constraints and the Soviet military presence, the program (which his sister Eleanor helped to administer) was probably the best course of action. Also, Dulles was able to accept the limited food relief program with magnanimity because, just days before the president approved it, the secretary learned that preparations were under way to execute a program in another arena of the cold war.

Iran had been in a state of turmoil since 1951, as what began as a British effort to retain control of Iranian oil quickly took on the cast of the cold war. Through the Anglo-Iranian Oil Company (AIOC), in which Her Majesty's Government owned a substantial interest, the British had a monopoly on pumping, refining, and shipping oil in most of Iran. The AIOC paid salaries to Iranian employees and rent and production royalties to the government of Shah Muhammad Reza Pahlavi, whom London had placed on the Peacock Throne in 1941. The company's earnings were ten times greater than its expenses.

Iranian nationalists demanded a more equitable financial arrangement. The AIOC replied that it had a binding agreement with the Shah until 1993 and conspired with its collaborators in the Iranian parliament to produce a report opposing Iran's nationalization of AIOC's assets. On February 19, 1951, the Iranian prime minister, perceived as complicit in the preparation of the report, was assassinated. His successor, the popular nationalist leader Dr. Muhammad Mossadegh, immediately discarded the report and presented legislation to parliament calling for the nationalization of AIOC. On May 2 the bill became law. Dulles, who by coincidence was in the Middle East at the time, concluded that the events in Iran indicated the growth of Soviet influence.

Moscow's involvement in Iran was negligible, but Dulles could not distinguish between indigenous nationalism and imported communism. Neither could Truman administration officials, who nevertheless counseled the British government not to resort to force. The repercussions could disrupt the global supply of oil, and struggling free world economies could ill afford to pay the resulting inflated prices. In addition, the Communist propaganda mill would doubtless churn out indictments of Western imperialism. There was even the danger that the USSR might intervene directly under the ruse of defending Iran's right to self-determination.

After Truman's endeavor to mediate a settlement between Teheran and the AIOC went nowhere, the crisis intensified. In mid-1952 the Shah's attempt to dismiss Mossadegh following the prime minister's request for parliamentary authority to rule by decree provoked rioting in the capital. The Iranian parliament responded by rejecting the Shah's effort and granting Mossadegh the authority he sought. The British responded by alleging that Iran's Communist Tudeh party had masterminded the incident. Mossadegh responded by severing diplomatic relations with London.

For the better part of a year the British Secret Intelligence Service (SIS) had been devising a covert plan to stage a coup d'état against Mossadegh, which it rapidly revised in the wake of the Shah's unsuccessful effort to dismiss the prime minister. Its premise was simple. Powerful interests in Iran remained loyal to both Britain and the Shah, and they recognized that the impasse between the AIOC and the Iranian government threatened the country with economic ruin. They would support another effort by the Shah to oust Mossadegh. Mossadegh would surely once again force a showdown, but this time the outcome would be different. Through the joint efforts of the SIS and CIA, Iranians would be hired to stage mass demonstrations in opposition to Mossadegh, and the Iranian military would be organized to demand his ouster. Parliament would be helpless to resist.

The SIS brought the plan to Kermit (Kim) Roosevelt, grandson of Theodore Roosevelt and the CIA's chief operative in the Middle East. Roosevelt's enthusiasm for it was not shared by Truman. As a lame duck still officially committed to mediation efforts, he refused to participate. Roosevelt was confident that the incoming Republicans would. Eisenhower had benefited from clandestine operations at several critical junctures during World War II, and he had ardently endorsed the efficacy of such operations ever since. Dulles had as well, although his reasons had more to do with personal ties than with personal experience. Allen Dulles's intimate connection to intelligence dated back to World War I. Less cerebral than his older brother Foster, he preferred operations to analysis. During World War II he had been a chief lieutenant in the Office of Strategic Services (OSS). He subsequently played an instrumental role in the 1947 establishment of the CIA; and when Eisenhower's former chief of staff, Walter Bedell Smith, became the agency's third director in 1950, Allen Dulles was appointed his deputy. Eisenhower promoted Allen to agency head because he wanted Smith to be Foster Dulles's deputy. Eisenhower intended this game of musical chairs to improve Department of State-CIA coordination. It did.

Allen Dulles knew that his brother identified Iran as a cold war battlefield, and thus would find the plan to oust Mossadegh intrinsically attractive. He also knew that his brother placed a premium on U.S. leadership, held the British in low regard, and deeply suspected their motives. He suggested that Roosevelt modify the plan to take into account the secretary of state's priorities. Roosevelt demanded that the British accept, on a take-it-or-leave-it basis, two essential new features. First, although by necessity SIS agents and communications facilities would be used for implementation, the operation would be orchestrated by the CIA, with him in charge. Second, lest there be any doubt that the purpose of the operation was to excise the Communist cancer from Iran and not simply to reinstate the AIOC's monopoly, the Shah would nominate the anti-British General Fazlollah Zahedi as the next prime minister.

Acquiescing to Zahedi was a particularly bitter pill for the British to swallow, but Roosevelt left them with no alternative. By the end of June 1953 the plan was ready for formal presentation. Allen Dulles arranged for Roosevelt to accompany him to a meeting with Foster Dulles and Walter Bedell Smith in the secretary's State Department office. Roosevelt laid out the plan, now code-named Project AJAX. Foster was delighted. In contrast to his experience with the East German uprising, he was now given a plan to operationalize the concept of liberation, and there were no Soviet tanks in the way. "So this is how we get rid of that madman Mossadegh," he commented, not entirely facetiously. "Let's get going."[5]

To get going required Eisenhower's approval. For more than a month Eisenhower delayed, fretting that the U.S. role in the operation would be exposed and that the United States would be branded throughout the Third World as merely another imperialist. Yet in the president's estimate, no less than in Dulles's, Mossadegh was either a Communist or the stooge of Communists. When in early August Moscow announced the start of negotiations with Iran, Eisenhower approved the plan. Roosevelt immediately entered Iran under secret cover, and except for the complication caused by the Shah's panicky flight to Italy, Project AJAX succeeded flawlessly. By the end of the month, Mossadegh was in prison, Zahedi was prime minister, and the Shah's power was greater than ever. The AIOC remained "nationalized"; indeed, it was renamed the

National Iranian Oil Company. It was operated, however, by an international consortium in which the United States had a 40 percent interest—equal to that of Britain.

Dulles was intoxicated by the stunning success. It meant nothing to him that Mossadegh had never appealed to the Soviets for assistance, or that the Soviets had never volunteered to provide it. It also meant nothing that Mossadegh was frequently at loggerheads with the Communist Tudeh party. Dulles simply assumed that Iran required liberation from the yoke of communism; Project AJAX demonstrated that the United States had finally developed the will to do the liberating. The downside, of course, was that because liberation was achieved by covert action, the demonstration could not be made public. Moreover, in the international cold war drama, Iran was but a sideshow. Korea remained at center stage, and Dulles was experiencing great difficulty with the final act.

In December 1952, immediately before Eisenhower fulfilled his pledge to "go to Korea," Dulles had sent the president-elect a memorandum underscoring the urgency of terminating the war. The conflict was a serious drain on U.S. resources, overtaxing its economy and overextending its military capabilities. The diversion of troops, arms, and equipment to a static front bred doubts throughout the free world about existing commitments to hold the line against Communist aggression, let alone doubts about the credibility of the incoming administration's vow to force Moscow onto the defensive. These doubts intensified the friction within the NATO alliance and encouraged neutralism and pacificism among nonaligned nations of the Third World and weak-willed ones, such as Japan. In sum, the United States would remain at an irreversible strategic disadvantage so long as the Korean War continued.

Eisenhower totally agreed, and during the campaign he had created the impression that he was working on a plan to bring closure to the war on terms favorable to U.S. interests. He had studiously avoided offering any specifics, however, because he had none to offer. His whirlwind tour of Korea brought him no closer to developing ideas for a breakthrough in the deadlocked negotiations at Panmunjom, nor did his discussions with his advisors on the return trip. After the *Helena* docked in Hawaii, Eisenhower's public statement merely borrowed Dulles's rhetoric. The Communists "would have to be impressed by deeds," he said, "executed under circumstances of our own choosing."[6]

What deeds should he choose to execute, and under what circumstances? A month into the administration, Eisenhower and

Dulles were still floundering for an answer. The most concrete suggestion came from the retired General Douglas MacArthur, who proposed atomic attacks on North Korea and Communist Chinese bases and installations in Manchuria. Eisenhower instinctively balked; the risk of igniting World War III seemed too great. Nevertheless, when the NSC met on February 11, 1953, to consider the request of General Mark Clark, the current commander of the UN coalition, for authority to launch a strike near Kaesong, Eisenhower broached the possibility of letting the atomic genie out of the bottle. The initial site of the armistice talks, Kaesong had been deemed a "sanctuary," and Chinese Communist troops were concentrated in the area. "[W]e should consider the use of tactical atomic weapons on the Kaesong area," Eisenhower advised. It seemed a "good target for this type of weapon. In any case," he added as if to stress that his frustration had reached the point of desperation, "we could not go on the way we were indefinitely."[7]

Dulles had apparently been waiting for such an opening. The Kaesong sanctuary, he explained, was but one of several arrangements the Truman administration had made with the Communists to facilitate the armistice negotiations. With negotiations at an impasse and the Chinese exploiting the sanctuary for military advantage, the time had come to declare these arrangements "defunct." More important, the time had come to confront head-on the "moral problem and the inhibitions on the use of the A-bomb." The Soviets had convinced much of the world's population that atomic weapons must be set apart from all others as a "special category." In Dulles's view, this was a "false distinction," and the sooner it was exposed as such and the taboo on atomic weapons removed, the better.[8]

Neither Eisenhower nor anyone else in the NSC disputed Dulles's premises and conclusions. All agreed, however, that the allies would be wary of escalating the fighting in Korea and unequivocally hostile to any escalation that included the use of atomic weapons. Eisenhower instructed Dulles to begin laying the diplomatic groundwork—very carefully. In the meantime, the Pentagon would estimate the danger an atomic attack on Kaesong would present to U.S. and other non-Communist forces in the theater. It would also evaluate the potential impact of bombing China north of the Yalu River. Eisenhower concurrently put the NSC Planning Board to work examining all contingency plans for ending the war.

The Eisenhower administration appeared to be headed toward intensifying the military effort in Korea, with or without atomic weapons, when Stalin died. Shortly thereafter, the Chinese Communists conceded on several issues related to the repatriation of prisoners of war (POWs), a key stumbling block in the Panmunjom negotiations. Foreign Minister Chou En-lai (Zhou Enlai) accepted unconditionally a UN proposal for the exchange of sick and wounded POWs who wanted to be repatriated.[9] Chou also suggested that in principle China no longer objected to previous U.S. proposals for the exchange of all POWs, although the details would still have to be worked out. China's concessions were simultaneous with the pronouncement by the new chairman of the Soviet Council of Ministers, G. M. Malenkov, that all existing international disputes could and should "be decided by peaceful means, on the basis of mutual understanding."[10]

Administration officials had to assess the sincerity of the apparent Sino-Soviet volte-face even as they struggled to draft Eisenhower's "Chance for Peace" speech. Predictably, the president's differences with Dulles surfaced. Eisenhower viewed the Chinese concessions as a promising development worth pursuing as long as there was progress. To Dulles, the Communists simply were stalling for more time while strengthening allied opposition to a military resolution of the war. Moreover, he vacillated, if the peace overtures were genuine, it meant that because of Stalin's death, exhaustion from the war, and/or fear of the new Republican administration, the Communists felt weak and vulnerable. Hence, it was "now quite possible to secure a much more satisfactory settlement in Korea than a mere armistice at the 38th parallel which would leave a divided Korea not economically nor politically viable to South Koreans."[11]

Dulles recognized that it was unrealistic to think in terms of uniting Korea under the Seoul government, and he appreciated the uproar that would be created in the United States and among its allies if Eisenhower's response to the Communist gestures was to terminate negotiations. He suggested that Eisenhower demand that the Communists agree to move the boundary between the two Koreas from the 38th parallel north to the peninsula's narrow "waist" between Sinanju and Hungnam. If they refused, the United States would break off armistice talks and settle the war on the battlefield.

Dulles's ultimatum scheme commanded scant support from his own State Department, and even less from Eisenhower. The negotiations continued, but each time the issue of repatriating POWs arose, the Communist Chinese equivocated. Eisenhower began again to muse about dropping some well-placed tactical atomic bombs, both to guard against a renewed Communist offensive and to impress the enemy with U.S. resolve. By May, however, the military had concluded that there were no suitable targets within Korea. If the United States really meant business, the JCS recommended, atomic strikes should be directed at Chinese air bases in Manchuria while a ground offensive secured the waist of Korea. Follow-up operations could then eliminate enemy forces from the peninsula.

The plan appealed to Dulles, and Eisenhower could not refute its logic. He "wished the record to show," the president announced as the May 20 NSC meeting drew to a close, "that if circumstances arose which would force the United States to an expanded effort in Korea, the plan selected by the Joint Chiefs of Staff was most likely to achieve the objective we sought." He remained gravely concerned, nevertheless, that the Soviets would retaliate, probably by atomic strikes on Japanese cities and U.S./UN supply centers in Pusan and Inchon. This road could only lead to general war.[12]

Eisenhower instructed the JCS to continue preparations for a D-day in about a year. But he would not idly allow circumstances to arise that would force D-day upon him. Both Eisenhower and Dulles were convinced that the Truman administration's failure to make unambiguous the U.S. commitment to defend South Korea had suggested to the Communists that they could invade with impunity. If World War III were to be avoided, these aggressors must not miscalculate again. They must be made to realize that the new administration was deadly earnest about its intention to end the hostilities in Korea without further delay.

Eisenhower decided to inform Peking (Beijing), and by extension Moscow, that he would extend the war to mainland China and use atomic weapons unless the Chinese agreed to a satisfactory armistice. Whether the idea was Eisenhower's or Dulles's may never be known. Logic would suggest that it originated with the president, although it might well have evolved from one of their informal get-togethers. Whatever the case, later in May Dulles visited with India's Prime Minister Jawaharlal Nehru in New Delhi. "If the armistice negotiations collapse," the secretary casually remarked, "the United States would probably make a stronger rather than lesser military exertion and this might well extend the conflict." Dulles well knew that Nehru's great nightmare was that the Korean War would grow to consume all Asia, and that he had an open channel to Peking. "I assume this [message] would be relayed," he wrote Eisenhower. But to make sure, Dulles arranged to convey to the Peking regime through other foreign intermediaries the more explicit warning that unless an armistice was concluded in the near future, the administration intended "to remove the restrictions of area and weapons."[13]

At Panmunjom the primary obstacle to achieving a cease-fire was removed. The Communists acquiesced to the fundamental tenets of the U.S. position on the repatriation of POWs, and despite South Korean President Syngman Rhee's attempt to sabotage the negotiations on June 18 by freeing 25,000 of the 35,400 prisoners he held, an armistice agreement was reached. Eisenhower, and doubtless Dulles as well, breathed a sigh of relief. From the secretary of state's point of view, a truce on U.S. terms was a victory, even if no additional territory was acquired. The Communists had backed down while the United States had remained resolute. Rather than compromise on its principles, it had flexed its military muscle.

There is reason to believe that Dulles's threat to extend the war beyond Korea's boundary and across the atomic threshold had little or no impact on the Communists. Even if Peking received the threat, and there is evidence that it never did, Mao Tse-tung (Mao Zedong) had already decided that the People's Republic of China's (PRC) economy could no longer sustain the war effort. Moreover, he was under mounting pressure to settle from the post-Stalin Kremlin, which wanted to end the turmoil and uncertainty in Korea in order to concentrate on consolidating its new regime (as it was, it had its hands full with the uprising in East Germany). Finally, Mao was convinced that because it enhanced PRC security and respect for his regime and military, the draw with the United States constituted a great victory. It was probably the synergy of these internal factors that accounted for the concessions. Dulles, however, publicly boasted that the United States had forced the enemy to the brink of war, attesting to the salutary consequences of the policy of boldness he recommended. Whether Eisenhower would adopt his recommendation was still to be decided.

On July 27, 1953, the adversaries signed the Korean armistice. On July 16, the Solarium task forces presented their reports to an all-day meeting of the NSC attended by the JCS, service secretaries, and Planning Board members, as well as by the Council's normal participants. The task forces had been briefed on recent developments but instructed to restrict their arguments to the general alternatives they were charged with advocating. Each task force proved itself a formidable advocate. He had "never attended a better or more persuasively presented staff job," said Eisenhower at the conclusion.[14]

For Dulles and most of the others in the room, the exercise was as frustrating as it was enlightening. The task forces had presented their respective arguments with such force and cogency that no single alternative appeared clearly superior to the others. Further, using the same intelligence reports and estimates, they reached diametrically opposite conclusions.

The most stark contrasts were between the positions of Task Forces A (continuation of containment) and C (a shift to liberation or rollback). The position of Task Force B, to draw the line and threaten retaliation against any trespassing, could be readily modified to buttress either. Task Force A maintained that although there was room for improvement (for example strengthening nuclear capabilities, defense systems, and foreign assistance programs), "sufficient deterrents [to Communist aggression] already exist." Unable to expand, the Soviet Union would stagnate, and over time the weaknesses inherent in its political and economic structure would bring about the retraction of Soviet power and influence until it lost its hold on its satellites and no longer posed an external threat. Hence, there was no need to risk provoking the Soviets by aggressively seeking to roll back its orbit.[15]

The proponents of liberation (Task Force C) argued against this patient, gradual approach. Its premise was unequivocal: The "U.S. cannot continue to live with the Soviet threat." The longer it did, the greater the threat of nuclear attack and nuclear blackmail. The threat to vital allies and the nonaligned nations would increase even more, and lacking the resolve and means to resist, they would gravitate or defect to the Soviet camp in increasing numbers. The United States could possibly survive as a state by hiding behind a Fortress America, but its economy and democratic institutions could not. There was but one alternative: The Soviet Union "will not fall apart"; it must be "shaken apart."[16]

From Dulles's point of view the Solarium exercise underscored the vast differences between the alternative policies and brought to the fore fundamental problems with each. Eisenhower's reaction was typically more positive. He stressed those areas about which the task forces agreed, and more important, he stressed the specific recommendations of each task force that the administration could develop and execute fruitfully. Eisenhower directed the NSC Planning Board, with the assistance of the task forces, to decide on "certain features of the three presentations as the best features and to bring about a combination of such features into a unified policy."[17]

It took until the end of September for the Planning Board to prepare for Eisenhower and the NSC a first draft of a new statement of basic national security policy. The draft reflected that in the interim the Korean Armistice was signed and the CIA had successfully orchestrated the overthrow of Mossadegh in Iran. Perhaps even more significant, it reflected a "new look" at U.S. military strategy and planning.

In May, following the debate over the defense budget, Eisenhower overhauled the Joint Chiefs of Staff. The most notable of his selections were Admiral Arthur Radford as chair and General Matthew Ridgway as Army chief of staff. A fiscal conservative with impeccable credentials as an Asia-firster and air and naval power enthusiast, Radford appealed to the GOP right wing and supported Eisenhower and Dulles's preference for greater reliance on the nuclear deterrent. Ridgway had served with distinction in both Asia and Europe, succeeding MacArthur as commander of the UN forces in Korea and then Eisenhower as NATO Supreme Commander. Filling out the reconstituted JCS were Air Force General Nathan F. Twining, Admiral Robert B. Carney as chief of naval operations, and General Lemuel C. Shepherd, Jr., who continued as commandant of the Marine Corps.

When announcing the appointments, Eisenhower promised that the new JCS would undertake a review of current military strategy "without any real chains fastening to the past." This study would evaluate current strategic concepts and implementing plans, the roles and missions of each service, the composition and readiness of present forces, the scale and effectiveness of military assistance programs, and the implications of nuclear weapons and delivery systems. "What I am seeking," Eisenhower explained to the JCS-designates at the same time that the NSC Planning Board began to draft the new statement of security policy, is a "fresh view" that would provide "interim guidance to aid the Council in developing policies for the most effective employment of available national resources to insure the defense of our country for the long pull which may lie ahead."[18]

After several "long and difficult" days sequestered aboard the yacht USS *Sequoia*, the new JCS completed the review in early August (the month its tenure officially began). Its "fresh view" turned out to be fresh in only two respects. First, it recommended that the president formulate and then announce "a clear, positive policy with respect to the use of atomic weapons." While this recommendation implied a policy congruent with Dulles's concept of "massive retaliation" and along the lines of what had been advocated by Task Force B during the Solarium exercise, the JCS left it imprecise and undeveloped.[19]

The second recommendation, which built on the first, was no more precise but significantly more developed—and radical. It accepted the premise of the preceding JCS: so long as the United States continued to place its "major emphasis in the military field on peripheral deployments overseas," its forces would remain gravely "overextended." This condition explained why currently "our freedom of action is seriously curtailed" and "the exercise of initiative severely limited."

As a solution, the JCS did not recycle its predecessor's request for more forces and more money to pay for them. Rather, it proposed that the administration "reverse our present strategic policy." It should not only rely more heavily on "the capability of delivering swift and powerful retaliatiory blows," but it should also drastically reduce the number of U.S. troops stationed abroad. In short, "Military commitments overseas—that is to say, peripheral military commitments—would cease to have first claim on our resources." The JCS appreciated that this redeployment "would involve a change in basic foreign policy of fundamental and far-reaching implications." In their opinion, nevertheless, it was the "only" course of action that offered a "reasonable promise of improving our general security position."[20]

Dulles was taken aback by what the administration labeled the JCS's "new concept," and profoundly conflicted about how to respond. On one level, its appeal was almost irresistable. He had time and again preached the benefits of a strategy that stressed the U.S. capacity for massive retaliation, and his dispair over Britain and France's lack of dynamism and resolve had reached monumental proportions. He soon made headlines by threatening that the Allies' continued reluctance both to shoulder more of the burden for defending themselves in Europe and to agree to Germany's rearmament by ratifying the EDC treaty would compel an "agonizing reappraisal of basic U.S. policy." The JCS's recommendations reinforced Dulles's own predispositions.[21]

On another, deeper level, the JCS's proposed redeployment of U.S. overseas forces propelled Dulles to come to grips intellectually with those predispositions. It was one thing to write a polemic for *Life* magazine or a platform for the Republican party, or even to lash out verbally at U.S. allies. It was quite another thing actually to promote a change in policy so drastic that it would approximate the Fortress America, unilateralist positions identified with the Republican right wing. Did he really want to give up on his effort to provide leadership to and "uplift" U.S. allies and win the trust and support of neutrals? Had he not argued that the alternative to collective security was free world paralysis, bankruptcy, and ultimately appeasement and defeat? What is more, virtually simultaneous with the JCS's proposal of a new concept, the Soviets successfully tested a thermonuclear bomb, thereby undermining, at least potentially and in principle, the credibility of America's nuclear shield. In Dulles's mind, theory and practice were in open conflict.

The NSC's initial discussion of the "new concept" on August 27 revealed deep divisions within the council and among the service chiefs themselves. At one extreme, among the JCS Radford alone endorsed it unambiguously; at the other extreme, Ridgway all but disavowed it entirely. If anything, the debate, which focused more on the concept's implications for the U.S. budget than for its foreign policy, exacerbated Dulles's distress. Only on the rarest of occasions did Eisenhower miss an NSC meeting, but he was on vacation at the "Summer White House" in Denver. Dulles was too impatient to await his return. He flew out to Denver in early September to discuss the problem.

Characteristically, as a means to shape his amorphous thoughts, Dulles rapidly prepared a memorandum in advance of seeing Eisenhower. He began by venting the pessimism that pervaded his remarks that had prompted the Solarium exercise and the frustration that had continued to build when the task forces presented their reports and the JCS their new concept. The memorandum made clear that in the aftermath of the NSC meeting, Dulles had concluded that America's allies would support neither the strategy that the JCS maintained held the only promise of enhancing U.S. security, nor the policy of boldness that he believed held the only promise of winning the cold war.

An "urgent reconsideration" of "our collective security policies" was required, Dulles wrote Eisenhower, because, the "NATO concept is losing its grip." Dulles proceeded to explain his judgment by forecasting a foreboding future. Regardless of the arguments the administration used to justify to its allies the new strategic concept, the allies would surely interpret the juxtaposition of relying more heavily on massive retaliation and redeploying U.S. troops back to the United States as "final proof of an isolationist trend." Moreover, because their "budget problems are even more acute than ours," they would cite America's behavior to exculpate their own "military economy." Add to this the combination of Europe's growing insecurity in the face of the Soviet Union's growing nuclear capability on the one hand and the Kremlin's efforts to appear more peaceful and accommodating after Stalin's death on the other, and the result, Dulles predicted, would be increased "wishful thinking" and "neutralism." This logic led inexorably to a single conclusion: "I doubt that any eloquence or reasoning on our part would prevent disintegration and deterioration of our position, with growing isolation through the reaction of our present allies." As a consequence, "the balance of world power, military and economic, would doubtless shift rapidly to our great disadvantage. . . . [E]xpenditures would have to mount very sharply."

Desperate situations demand desperate measures, and Dulles had one in mind. As if he had finally come around to the point of view Eisenhower had expressed during the debate over the "Chance for Peace" speech, he recommended that the president "make a spectacular effort to relax world tensions." In essence, Eisenhower would propose that the United States and Soviet Union mutually withdraw their forces from Western Europe and the satellites and agree to some formula for international control of nuclear weapons and missiles.

Panic had led Dulles to so radically reverse his previous positions. Something had to be done before NATO lost its grip entirely, and the balance of power shifted decisively in favor of the Communists. Further, he assessed the "present" as a "propitious time" for the proposal. The Communists had just suffered a "major reversal" with the overthrow of Mossadegh in Iran, and they had agreed to cease hostilities in Korea "in an atmosphere of our willingness to enlarge the war unless the armistice was accepted." In addition, Konrad Adenauer, West Germany's great champion of its alignment with the West and its contribution of forces to the European Defense Community, had recently been reelected chancellor despite the Kremlin's concerted efforts to subvert his candidacy. Finally, the "full impact of Soviet advances in non-conventional weapons has not yet been felt" in either Europe or Asia. Hence, for the time being, but only temporarily, Dulles concluded, "we will be speaking from strength rather than weakness."[22]

On several previous occasions Eisenhower had tried to impress upon Dulles that he disagreed with Dulles's pessimistic opinion of

America's allies and, by extension, his prognosis for NATO's future. In contrast to Dulles's views, the president's experiences during his World War II and NATO commands suggested that, although frequently insecure and occasionally critical of its government policies, the leaders and publics throughout Western Europe greatly respected the United States and shared virtually all its values. They took the ideal of an Atlantic community very seriously and genuinely wanted it to reach fruition (indeed, in many ways to a greater extent than they wanted to build a European community). Obviously, Eisenhower had made little headway in changing Dulles's outlook.

The president now decided to take a different tack: to administer some shock therapy. Reversing Dulles's intent, Eisenhower expressed "emphatic agreement" with the notion that "renewed efforts should be made to relax world tensions on a global basis." Nevertheless, it would be dangerously premature to implement anything along the lines Dulles proposed until the pluses and minuses of a mutual withdrawal, and consequently a fundamental revision of U.S. policy and strategy, had been subjected to "intensive study by the ablest group of individuals we can possibly assemble."

Eisenhower could have abruptly terminated the discussion by suggesting another Solarium-type exercise or by turning Dulles's proposal into additional grist for the NSC's mill as it reviewed current security policy. Instead, he confronted Dulles with a scenario that he considered a reasonable finale to the secretary of state's premises. Eisenhower inferred from the Kremlin's passive response to his "Chance for Peace" speech that there was little likelihood of the new regime's imminent agreement to either a limit on nuclear weapons or a mutual withdrawal of conventional forces from Europe. Thus, if the administration resigned itself to the collapse of the Atlantic Alliance, what should it do next? Logic would dictate, Eisenhower continued, that it should assume that the Soviets' rejection of the U.S. offer to control arms meant that they were "contemplating their aggressive use." This estimate would demand an expansion and acceleration of the West's defenses, but the United States would have to pay the cost unilaterally. The effort would destroy the economy and require "some form of dictatorial government" without providing a guarantee against war. In Eisenhower's judgment, the conclusion was inescapable. Rather than confront such a bleak future, it would make sense for the United States to initiate a preventive war.

Eisenhower had repeatedly stressed to Dulles and his other advisors that preventive war was not an option. He resolutely believed that any military confrontation with the Soviet Union would inevitably involve nuclear weapons and leave in its wake such massive destruction as to preclude victory. The president was raising the specter of Armageddon now in order to bring Dulles face to face with reality. The alternative to collective security was nuclear holocaust. Hence, the administration must focus its time, energy, and resources on reducing strains and stresses within the alliance by bolstering the strength and morale of the allies. If "your memorandum proves nothing else," Eisenhower ended his "lesson" to Dulles, "it proves that we must get our thinking on these vast problems organized and coordinated so that as a first step all in responsible positions can have confidence that our conclusions are essentially correct."[23]

It is impossible to determine whether Dulles was influenced more by Eisenhower or his own subordinates in the State Department, who were as resistant to his proposal as was the president. In addition, while in Europe a few weeks later, conversations Dulles had held with allied leaders made it emphatically clear that regardless of the terms of an agreement for the mutual withdrawal of forces, such an agreement would destroy Western European confidence in the U.S. commitment to the defense of Europe. Whatever the impetus, Dulles soon abandoned his proposal for a mutual withdrawal. As the NSC's process of preparing a new statement of security policy progressed through September and October, Dulles aligned himself firmly with Eisenhower about the need to enhance collective security. At meeting after meeting the secretary of state argued that, although for both strategic and economic reasons the administration must base military planning on its nuclear arsenal, the primary deterrent to Communist aggression remained the vitality and cohesion of the free world alliance.

In this regard the most heated debate in the NSC concerned the JCS's proposed redeployment of U.S. overseas forces. The NSC Planning Board had defined the problem by writing in its initial draft that "under present conditions . . . any major withdrawal of U.S. forces from Europe or the Far East would be interpreted as a diminution of U.S. interest in the defense of these areas and would seriously undermine the strength and cohesion of the coalition." Cutler, however, considered this innocuous statement an inadequate reflection of the JCS's "fresh look" because it took insufficient account of the overextension of U.S. forces. In his capacity as custodian of the NSC process, he proposed as an alternative to the Planning Board draft a sentence to the effect that, "with the understanding of our allies," the government should over the next few years incrementally redeploy to the United States most of its forces currently stationed abroad.[24]

Representing the JCS, Radford endorsed Cutler's suggested revision. Dulles did not. Unless implemented "under cover of another and larger operation," he "felt obliged to say," probably thinking again about a "spectacular effort" toward a mutual withdrawal, "the redeployment could bring about the complete collapse of our coalition in Europe." It "simply could not be done as a separate and distinct move." A sentence that projected a future redeployment was not inherently objectionable, Dulles continued, and it was a goal that should be pursued. It should not be pursued with "undue haste," however. Moreover, it was imperative to precede any reference to redeploying U.S. forces with the Planning Board's original warning about the grave damage a withdrawal might do to the coalition under conditions as they stood.[25]

In the end Dulles (of course, supported by Eisenhower) carried the day. As approved on October 30, NSC 162/2 made clear the administration's intention to stress the "capability to inflict massive retaliatory damage by offensive strategic striking power" both as a deterrent to Soviet aggression and, if deterrence failed, as a counter to an attack on a vital interest. It made equally clear that it did not intend for this capability to substitute for collective security. "Our allies must be genuinely convinced that our strategy is one of collective security," the statement read. For this purpose, "the presence of U.S. forces" abroad "makes a contribution other than military to the strength and cohesion of the free world coalition." That contribution was as a symbol of U.S. commitment and leadership and, most fundamentally, a symbol of the "strong sense of community of interest" that united all peoples and nations opposed to communism. For the foreseeable future there would be no redeployment.[26]

Dulles was satisfied. Whereas at the start of the NSC's effort to formulate basic national security policy he was prepared to all but bury the concept of collective security, he emerged at the end as the administration's foremost proponent of it, except for Eisenhower. In fact, when NSC 162/2 came up for review the next year, it was Dulles, even more than the president, who fended off proposed revisions that could fracture the international alliance. Dulles's arguments were more consequential because they addressed the issue on which he had for so long been identified: liberation.

The process of writing NSC 162/2 rapidly produced a consensus that the United States should take "feasible political, economic, propaganda and covert measures designed to create and exploit troublesome problems for the USSR, impair Soviet relations with Communist China, complicate control in the satellites, and retard the growth of the military and economic potential of the Soviet bloc." Further, and before the Planning Board submitted the policy statement's first draft, the CIA engineered Mossadegh's overthrow in Iran. Led by the JCS, nevertheless, some of Eisenhower's advisors advocated what, borrowing Dulles's jargon, they euphemistically called a more "positive" or "dynamic" policy. The Joint Chiefs asserted that it was vital to roll back the Communist bloc by means of coercion or even direct force (as had been recommended by Solarium's Task Force C) before the Soviets achieved the capability to strike a crippling nuclear blow against the United States. Otherwise, the resultant strategic stalemate would enhance Moscow's capacity for both nuclear blackmail and conventional aggression.[27]

Eisenhower strenuously disagreed. During the 1952 campaign he had insisted that Dulles qualify his references to liberation with the phrase "by peaceful means," and, if anything, as president he was more determined to lessen the risk of general war. A paramilitary intervention in a peripheral region of the globe was one thing, as was the possible use of tactical atomic weapons on a battlefield such as Korea where the Soviets were not openly engaged. But other than to deter an attack or to retaliate against one, the use of nuclear weapons in an area vital to Soviet interests, or an overly aggressive threat to use them, was too dangerous. It was also pointless. If, as the JCS estimated, the urgency stemmed from the development of Soviet nuclear and missile capabilities, what immediate strategic advantage would be derived from liberating the satellites, or even Communist China? A strike could be launched from Soviet soil. In Eisenhower's view the cost of a more "dynamic" policy—exacerbating the fears of America's allies and the insecurities of the Kremlin—far outweighed the benefits.

While Dulles and most of the NSC members accepted the president's analysis, the military representatives continued to favor a more aggressive posture in order to seize the initiative. Liberating a single Soviet satellite might not diminish Soviet capabililties, they responded, but it "might well initiate a chain reaction" that would in the process generate instability and lead to a "major retraction of the Soviet sphere of influence and control." In the end, Eisenhower relented—somewhat. At Dulles's urging, he agreed to delete from NSC 162/2 a sentence prohibiting the use of force against the Soviet bloc, but only with the understanding that any such action required NSC consideration and the president's express approval.[28]

The deletion of the prohibition against the use of force provided a loophole that the Joint Chiefs sought to exploit. Reiterating their previous arguments, they proposed in 1954 that NSC 162/2 be amended to include "more positive measures to be undertaken [to reduce the Soviet orbit] 'even at the risk of but without deliberately provoking war.' " This time it was Dulles, not Eisenhower, who led the opposition. The secretary of state went directly to the heart of the matter. Not only did the JCS recommendations entail great risks, but if the United States accepted them, "very few of our allies will follow us." Besides, Dulles commented shortly thereafter, "our basic policy on the whole was pretty good," adding sarcastically, even "if it hasn't got us into war."[29]

Dulles's remarks reveal how dramatically his perspective had changed since as late as the summer of 1953. He stressed that change to amplify the force of his arguments. He "could not help but have some sympathy for the general view of the Joint Chiefs of Staff in favor of greater dynamism in the American attitude toward the Soviet Union and Communist China," Dulles conceded to the NSC. "After all," as if anyone needed reminding, "during the course of 1952 he had himself called for a more dynamic U.S. policy vis-à-vis Communism." But he had learned from subsequent experience to think differently. He no longer believed that a "more dynamic and aggressive policy" would substantially mitigate the Soviet threat "unless it eventuated in a general war." The United States would win this war, Dulles said, echoing Eisenhower, but the cost would be intolerable. Most important, while "these more aggressive policies, if successful, *might* result in the disintegration of the Soviet bloc, they would *almost certainly* cause the disintegration of the free world bloc, of which we were the leaders, for our allies in the free world would never go along with such courses of action as these." This cost/benefit analysis alone was reason to "conclude that this kind of aggressive policy was not in the best interests of the United States."[30]

What a contrast with the Dulles who had written a "Policy of Boldness" in 1952, who had implored Eisenhower to pursue liberation in the White House Solarium, and who in Denver had urged the reconsideration of U.S. policy because NATO was "losing its grip"! Although his confession of conversion was insufficient to silence the JCS, it did disarm them. The basic national security policy remained intact. It is therefore ironic that when Dulles sought to articulate that policy to the U.S. public and its allies, he came across as the crusading saber rattler of old. That he did so because of Eisenhower's advice added to the irony.

At the beginning of 1954, following the administration's formulation of its "New Look," Dulles arranged to deliver and have broadcast over television and radio a "major address" to the Council on Foreign Relations entitled "The Evolution of Foreign Policy."[31] While the speech dealt with a variety of issues, it focused on the role of nuclear weapons. Dulles assumed that this was the element of strategy that a nonexpert audience (including many congressmen) could most easily understand and that it best illustrated the administration's promotion of both security and economy. Eisenhower concurred, but when, as usual, he read the draft Dulles submitted to him for comments and approval, he determined that it was too complex and nuanced. He recommended that Dulles insert in the text the simple and clear sentence: "The basic decision [of the administration] was to depend primarily upon a capacity to retaliate, instantly, by means and at places of our choosing." This sentence, Eisenhower advised, could be followed by the explanation that this decision would allow the JCS to "shape our military establishment to fit what is our policy, instead of having to be ready to meet the enemy's many choices. That permits a selection of military means instead of a multiplication of means."[32]

Dulles incorporated Eisenhower's suggestions verbatim. Public reaction was immediate and intensely critical, centering on the very sentences the president had written. Commentators in the domestic and foreign press, doubtless conditioned by their preconceived image of Dulles as a reckless crusader, interpreted the speech to mean that the administration conceived of massive retaliation as a panacea. It would rely on nuclear weapons both to deter and combat all forms of aggression whenever and wherever it occurred, abandoning the allies to fate.

Dulles told Eisenhower that he hoped to repair the damage by preparing an article that clarified "a few points which had led to some misconception, particularly in relation to 'massive retaliatory power.'" The article explained that the capacity for instant nuclear retaliation was the most effective deterrent against a surprise attack by the Soviets on either the United States or one of its vital interests. A "potential aggressor must not be left in any doubt that he would be certain to suffer damage outweighing any possible gains from aggression." Further, because the free world cannot match "Communist forces, man for man and tank for tank, at every point where they might attack," it must develop a strategy "based on its own special assets. . . . especially air and naval power and atomic weapons." This was what the administration had done.[33]

Nevertheless, Dulles stipulated, the phrase "by means and at places of our own choosing" was intended to cover localized aggression, especially on the periphery. In these cases a nuclear response would not be automatic. To the contrary, in order to avoid "the position where the only response open to it is general war," the United States had to "have the flexibility and the facilities which make various responses available." This capability required developing "a system in which local defensive strength is reinforced by more mobile deterrent power." This system would afford the "means," Dulles stressed, for "responding effectively on a selective basis." Of course, the "method of doing so will vary according to the character of the various areas."

The intent of Dulles's article was not merely to provide assurance that neither he nor the administration perceived the capacity for massive retaliation as an all-or-nothing nuclear straitjacket. Perhaps even more important, Dulles sought to provide assurance that the principle of collective security remained central and inviolate. For this reason, the secretary of state elaborated on the Eisenhower-crafted clause—the "basic decision was to depend primarily upon a great capacity to retaliate." Administration strategy placed "primary reliance," he now wrote, on the "combining of two concepts, namely, the creation of power on a community basis and the use of that power so as to deter aggression by making it costly to an aggressor." Although these concepts shared pride of place, Dulles made it clear that without community there could be no power: "No single nation can develop for itself defense power of adequate scope and flexibility." What is more, because the United States lacked an intercontinental delivery system and hence required foreign bases to reach strategic targets, "Without the cooperation of allies, we would not even be in a position to retaliate massively." Dulles then arrived at the conclusion to which he had been aiming: "The cornerstone of security for the free nations must be a collective system of defense."[34]

Dulles called the article "Strategy for Security and Peace" and published it in the April 1954 issue of *Foreign Affairs*. It remains an exceptional encapsulation of the Eisenhower New Look, and compelling testimony to the maturation of Dulles's thinking. Yet relative to the hue and cry his earlier speech had provoked, it was largely ignored. The misconceptions surrounding both Dulles and the New Look endured. This was in part because articles rarely attract the attention of a public address. But in greater part, it was because concurrent with its publication, worldwide attention was riveted on a small fortress in remote Vietnam, where Dulles, the New Look, and collective security were facing their most severe test yet.

Notes

1. Memorandum of conversation, [probably by Cutler], "Solarium Project," May 8, 1953, lot 66D148, SS-NSC files, RG 59, National Archives II, College Park, MD.

2. Cutler memorandum for the record, "Solarium Project," May 9, 1953, *FR, 1952–54* 2:323–26

3. Summaries Prepared by the NSC Staff of Project Solarium Presentations and Written Reports, n.d., ibid., 399–400, 412.

4. "A Report to the National Security Council by Task Force 'C' of Project Solarium," July 16, 1953, "Project Solarium—Report by Task Force 'C' (1–10)," NSC Series, Subject Subseries, Records of the Office of the White House Special Assistant for National Security Affairs, Eisenhower Library, Abilene, KS; Summaries prepared by the NSC Staff, 416.

5. Quoted in Kermit Roosevelt, *Countercoup: The Struggle for Control of Iran* (New York, 1979), 8, 18.

6. Quoted in Edward C. Keefer, "President Dwight D. Eisenhower and the End of the Korean War," *Diplomatic History* 10 (Summer 1986): 270.

7. Memorandum of NSC meeting, February 11, 1953, *FR, 1952–54* 15:769–70.

8. Ibid.

9. I use the Wade-Giles system of romanization because it remains most familiar and was used at the time. Names as romanized in the pinyin system common today and preferred by the PRC are enclosed in parentheses.

10. Quoted in Stephen E. Ambrose, *Eisenhower: The President* (New York, 1984), 91.

11. Quoted in Keefer, "Eisenhower and the Korean War," 275.

12. Quoted in ibid., 278.

13. Quoted in ibid., 280; quoted in William Stueck, *The Korean War: An International History* (Princeton, NJ, 1995), 329.

14. Memorandum by Cutler, July 16, 1953, *FR, 1952–54* 2:397.

15. Summaries Prepared by the NSC Staff, July 16, 1953, ibid., 432–34.

16. Ibid.

17. Memorandum by Cutler, July 16, 1953, ibid., 397.

18. Quoted in Robert J. Watson, *History of the Joint Chiefs of Staff*, vol. 5, *The Joint Chiefs of Staff and National Policy, 1953–1954* (Washington, DC, 1986), 16–17.

19. Arthur W. Radford, *From Pearl Harbor to Vietnam: The Memoirs of Admiral Arthur W. Radford*, ed. Stephen Jurika, Jr. (Stanford, CA, 1980), 321; Memorandum by Radford, Ridgway, Carney, and Twining to the secretary of defense, August 8, 1953, author's possession. I am indebted to David Alan Rosenberg for providing me with a copy of this document.

20. Memorandum by Radford, Ridgway, Carney, and Twining to the secretary of defense, August 8, 1953.

21. Memorandum of NSC meeting, August 27, 1953, *FR, 1952–54* 2:443–55; quoted in Louis L. Gerson, *John Foster Dulles* (New York, 1967), 141.

22. Dulles memorandum to Eisenhower, September 6, 1953, *FR, 1952–54* 2:457–60.

23. Eisenhower memorandum to Dulles, September 8, 1953, ibid., 460–63.

24. NSC 162, "Draft Statement of Policy Proposed by the NSC," September 30, 1953, ibid., 508–9.

25. Memorandum of NSC meeting, October 7, 1953, ibid., 526–28.

26. NSC 162/2, "Statement of Basic National Security Policy," October 30, 1953, ibid., 582, 592, 585–86.

27. Ibid., 595; JCS memorandum for the Secretary of Defense, "Review of Basic National Security Policy (NSC 162)" and Appendix, October 6, 1953, Records of the Office of the Secretary of Defense, RG 330, National Archives II, College Park, MD.

28. Appendix to JSC memorandum to Secretary of Defense, October 6, 1953, 2–3.

29. Memorandum by the secretary of defense to the executive secretary of the NSC, November 22, 1954, *FR, 1952–54* 2:785–87; Memorandum of NSC meeting, June 24, 1954, ibid., 694–95; Memorandum of NSC meeting, November 24, 1954, ibid., 788–90.

30. Memorandum of NSC meeting, December 21, 1953, ibid., 832–36. (emphasis in original.)

31. Foster Dulles telephone conversation with Allen Dulles, December 28, 1953, "December 1953 [Telephone calls] (2)," Chronological File, DP—Eisenhower.

32. Eisenhower to Dulles, January 8, 1954, "Dulles—January 1954," Dulles-Herter Series, Whitman File; Draft #8, Speech Before Council on Foreign Relations, January 7, 1954, "Re: 'The Evolution of Foreign Policy,' " Selective Correspondence and Related Material, DP—Princeton.

33. "Dulles memorandum of luncheon conversation with the president," February 24, 1954, "Meetings with the President 1954 (4)," White House Memoranda Series, DP—Eisenhower; Dulles, "Policy for Security and Peace," *Foreign Affairs* 32 (April 1954): 353–64.

34. Dulles, "Policy for Security and Peace," 353–64.

5

United Action

E ven as Dulles was preparing the speech to the Council on Foreign Relations that generated serious misconceptions about the fundamental precepts of the Eisenhower New Look, Communist-led Vietminh forces under the command of the formidable General Vo Nguyen Giap were laying siege to 12,000 elite French troops isolated in the fortress of Dien Bien Phu in the far northwest corner of Vietnam in French Indochina. By the time Dulles published his "corrective" in *Foreign Affairs*, the siege had produced one of the most severe crises faced by any administration during the cold war. Dulles was at the center throughout. He served the president as ramrod and lightning rod; he proposed policies, publicly defended them, and personally bore the burden for most of the tortuous negotiations—during and after, with friends and foes.

Like the cold war, the Dien Bien Phu crisis emerged from the rubble of World War II. The linchpin of France's empire in Indochina, Vietnam was occupied by the Japanese in 1941. Their abrupt surrender following the atomic bombing of Hiroshima and Nagasaki created a political vacuum, which the Vietnamese nationalist leader Ho Chi Minh sought to fill. At the end of August 1945 he declared the establishment of the independent of state of Vietnam. France could not tolerate Ho's nationalism; war broke out. The United States could not tolerate Ho's communism; it supported France. When Eisenhower took office the United States was paying for roughly one-third of the French counterrevolutionary effort.

It was getting little return on its investment. Giap's mobility and hit-and-run tactics kept the French off balance and on the defensive. The United States urged them to fight more aggressively and allow U.S. military advisors a greater role in planning and training. France accepted U.S. money but not its advice. The French particularly resisted appeals that they promise to grant Vietnam independence, which Americans advocated for reasons of both principle and pragmatism. To Dulles and Eisenhower, colonialism was anathema both to U.S. (and Christian) ideals and to stability and security. Further, France's imperial goals denied it the indigenous support essential to combat Giap's strategy of "people's war."

Dulles had held the French in low esteem since the Versailles conference, and his regard for them plummeted as the situation in Vietnam deteriorated. Yet he assessed the repercussions of a Vietminh victory as almost too horrific to contemplate. To "lose" more territory in Asia so soon after the Communist success in China would make a mockery of the Republican platform he had written and leave the administration vulnerable to crippling attacks from its own party's right wing. Just as Vietnam had been the launching pad for Japan's aggression during World War II, so a Vietminh triumph would lead to Communist control of all Southeast Asia. The West would be deprived of bases, sea lanes, and raw materials. Japan, the "workshop of Asia," would lose access to indispensable resources in Southeast Asia and confidence in America's protection, undoing all that Dulles had accomplished through the treaty ending the occupation. "The situation of the Japanese is hard enough with China being commie," Dulles commented. If Indochina and thus Southeast Asia also fell, "the Japs would be thinking how to get on the other side."[1]

There seemed no end to Dulles's nightmarish list of repercussions. British control of Malaya would be placed in jeopardy, and with it, the vital dollars Britain received through the sale of Malay rubber and tin. As its economy foundered, so also would Europe's recovery and the economic foundation of the Western alliance. Perhaps worst of all, the military foundation of the alliance would founder as well. The French government of René Mayer could probably not survive defeat in Vietnam. Its fall could doom the European Defense Community treaty. In sum, read a memorandum Dulles wrote following a conversation with Eisenhower in March 1953, "the Indochina situation" was even "more important than Korea because the consequences of loss there could not be localized, but would spread throughout Asia and Europe."[2]

Dulles was confident that the catastrophe could be prevented if the French demonstrated more courage and determination, and he tried to coerce them to do so by threatening to withhold future U.S. assistance. The French government appeared to succumb to his pressure. Mayer promised to "perfect" Vietnamese independence, and his successor as prime minister, Joseph Laniel, appointed a new commander for the French forces in Indochina, General Henri Navarre. Navarre quickly devised a military plan intended to satisfy the United States. If provided additional economic aid, he pledged to improve the training of a Vietnamese National Army to enable it to maintain security in French-controlled territory. He would also mass his scattered forces and launch a concentrated offensive to drive the Vietminh from the Red River Delta. Dulles and Eisenhower were skeptical about both the meaning of "perfecting" independence and the potential of Navarre's plan to achieve victory (as was Navarre). But neither of the alternatives—direct U.S. intervention or France's suing for peace—was acceptable. Navarre got his money.

The United States soon came face-to-face with the alternatives nevertheless. Navarre never implemented his plan. Soon after he began to combine his forces in Vietnam, Giap's invasion of France's neighboring colony of Laos (which, as part of Indochina, was also Navarre's responsibility to defend) forced the commanding general to disperse his troops again. Navarre then improvised. He garrisoned twelve French battalions at Dien Bien Phu on the premise that the Vietminh would be lured from Laos into a set-piece battle. Giap was lured. In numbers far superior to the French, and better equipped than in 1953 because of matériel the Korean armistice had freed the PRC to provide, the Vietminh circled back through Laos to tie a noose around the fortress.

The NSC spent much of January 1954 debating its options. None seemed good, and Eisenhower appointed a special committee to study what circumstances might demand direct U.S. intervention and what would be the requirements for an effective intervention. As the committee pondered and analyzed, the situation deteriorated. Despite U.S. warnings that negotiating from weakness produced disaster, France's weariness of the war convinced Prime Minister Laniel that he must negotiate. At a February meeting of foreign ministers in Berlin held to discuss Germany's future and European security, the French pried from Dulles an agreement to add Indochina to the agenda of the Geneva Conference scheduled for April to discuss the Korean Armistice (at which for the first time the Chinese Communists would be officially represented among the "Great Powers"). Dulles feared a French sellout, but he felt compelled to accede. "If we had vetoed the resolution regarding Indochina," he explained on his return, "the Laniel government would have fallen at once, and would have been replaced by a government which not only would have a mandate to end the war in Indochina on any terms, but also to oppose ratification of EDC." Besides, if "the French were completely honest they would get out of Indochina, and we certainly didn't want that."[3]

Giap was determined to leave France no choice. Confounding both French and U.S. military experts, the Vietminh, like colonies of ants, transported heavy artillery up the steep hills overlooking the beleaguered fortress of Dien Bien Phu. In mid-March they began shelling, knocking out the airfield the French had laboriously built. Henceforth, parachute drops were the sole means of resupply. Simultanously, waves of Vietminh soldiers overran the outposts that ringed the fortress. Although the French fought bravely, the CIA estimated their chance of holding on as at best even. The United States had to confront head-on the prospect of intervening to help them out, or even of carrying on the fight alone.

France's chief of staff, General Paul Ely, flew to Washington to sound out the administration. Ely asked about what he could expect if, as in Korea, Communist China committed its forces. Dulles suspected he was not inquiring about just that contingency. Because "to suffer a defeat" would produce "worldwide repercussions," he emphasized, under no circumstance would the United States put its prestige on the line in Indochina unless it was sanguine about the prospect for success. If "the French wanted our open participation in the Indochina war," they would have to grant the U.S. military a "greater degree of partnership" regarding both strategic planning and the training of indigenous forces. They would also have to provide a timetable for "perfecting" Vietnamese independence.[4]

Ely later reported that at a last-minute meeting with Radford, the JCS chair assured him that if necessary the United States would launch massive bombing strikes on the Vietminh positions. Possibly he did. Along with Vice President Richard Nixon, Radford was the most zealous proponent of intervention among Eisenhower's top advisors. He was aware that a bombing plan, codenamed Operation VULTURE, had been formulated in Saigon. Yet

Radford was also aware that neither Eisenhower nor Dulles was close to approving it.

Dulles, although widely perceived as hawkish on intervention, was in truth quite conservative. He doubted that a VULTURE-like operation would succeed unless followed up by U.S. ground forces. He also feared that if the U.S. committed its forces, so would the Communist Chinese. The administration could not afford, and the American public would not tolerate, another Korea. But Dulles believed that the United States had to do something to strengthen the West's hand at the forthcoming Geneva talks.

Dulles formulated a plan, which he called United Action, based on the regional security program he had unsuccessfully promoted while working on the Japanese Peace Treaty. The heart of the plan was the formation of a collective security arrangement for Indochina and the rest of Southeast Asia. The coalition would include the ANZUS Pact powers (Australia, New Zealand, and the United States), France, Great Britain, Thailand, the Philippines, and the Associated States of Indochina. If the United States did intervene, it would have allies—nonwhites from Asia and the Pacific as well as European Caucasians. The administration could thereby avert being charged with spearheading a white man's crusade. But Dulles's objective was to make intervention unnecessary. He hoped that the very existence of this coalition would bolster French morale, deter the Communist Chinese from intervening, and furnish the West with a powerful bargaining chip at the Geneva Conference. The United States could thereby remain out of harm's way.

With the president's blessing, Dulles unveiled his concept in a widely publicized speech on March 29. His menacing tone effectively masked his intent. "The imposition on Southeast Asia of the political system of Communist Russia and its Chinese Communist ally, by whatever means, would be a grave threat to the whole free community," he warned. He then moved to the speech's core. "The United States feels that possibility should not be passively accepted but should be met by united action. This might involve serious risks."[5]

Although Dulles assiduously avoided committing the United States to any specific course of action, as he intended, most observers interpreted the speech as suggesting direct U.S. intervention was in the offing. The next step was to put together the coalition, which Dulles recognized would not be easy. His strategy was to present the prospective member nations with tangible evidence that

Congress had already granted Eisenhower the authority to intervene. With this assurance of U.S. commitment and leadership, they would be more likely to fall in line. Dulles had the State Department draft a resolution providing the president with a blank check.

Congress, however, refused to write the check. At a secret meeting with Dulles and Radford on Saturday April 3, leaders from both parties made it clear that they would sanction the use of U.S. force only after the administration had obtained "satisfactory commitments" of support from the other nations, especially Britain. There must be "no more Koreas with the United States furnishing 90 percent of the manpower." They also made congressional approval of the resolution conditional on France's agreeing to "internationalize" the war and to extend independence to the Indochinese. After the meeting adjourned, Dulles confided to Eisenhower that although it "went pretty well," the outcome did raise "some serious problems." He did not object to the conditions Congress imposed. But now that U.S. participation in United Action was inextricably tied to them, the task of inducing allies to go along would be more difficult.[6]

Eisenhower did his part to provide allies with the proper incentive. Expounding on what became notoriously known as the domino theory at a press conference several days later, he warned that if Indochina fell the rest of Southeast Asia would "go over very quickly." The resultant economic and strategic losses to the free world would be "incalculable." Dulles then flew off to Europe for weeks of shuttle diplomacy in search of "satisfactory commitments" to head off the potential calamity. In London he was told not to count on British participation; they would not even consent to planning for a joint military operation. In Paris he was told not to count on France agreeing both to fight and give up its empire. Foreign Minister Georges Bidault later alleged that to encourage the French to persevere, the U.S. secretary of state offered the "loan" of two atomic bombs. Bidault loathed Dulles, and the allegation is almost certainly false. He would never have made this offer without Eisenhower's authorization. The president discussed the possibility with the NSC after Dulles's return from Europe, but he never approved it.[7]

What is certain is that Dulles categorically rejected Bidault's request that the U.S. intervene unconditionally and independent of other allies. The secretary estimated that the fall of Dien Bien Phu was preferable "under present circumstances." It was in a last-ditch effort to change the circumstances that he traveled once more to London. If he could persuade the British to sign onto United Action, Dulles thought that concessions might be wrung from the Communists at Geneva by the threat of intervention regardless of the fate of Dien Bien Phu. But Churchill's resistance had not waned. He would agree to cooperate with the United States only in guaranteeing any settlement reached at Geneva and securing the remainder of Southeast Asia should the Communists renew aggression in the future. "I have known many reverses myself," said the old warrior. "I have suffered Singapore, Hong Kong, Tobruk; the French will have Dien Bien Phu."[8]

They did. On May 7, after fifty-five days of resistance, the French forces surrendered. For Dulles, the timing could not have been worse. By May 7 he was already in Geneva; the next day the Indochina phase of the conference began. Dulles was afraid that France, having suffered such a humiliating defeat, would cave in to any Communist demands. And without the threat of United Action on the part of the West, the Communists would demand all of Indochina.

Dulles's best-case scenario was that the negotiations would acrimoniously collapse before the Communists gained anything diplomatically that they had not already acquired militarily. The French and British might then be convinced to change their minds. He recognized that such a development was unlikely. Still, if he could keep alive a credible threat of intervention by either resurrecting United Action or perhaps making the Communists believe that unilateral U.S. action was possible, some portion of Vietnam and the rest of Indochina might be salvaged. As his backup plan, Dulles intended to disassociate the United States from any agreement that approximated appeasement in order to insulate himself and Eisenhower should they be pilloried by right-wing Republicans.

At Geneva, Dulles behaved in a manner that signaled that he found the proceedings intrinsically—and profoundly—distasteful. He refused to shake the hand of Chinese Foreign Minister Chou En-lai (Zhou Enlai). His refusal to be seated anywhere near him or any other Communist delegate caused logistical problems for everyone. He also seemed to take exception to whatever was said, no matter who said it. "[A]lmost pathological rage and gloom" were the words used by Evelyn Shuckburgh, British Foreign Minister Anthony Eden's secretary, to describe Dulles's attitude. He sat around the table with his "mouth drawn down at the corners, and his eyes on the ceiling, sucking his teeth." Dulles remained at Geneva only long enough to demonstrate his contempt and thereby reinforce his image as someone champing at the bit to do battle against the Communists, preferably with atomic weapons. On May 3 he returned to the United States.[9]

With Undersecretary of State Walter Bedell Smith taking over his chores in Geneva, Dulles turned his attention to promoting United Action from Washington. Even if the British remained resistant, he opined, the agreement of Australia and New Zealand would be sufficient to keep the threat of intervention alive. But Australia made its participation contingent on that of Britain. France, moreover, persisted in playing hardball. It demanded a U.S. commitment to use ground forces as a condition for its fighting on. Dulles was convinced the French was either trying to maneuver the United States into assuming primary military reponsibility for a renewed conflict or to set up an alibi to explain its capitulation. He could not decide which of the two would be worse. Meanwhile, U.S. officials continued developing plans for intervention under a variety of circumstances and with a variety of allies.

Dulles's hopes rose somewhat as May turned into June. He was not making any progress toward United Action, but neither were the Geneva conferees progressing toward a settlement. Negotiations deadlocked over a spectrum of issues, most notably the possible partition of Vietnam and the withdrawal of Vietminh troops from Laos and Cambodia. But even as Dulles wrote Smith that it was probably "in our best interest" for the conference to break down without settling anything, British Foreign Minister Eden proposed a series of promising compromise measures. At the same time the French ran out of patience and replaced the Laniel government with one headed by the Socialist Pierre Mendès-France. Mendès-France, who served as both prime and foreign minister, set a deadline of July 21 for achieving an accord.[10]

These developments forced Dulles to shift gears. The apparent determination of both Britain and France to reach an agreement with the Communists at virtually any cost not only dashed his hope that the negotiations might collapse, but it also effectively ended any prospect for resurrrecting United Action in any form. Dulles resigned himself to a settlement that, he told Eisenhower, "we would have to gag about." All the United States could do was to seek to control its consequences.[11]

Dulles thought it imperative that the administration at a minimum avoid identification with either outright appeasement or a settlement that "might come about through the Communist habit of using words in a double sense and destroying the significance of good principles with stultifying implementations." Had he had his way, the U.S. delegation would be led by no one above the rank of ambassador for the duration of the conference. By maintaining this low-level representation, Washington could distance but not completely divorce itself from its allies. For the first time during the Indochina crisis, Eisenhower overruled his secretary of state. "We do not want to have an apparent parting of the ways among us occur in the spotlight of the Geneva conference," he explained. Further, the president feared that Mendès-France might charge that U.S. indifference toward the negotiations deprived him of the leverage he needed to obtain valuable concessions from the Communists. Eisenhower insisted that Smith remain as head of the U.S. delegation. He sent Dulles to Paris, where he worked out with Mendès-France a convoluted arrangement by which the United States pledged to support the French without endorsing their position unconditionally.[12]

To Dulles's surprise, the Communists acceded to terms much more favorable than he had predicted. He evidently had succeeded in convincing the Soviets that the United States might still intervene, and the Kremlin refused to accept the risk of being drawn into an expanded conflict. For their part, the Chinese Communists feared that a unified, independent Vietnam would be less susceptible to their influence and perhaps become their future rival. Both Moscow and Peking pressured the Vietminh to withdraw their forces from Laos and Cambodia and agree to Vietnam's partition at the 17th parallel (the boundary proposed by the West in contrast to Ho Chi Minh's proposal of the 13th parallel) until 1956, when elections would be held to unify the country. An international commission would supervise the accord and the election. The Vietminh believed they had been sold out, but without Soviet and Chinese support they had to relent. As for the United States, it refused to sign the Final Declaration but pledged not to "disturb" its provisions.

Dulles was already at work on another scheme when the Geneva Conference concluded on July 21. The U.S. statement promising not to disturb the accords had been carefully worded so as to allow great latitude in subsequent actions. The "important thing," Dulles commented several days later, was "not to mourn the past but to seize the future opportunity to prevent the loss in Northern Vietnam from leading to the extension of communism throughout Southeast Asia and the Southwest Pacific." No longer did the United States "want to operate on what has been referred to as the domino theory, where the loss of one area will topple another and another," Dulles explained. "I think there is a good chance, if we can get some cooperation, to prevent the situation from continuing."[13]

Toward this end, Dulles reformulated his United Action blueprint to produce a proposal for a regional collective security pact whose purpose was to quarantine the Communists. While it formally included the same members, it incorporated a separate protocol stipulating that any threat to southern Vietnam, Laos, or Cambodia by definition threatened the peace and security of the signatory nations. This device brought these areas under a protective umbrella. The part of Vietnam below the 17th parallel was implicitly acknowledged to be independent, at least to a degree, thereby contravening the spirit if not the letter of the Geneva Accords and foreshadowing future developments.

Although Dulles was the prime force behind the creation of a regional security pact, he did not embrace the concept without reservations. He would have preferred to exclude Britain and France in order to prevent Communist charges that the organization was merely a more sophisticated vehicle for perpetuating Western colonialism. He recognized, however, that neither country would countenance being left out. Besides, the nations of the area themselves were too weak and distrustful of one another to stand alone, particularly because stronger powers such as India and Indonesia were avowedly neutral and would not participate in the pact.

Dulles was equally concerned that U.S. participation would lead to its overcommitment. He envisioned that rather than a specific obligation of troops, a mobile strike force would support a consultative arrangement similar to that of the Organization of American States (OAS) in the Western Hemisphere. He was even reluctant to call the pact the Southeast Asia Treaty Organization (SEATO) because it suggested too many parallels with Europe's NATO. Dulles also stressed that unlike the Marshall Plan, U.S. economic assistance to Southeast Asia would remain limited and be dispensed on the basis of individual need.

Throughout the negotiations in Manila that established SEATO in September, Dulles led the U.S. delegation. By design the final provisions were so vague that the organization lacked real strength. Dulles believed that the pledge of SEATO's members to consult together if confronted by aggression, albeit only on paper, would give the Communists reason to pause. Should they attack, the United States would have at its disposal a legal foundation to respond with its own forces and, in theory, allies to fight by its side.

Dulles knew that the most effective deterrent to Vietminh aggression was a strong and stable regime south of the 17th parallel. If such a regime attracted significant popular support, the 1956 elections might result in a unified Vietnam aligned with the West. Dulles was sufficiently realistic to evaluate this possibility as highly doubtful. Ho Chi Minh's appeal was widespread and enthusiastic. Still, there was no guarantee that the elections would take place. A lot could happen before 1956 to justify calling them off, and the SEATO treaty accorded a measure of independence to southern Vietnam. Further, exhausted from efforts against the French and uncertain of much assistance from the Soviets and Chinese, the Vietminh would have to think long and hard about reigniting hostilities against an "entity" in the south that could offer formidable resistance.

Standing in the way of Dulles's objectives were both the southern Vietnamese and the French. Chaos reigned supreme among the former. In the midst of the Geneva Conference, the Vietnamese Emperor Bao Dai, the titular head of France's puppet state, had invited Ngo Dinh Diem to form a new government. Of mandarin stock, Diem had the appropriate administrative experience, had not collaborated with the French, and was fanatically anti-Communist. He was also a reclusive Catholic in a largely Buddhist country who lacked political judgment and skill. Rather than seek to build a dependable constituency, he preferred to govern through his family network, especially his drug-addicted, meglomaniacal younger brother, Ngo Dinh Nhu. Diem's effort to consolidate his rule was also impeded by the autonomous power wielded by the Cao Dai and Hoa Hao, two feudalistic, political-religious sects, and the Binh Xuyen, who ran Saigon's police force as well as its organized gambling. Diem's military was weak, disorganized, and disloyal. Dulles admitted that Diem suffered from serious shortcomings, but he judged him more capable of "rallying and holding nationalist sentiment than most of the Vietnamese who seem now to be on the scene, or in the wings."[14]

The secretary of state saw the continued presence of the French as part of the problem, not its solution. They were understandably reluctant to support the Francophobic Diem. More fundamentally, their objectives were uncertain and conflict-ridden. Their commitment to implementing the Geneva Accords and safeguarding Vietnamese independence collided with what they considered a colonialist entitlement to retaining overarching influence. In addition, although in principle they agreed to work toward creating a viable regime in the south and to coordinate their efforts with the United States, the French estimated that unification under the Communists was all but inevitable. Thus, the protection of their remaining interests in Vietnam required their mending fences with the north. When U.S. officials objected to France's attempts at conciliation, the French accused the United States of "meddling," "ineptitude," and "total ignorance of the country and people."[15]

Dulles's strategy was to reduce the French role in Vietnam. This had to be done gradually. Not only was France pivotal to the free world alliance, but in southern Vietnam it retained many indigenous allies and remained a potential source of stability. What is more, Dulles was not prepared for the United States to assume full responsibility for an area until he could be more certain about its future. For the time being, he counseled that the United States exercise patience and try to cooperate with the French to strengthen both Diem and his army.

Through early 1955, U.S. policy appeared to be making headway. In November 1954, Eisenhower had sent to Vietnam as his personal representative General J. Lawton ("Lightning Joe") Collins. After a rocky start, Collins developed a productive relationship with General Paul Ely, the former French chief of staff who now served as Paris's High Commissioner in Indochina. In concert they succeeded in improving the indigenous army. Further, although the French continued to suggest alternatives to Diem, they no longer seemed as unalterably opposed to his rule.

They still resisted Diem, however, and after the prime minister was almost overthrown Dulles decided the time had come to ease France out of Vietnam. What forced the issue was the so-called "sects crisis" in the spring of 1955, when the simmering antagonism between Diem and the Binh Xuyen, Cao Dai, and Hoa Hao boiled over into open warfare. Dulles blamed the sects and accepted Diem's claim that they had been goaded by the French. Ely blamed Diem's misrule. This Dulles expected. He did not expect the support Ely received from Collins. The key U.S. official on the scene cabled Washington that the crisis proved Diem's incompetence. He recommended his replacement.

Dulles was so shocked that his patronage of Diem momentarily wavered. He confided to his brother at the CIA that it "looks like the rug is coming out from under the fellow [Diem] in Southeast Asia." And he wrote Foreign Relations Committee Chairman Walter George that although he was reluctant to acquiesce to a change in the Saigon government, "we may have to do so at any rate." Dulles then summoned Collins to consult about how to remove Diem at a minimum cost and whom the U.S. should sponsor as a successor.[16]

Dulles never had to arrive at answers to either question. While Collins was in Washington, Diem, with aid from the CIA, turned the tide of the civil war decisively in his favor. After securing Eisenhower's clearance, Dulles instructed Collins to return to Saigon and back the prime minister without qualification. The secretary immediately flew to Paris to take care of the French end of the problem himself. At a scheduled NATO meeting, he told Prime Minister Edgar Faure, who had a few months before succeeded Mendès-France, that U.S. support for Diem was unequivocal. When Faure replied that France remained committed to Diem's removal, Dulles said that he regretted the difference of opinion but the U.S. position was fixed. Diem and southern Vietnam will then be your responsibility, not ours, Faure retorted. Dulles shrugged, and that was that. As Dulles had desired, U.S. policy toward Vietnam would no longer be held hostage to the French. Washington flooded the south with aid and advisors. The 1956 elections were never held.

It was no coincidence that Franco-American differences over Vietnam reached their climax at a NATO meeting in Paris. Since September 1950, when NATO planners decided to rearm the Federal Republic of Germany (the FRG had been formed the year before by the merger of the three postwar Western zones), the future of the European military alliance and the future of Indochina had been inextricably intertwined.

From the U.S. perspective, the viability of any collective security blanket for Europe required the contribution of West German troops. This objective took precedence over the settlement of any other dimension of the "German Problem," reunification above all. In addition, U.S. policymakers during both the Truman and Eisenhower administrations assumed that only the watchful eye of the Atlantic Alliance provided an adequate safeguard against the German military's reemergence as an independent force and a threat to its European neighbors—America's vital allies.

While avowedly supportive of the U.S. position, France was still scarred by the experience of World War II and feared German rearmament regardless of the circumstances under which it occurred. In order to deflect and dilute U.S. demands, it advanced a concept (the Pleven Plan) that evolved into the European Defense Community. As an alternative to incorporating an autonomous West German national force into NATO, France proposed the creation of an integrated European army with a unified command and procurement procedure. This arrangement enhanced French control over the German contribution. After labyrinthine negotiations, France, the FRG, Italy, Belgium, the Netherlands, and Luxembourg signed the EDC treaty in May 1952. Tied to the treaty were contractual agreements to end the occupation and restore full FRG sovereignty. Three months earlier the West Germans had agreed to integrate their coal and steel industries with those of France.

To America's great consternation, it rapidly became apparent that France remained deeply suspicious of its historic enemy. Although the EDC army was to be wholly dedicated to NATO, the absence of direct U.S. and British participation in it bred anxiety in France as to whether its structure was sufficient to bridle the Germans. As the Indochina War consumed its troops and officers corps in ever increasing numbers, this anxiety intensified. By the time the Eisenhower administration took office, France was continually postponing a vote on EDC and demanding more and more U.S. assistance in Vietnam as the price for its agreeing to German rearmament. There was no question in either Washington or Paris that French ratification of the treaty was contingent on the quantity and form of this aid.

France's foot-dragging on EDC ratification, thus putting on hold German rearmament and sovereignty, was a primary cause for Dulles's growing pessimism about the prognosis for European collective security in 1953. "If France and Germany cannot be woven together in a European fabric of mutual understanding and common endeavor," there could "be no real strength in Europe," he insisted. France's attitude also bedeviled his efforts to balance U.S. policies and objectives in Europe and Asia. Through the initial stages of the Dien Bien Phu crisis, Dulles believed that any chance to secure French ratification of the EDC treaty rested on assisting the French to win the Indochina War. After the Berlin conference in February, he concluded that any chance of securing French ratification of the EDC treaty rested on agreeing to negotiate an end to the Indochina War.[17]

Dulles was correct, but only in a limited sense. What doomed EDC ratification in France was neither the French defeat at Dien Bien Phu nor the outcome of the negotiations at Geneva. Nevertheless, Dulles was correct in recognizing that both affected the political landscape, and consequently the prospects for EDC's approval, in Paris. Indeed, the grief the French suffered in Vietnam on both the military and diplomatic fronts was the decisive factor in the fall of the Laniel government to one headed by Mendès-France. As

Dulles had repeated predicted, Mendès-France was more eager than Laniel to reach a settlement on Vietnam, and less eager to persuade the French Assembly to approve the EDC treaty in its current form. There was little he could do about the former, but he was determined to influence the latter.

In early July 1954, Dulles flew to Paris to meet with Mendès-France and British Foreign Minister Anthony Eden. His primary purpose was to discuss the level of U.S. representation at the Geneva Conference and to arrive at a formula that bridged the gap between the U.S. position and the position of its allies. Dulles considered the need to confer about the EDC no less pressing. He told Mendès-France as forcefully as he could that the French delay in ratifying the treaty was jeopardizing the security of the entire free world.

The problem, Dulles explained, went beyond the vital role assigned to German troops in plans to defend Europe. More fundamentally, the chief objective of the Soviet Union's global strategy was, preferably, to gain control of West Germany's resources and manpower, and, minimally, to deny them to the West. France's procrastination played directly into the Kremlin's hand. The longer the delay in restoring the FRG's sovereignty, the stronger would become its public's sentiment in favor of Soviet proposals for a reunified but neutral independent German state. If this momentum proved unstoppable, the West would forfeit its guaranteed access to German assets and, no less important, its guaranteed influence over Germany's destiny. Was Mendès-France, Dulles asked, willing to risk Germany's remilitarizing in the future without Western supervision or its gravitating toward the Soviet orbit? Neither the secretary of state nor anyone in the Eisenhower administration was willing to take the risk.

A year earlier Dulles had proclaimed that "our policy with respect to Europe" must not "involve a choice between France *or* Germany. It is based on France *and* Germany." Now he warned Mendès-France that the French would suffer the consequences of forcing the United States to choose. Dulles threatened that the United States would be compelled to work out with the British and the countries who had already ratified the EDC treaty a new collective security pact that left out the French completely. Eden nodded his agreement. In Washington several weeks earlier, he had pledged Dulles Britain's support.[18]

Mendès-France replied plaintively, and sincerely, that his goals did not differ from Dulles's. His government would promote the EDC, but it was imperative to postpone a vote in the Assembly. At present he was not confident that there was a majority in favor, and its defeat could irreparably cripple NATO and European unity. In the best case, the treaty would be approved by a slim majority, but that would be a Pyrrhic victory. France would be left weak and divided. Mendès-France assured Dulles that the prospects for EDC ratification would be much approved after a settlement on Indochina was achieved. He did not explain why, however. The conclusion of the Geneva Conference shed no new light on his strategy. The "tension is mounting in Paris on both sides of the EDC question," U.S. Ambassador to France Douglas Dillon cabled Dulles, "as Mendès continues successfully to conceal his views and intentions."[19]

Mendès-France finally made his move the second week of August, but it was not what Dulles had hoped for. On August 4, the Soviets proposed to meet with the United States, Britain, and France to prepare for a four-power conference on general European security. This was precisely the type of meeting that Dulles had vigorously opposed following Stalin's death because of its potentially adverse affect on progress toward rearming West Germany and anchoring it firmly to the West. The Soviets had revived their plan for a reunified, demilitarized, and neutral Germany at the Berlin Conference in February, and the EDC treaty was still in limbo; Dulles's objection to a conference was consequently even more intense. Mendès-France claimed he could exploit the meeting to secure greater support for EDC ratification. He planned to schedule a vote in the French Assembly after negotiations on Germany exposed Soviet hypocrisy.

Dulles was "deeply shocked and disheartened." He never trusted Mendès-France and suspected, unfairly, that the prime minister's true intention was to trade a French vote against EDC in exchange for Soviet agreement to reunify Germany on the basis of a free election and its neutrality. The result, Dulles cabled Ambassador Dillon in Paris, would "completely destroy NATO defense plans" and "probably destroy [FRG Chancellor Konrad] Adenauer," whose political opposition maintained that his support for EDC was antithetical to reunification. Moreover, if Mendès-France exchanged EDC for German neutralization, he would "split [the] basic Western position and [its] solidarity, thereby providing [the] Soviets with [the] opportunity they have sought for years."[20]

Eisenhower backed Dulles's protest, and Mendès-France yielded. He agreed not to await a four-power conference before submitting the EDC treaty to the French Assembly. He proposed several modifications, however, that he claimed would boost the prospects of a favorable vote. The most significant were that any member of the EDC would have the right to veto all its decisions, and that only within the FRG itself would West German forces be integrated with those of the other European allies. Most important, the treaty would explicitly stipulate that should German reunification come about, the EDC member states would be free to withdraw from the community.

Dulles immediately objected. To amend the EDC treaty at this time would require those nations that had already ratified it to begin the process anew. This would cause additional, and unacceptable, delay. What is more, the revised treaty would blatantly discriminate against the West Germans. Did the French really need to be reminded of the developments that had ensued following Versailles? Finally, granting each member veto power would gut the community of its supranational character. Mendès-France was sabotaging the treaty's political purpose of promoting European integration. The provision concerning withdrawal signaled that the EDC was but a temporary expedient. Dulles presented Mendès-France with an ultimatum: Either he drop his proposals to amend the treaty and submit it unaltered to the French Assembly without more dawdling, or the United States would immediately take steps to rearm West Germany and restore its sovereignty.

Dulles's ultimatum was both unnecessary and disingenuous. It was unnecessary because none of the nations who had already ratified the treaty would agree to consider amending it. It was disingenuous because Dulles refused even to contemplate a mechanism other than the EDC for anchoring the FRG to the West. When the British suggested that it was prudent to begin some contingency planning, such as to invite West Germany to join NATO, Dulles replied: "We must while there is still a chance for EDC keep our eyes exclusively on the EDC." Bending to U.S. pressure, Mendès-France put the treaty to a vote on August 30. He had predicted its rejection unless it was modified. He predicted correctly.[21]

Dulles could not contain his gloom. Within hours of the French vote he drafted a statement that one of his assistants described as the secretary's "lament on the death of EDC." Dulles began by reasserting that, on the one hand, "there cannot be an effective defense of Continental Europe without a substantial military contribution from the Germans," and, on the other, that "Germany cannot be indefinitely neutralized or otherwise discriminated against in terms of her sovereignty." Dulles, as he did so often, went on to present a lesson in history. The United States since the end of World War II "had assumed that, given U.S. aid and support, Western Europe would at long last develop a unity which would make it immune from war as between its members and defensible against aggression from without." Toward this end, "on the economic and military side we made massive contributions." France's vote against the EDC treaty "without provision of any alternative means of dealing with the basic ills of Europe," therefore, was not only inimical to "international peace and security," but also tantamount to rejecting the "premise" of "U.S. post-war policy." This "tragedy," Dulles concluded, "compels the U.S. to reappraise its foreign policies and to adjust them to the resultant situation."[22]

Until this point Eisenhower had supported Dulles without reservation. After reading the draft, he counseled that "we cannot sit down in black despair and admit defeat." He joined with Dulles's subordinates in urging the secretary to revise the statement to "remove the tone of bitterness and preserve our position of leadership." Having partially recovered from his depression, Dulles agreed. He also added to his statement a summons for the NATO Council, which of course included France, to convene a special meeting to address the "emergency" and determine a course of action to mitigate the consequences of the French vote.[23]

The British, who had concluded that French rejection was a certainty long before the vote on August 30, had on hand a course of action to propose. Despite U.S. advice to the contrary, Britain had continued its effort to formulate a procedure for rearming West Germany and restoring its sovereignty directly through NATO. The key was to persuade France that the FRG was going to be rearmed regardless of French opposition, and that the most effective safeguard against its ever again threatening the continent would be for this rearmament to occur within a framework in which the United States and Britain as well as France were directly involved. In addition, the Germans would have to agree that FRG rearmament would be subject to restrictions decided upon by the original NATO powers.

Lest the United States have time to come up with a different formula that "might not seem to us wise," British Foreign Minister Eden suggested that rather than a meeting of the NATO Council, the four powers most directly involved—France, the FRG, the United States, and Britain—assemble in conjunction with all the EDC signatory nations. This Nine-Power Conference, which Eden wanted held in London, could move directly to consideration of the British proposal and provide "the opportunity to wind this up." Dulles hesitated. He fully understood the reason for Eden's urgency because his distrust of Britain mirrored that of Churchill's foreign minister of the United States. He suspected that the British were "deliberately attempting to rush us in order to put across some plan of their own which we may or may not approve."[24]

His need to go to Manila to finalize SEATO provided Dulles with an excuse to defer the meeting. Eden used the additional time to broach his idea to Adenauer and Mendès-France. Encouraged by their responses, he wrote Dulles on September 13 that "I think we now have the foundation for a practical plan which our experts in NATO could work out quickly with German participation." Dulles still had doubts. But if "there was a better way," he conceded, "he had not thought of it." After another quick trip to Europe to visit with Adenauer and Eden on September 16 and 17, Dulles went further. The "general scheme or conception Mr. Eden had developed," read the secretary of state's memorandum of his conversations, "seemed the best that could be devised to meet the situation which confronts us."[25]

Dulles remained unenthusiastic in no small measure because the United States had ceded the initiative to the British. In his remarks to the NSC the next week, he refused to credit Churchill and Eden with either foresight or imagination. Instead, Dulles advocated that the United States follow Britain's lead in order to placate its rather childlike craving to "throw [its] weight around a little" and not "seem tied to U.S. coattails." It will not "take kindly to any plan 'made in America'," Dulles elaborated, as if the administration had formulated one. The United States would lose nothing by playing along, and if doing so reinforced Atlantic unity at the same time that it rearmed Germany, it had everything to gain. "National pride may do more to assure a successful defense of Europe than U.S. tutelage," Dulles concluded. Eisenhower "heartily" concurred. The "Europeans should make the plan and do most of the talking," he said.[26]

On September 25, Dulles flew to London for the Nine-Power Conference. He had scripted the role he intended to play at the previous day's NSC meeting, and he followed it religiously. Dining with Eden prior to the start of the conference, he asserted that his "attitude would be that the U.S. was there as a friend and counselor and was deeply interested in the results but looked to the Europeans to put forward proposals."[27] To Mendès-France he said much the same thing. The U.S. position was that "even though there was indeed no good alternative to the EDC, nevertheless we could find a solution. . . . We came here with no plan of our own but only the desire to be helpful."[28]

The Nine-Power Conference stretched over fourteen plenary sessions from September 28 to October 4, 1954. Throughout, Dulles was purposefully but uncharacteristically subdued, even deferential. At the secretary's invitation Eden served as the conference's permanent chairman, and it was British proposals that framed the discussions from beginning to end. The result was to accomplish in a matter of days what had eluded the NATO powers for years, and to do so in a manner probably superior to the EDC. The conferees agreed to resuscitate the Brussels Treaty, the collective security pact signed by Britain, France, Belgium, the Netherlands, and Luxembourg in 1948 that had laid moribund since NATO's establishment a year later. The name of the Brussels Pact's executive organ, the Western Union, was changed to the Western European Union (WEU) and enlarged to include Italy as well as the FRG. As had been planned for the EDC's integrated army, the WEU's entire military force structure was dedicated to NATO. Consequently, the size and shape of the FRG national army was restricted by decision of the NATO Council, and it was enveloped within and was subordinate to an American-led supreme command. In exchange for the restoration of West German sovereignty, Adenauer declared that the FRG would manufacture neither atomic, biological, and chemical (ABC) weapons, nor warships and strategic bombers.

A month later the nine powers met again in Paris, this time joined by all the NATO ministers. Over the previous weeks the details of the outline decided upon at London were worked out. Although the discussions dragged out over three days, they were comprised virtually entirely of declarations of support for agreements already reached. With great pomp and circumstance, the Paris Agreements were signed on the afternoon of October 23, 1954. By the new year they had been ratified by the French Assembly. In May 1955, the occupation of the Federal Republic of Germany officially ended, and it formally joined the NATO alliance.

Dulles had long since turned his attention to other cold war battlefields. Notwithstanding his contribution to and support for the administration's New Look, his hectic agenda and peripatetic behavior were the product more of crisis management than strategic doctrine. In the midst of the Vietnam and EDC imbroglios he was forced to find time to put out another fire. This one flared up in the Western hemisphere itself, in Guatemala, where the United

States had much greater latitude to respond unilaterally—and covertly. Even in this case, Dulles found himself yet again knocking heads with the European allies.

As with their other foreign policy challenges, Eisenhower and Dulles inherited the problem with Guatemala from Truman. For the decade prior to World War II, Guatemala's strong-arm ruler (caudillo), Jorge Ubico Castañeda, had put the country at the service of the United States. Diplomatically, he marched in lockstep with Washington's hemispheric policies. Economically, he acceded to the wishes of the North American United Fruit Company (UFCO). In 1944 a loose coalition of middle-class intellectuals and junior army officers overthrew Ubico, who had severely curtailed their economic opportunities and political freedoms. The revolutionaries proclaimed their intention to liquidate the agrarian system that privileged the small minority of large landowners and depended on volatile external markets, to introduce modern technologies to expand production, to establish representative governing institutions, and to end the economic disparities and racial oppression (a majority of Guatemalans were Mayan Indians) that defined the country's stratified social structure.

Juan José Arévalo Bermej dedicated his administration to fulfilling this very ambitious agenda. Elected president in a landslide at the end of 1944, Arévalo was a civilian intellectual. He repudiated Marxism's emphasis on the "disingenuous distribution of material goods for the silly economic leveling of men who are economically different," but he promoted the ideal of harmony between the individual and society. He also believed that it was the responsibility of government to prevent the interests of the few from standing in the way of the needs and progress of the many. Arévalo called his philosophy "spiritual socialism."[29]

While Arévalo's writings and rhetoric were amorphous and idealistic, his policy initiatives were concrete and pragmatic. At his urging, Guatemala's National Assembly ratified a constitution with a myriad of provisions for strengthening democratic processes and fostering social, political, and economic reform. Power was no longer vested in a single authority but was divided among an executive, a legislature, and a judiciary. The constitution explicitly guaranteed freedom of speech, of the press, and of assembly, and extended the franchise to all adults, excluding illiterate women. It also granted political parties the right to organize and operate without restriction, with the explicit exception of those either based abroad or beholden to a foreign government.

Arévalo directed most of his effort to redressing Guatemala's social and economic ills. He launched massive public health and literacy campaigns, and established government-funded agencies to stimulate indigenous investment and economic diversification. He won legislative approval for a Law of Forced Rental, which controlled land rents by compelling large landowners to lease uncultivated property at a rate not to exceed 5 percent of the market value of the crops produced. Most significant, he promulgated a Labor Code that gave workers the right to unionize, established minimum wages and made contracts compulsory, set standards for improved labor conditions (especially for women and children), and mandated preferential hiring for native workers.

Arévalo also appointed commissions to study Guatemala's historic land tenure problems and investigate efforts at agrarian reform in other countries. His term in office expired before he could act on any recommendations, but he left office confident that his successor, Jacobo Arbenz Guzmán, would do so. An army colonel, Arbenz had played a leading role in the 1944 revolution, served as Arévalo's minister of defense, and enthusiastically embraced the program of social reform and economic renewal. He was Arévalo's candidate of choice in the 1950 election, and although his overwhelming victory was tainted by the assassination of his most formidable opponent, it was all but foreordained. For the first time in the 130-year history of the Guatemalan Republic, the transfer of executive power took place peacefully and on schedule.

Arbenz immediately set to work to expand upon the legacy that he inherited. His "pet project" was implementing the recommendations of Arévalo's commissions on agrarian reform. The most fundamental and explosive feature of the Agrarian Reform Bill that Arbenz proposed was its provision for the expropriation and redistribution of land not presently under cultivation. The bill stipulated that, with certain exemptions, a percentage of the idle land of the largest estates be nationalized and rented to landless Guatemalans at an affordable rate. Owners of land that was expropriated would receive compensation in the amount they had declared the land worth for tax purposes, paid over twenty-five years with 3 percent interest. On June 17, 1952, the National Assembly approved the Agrarian Reform Bill by an unanimous vote.[30]

The enactment of agrarian reform reinforced U.S. suspicions of Communist influence in Guatemala that had been building since the early years of Arévalo's tenure. The United States had been surprised by the 1944 revolution and uncertain what to make of

Arévalo's "spiritual socialism." It became increasingly apprehensive as the cold war escalated and the pace and scope of the reform measures grew. The Truman administration was inundated by alarming reports of Communist subversion, most notably from the United Fruit Company. UFCO, or the "Octopus" as the company was called in Guatemala, had received preferential treatment from Ubico, was the country's largest landowner and employer, and was the most prominent target—it claimed victim—of the reform program. It alleged to the United States and in the press that Arévalo was either a Communist or the dupe of Communists, and in the climate of the time the burden of proof was light indeed. As Richard Patterson, Truman's ambassador to Guatemala, explained in 1950:

> Many times it is impossible to prove legally that a certain individual is a Communist; but for cases of this sort I recommend a practical method of detection—the "duck test." The duck test works this way: suppose you see a bird walking around in a farm yard. This bird wears no label that says "duck." But the bird certainly looks like a duck. Also, he goes to the pond and you notice he swims like a duck. Then he opens his beak and quacks like a duck. Well, by this time you have probably reached the conclusions that the bird is a duck, whether he's wearing a label or not.[31]

The enactment of agrarian reform removed lingering doubts that Guatemala was ruled by ducks.

Truman, however, was a lame duck. Besides, Guatemala was far down on his list of priorities. Eisenhower took office determined to elevate the issue, and Dulles agreed. His first diplomatic assignment for Woodrow Wilson had been to secure Central American support for safeguarding the Panama Canal, and at Sullivan & Cromwell he had provided legal counsel to many clients with interests in the region, including the UFCO. This assured his awareness of their problem, but had little effect on his definition of it.

In Dulles's view, Communists in Guatemala, whether homegrown or imported, were spearheading the Kremlin's campaign to establish outposts throughout Central and South America in order to threaten strategic assets like the Canal and hemispheric collective security, to force the United States to circle its military wagons in its backyard at the expense of overseas commitments, and to sabotage vital inter-American trade and investment. At stake were the principles of the Monroe Doctrine and, by extension, the principles that underlay the United States' global posture and its capability and resolve to promote and protect them. Dulles warned Eisenhower's NSC at the start of the administration that

Guatemala's contamination by communism was already a crisis of the first magnitude. To the public he was more expansive. "If the United Fruit matter were settled, if they gave a gold piece for every banana, the problem would remain just as it is today as far as the presence of Communist infiltration in Guatemala is concerned. That is the problem, not United Fruit."[32]

To no avail did Arbenz and his emissaries try to convince U.S. officials that his policies and programs, the agrarian reform in particular, had nothing to do with some international conspiracy masterminded by the Soviets. Dulles's assessment was shared by the entire administration, and his mind was made up. To liberate Guatemala, Arbenz had to be overthrown. The CIA project against Mossadegh in Iran provided a precedent. A covert operation could be effective, pose little risk, and conceal from Latin Americans that the United States had broken its promise not to intervene in their internal affairs. In the latter months of 1953 the CIA, buoyed by its success in Iran, began to plan a repeat performance in Guatemala.

The plan, code-named PBSUCCESS, was an exercise in psychological warfare. Its premise was that the army was the ultimate arbiter of power in Guatemala, and that it would defect to any counterrevolutionary force rather than risk endangering its safety and autonomy by defending the Arbenz government. The wealthy landed oligarchy would enthusiastically embrace a counterrevolution. The peasant majority was too insular and atomized, and the middle class, students, and intellectuals were too small in number and feeble, to resist. The CIA estimated that Arbenz would surrender once he recognized his vulnerability and isolation. His regime would collapse, eradicating the Communist threat to Guatemala.

As a catalyst to set off this chain of events, the CIA organized in neighboring Honduras what it symbolically called an "Army of Liberation." For its leader, it selected after some hesitation Colonel Carlos Castillo Armas, Arbenz's former colleague in the military and already a veteran of one attempted coup. For its rank and file, mercenaries were recruited from throughout the region. By early 1954 the CIA had set up a clandestine radio station, the "Voice of Liberation." It broadcast grossly inflated accounts of the size and quality of the Army of Liberation's forces and reported that its preparations to invade Guatemala were nearing completion.

The objective was to generate the essential climate of anxiety by creating the "impression of very substantial miltary strength" (although there might be a need for some selective assassinations as well). As the CIA explained, the entire effort was "dependent upon psychological impact," and the invasion was not intended "in any sense [as] a conventional military operation." Allen Dulles was more explicit. It was critical, he wrote, "to exert all possible influence to persuade the [Guatemalan] Army that their next target must be Arbenz himself if they are themselves to survive.[33]

Dulles cooperated closely with his brother as the CIA's plan unfolded, and, despite competing demands on his time, his contribution went beyond advice and encouragement. From his global point of view, overthowing Arbenz was necessary but far from sufficient. It was crucial that the court of world opinion judge Castillo Armas and his Army of Liberation as crusaders for freedom against tyranny, not agents of the United States or, worse, of the United Fruit Company.

With this objective in mind, in the midst of the Dien Bien Phu crisis Secretary Dulles decided to head personally the delegation to the Inter-American Conference that convened in Caracas, Venezuela, in March 1954. His initial plan was formally to indict the Arbenz regime for conspiring with the Kremlin and to induce the other members of the OAS to render a guilty verdict. His advisors warned, however, that such a verbal assault would revive the image of the bully from the North and refresh memories of its military interventions earlier in the twentieth century. Consequently, without mentioning Guatemala specifically, Dulles introduced a broad resolution to unite the OAS against the "alien intrigue and treachery" that so gravely threatened the hemisphere's peace and security. He called the resolution a "Declaration of Solidarity for the Preservation of the Political Integrity of the American States against International Communism."[34]

That Dulles was pointing the finger at Guatemala was clearly understood by all. Arbenz's foreign minister, as the State Department expected, denounced the Declaration as "the internationalism of McCarthyism" and "merely a pretext for intervening in our internal affairs." The ensuing debate was predictably rancorous, and, as Guatemala attracted a good deal of sympathy if not support, for a time it appeared that Dulles would lose. After more than a little arm twisting, the OAS members finally approved the declaration; only Guatemala dissented (Mexico and Argentina abstained). The conferees turned to the economic items on the agenda. His work done, Dulles flew off to promote United Action against the Communists in Vietnam.[35]

As with the rest of PBSUCCESS, Dulles's brief appearance at Caracas was essentially a publicity stunt. In the United States it generated additional attention to the problem; in Guatemala it generated additional anxiety. Because the United States embargoed arms sales to his government, a very nervous Arbenz arranged to purchase matériel from behind the Iron Curtain and vowed to distribute arms to the peasant and workers' militias. Eisenhower trumped him by giving the go-ahead to Castillo Armas's invasion.

What also influenced the timing was the approach of the off-year U.S. elections in November. The Indochina negotiations were reaching a climax, and it was evident that the most the administration could hope for was a "tie." The Democrats would be sure to contrast this result with the Republicans' rollback rhetoric. Further, the GOP's Old Guard was furious with Eisenhower's use of executive privilege to thwart Joseph McCarthy's investigation of alleged Communist infiltrators in the Army, which significantly contributed to the Wisconsin senator's self-destruction over nationwide television in June. Whatever chance there was of retaining the slim Republican majority in Congress depended on the party's wings agreeing to cooperate and their running on a scorecard that included at least one illustration of successful liberation.

On Eisenhower's order PBSUCCESS began on June 18, but what transpired hardly constituted an "invasion." While the Army of Liberation (composed in reality of less than 500 troops without either rockets or artillery) primarily hid near the Honduran border, the CIA jammed Guatemala's radio communications. Fabricated Voice of Liberation accounts of divisions of anti-government troops closing in on the capital monopolized the air waves. Meanwhile, U.S. pilots under contract to the CIA bombed urban targets from unmarked planes. The Guatemalan army went on alert and decisively defeated the counterrevolutionary forces in the few border skirmishes that were actually fought. In the main, however, Arbenz's military, fearful that U.S. forces were looking for a pretext to intervene directly, was reluctant to place itself in danger to defend the regime.

A shell-shocked Arbenz retained sufficient wit to complain to the UN that the Army of Liberation was sponsored by foreign powers (the complaint tactfully cited only Honduras and Nicaragua) and to demand an emergency meeting of the Security Council so that "it may proceed to take the necessary measures to prevent a breach of international peace and security in this part of Central America." On Dulles's instructions Henry Cabot Lodge, Jr., the U.S. delegate to the UN, who by coincidence of the rotation currently presided over the Security Council, countered by describing the events in Guatemala as a civil war. If Arbenz insisted on alleging foreign aggression, Lodge argued that the proper forum to consider the matter was the OAS (where, he, of course, did not mention, the United States exercised greater control).[36]

There was nothing Lodge could do to prevent the Security Council from at least discussing the Guatemalan complaint and ruling on its request that UN observers be sent to Guatemala to investigate. For this purpose it met on June 20, its first Sunday meeting since the outbreak of the Korean War. Adding insult to the U.S. injury, Guatemala began its presentation by augmenting its list of foreign aggressors to include the United States. Lodge both denied the charge and reiterated that the OAS held jurisdiction over regional disputes. When the Soviet representative rose to Guatemala's defense, Lodge pointed an accusing finger: "Stay out of this hemisphere and do not try to start your plans and conspiracies over here."[37]

What irked Lodge most of all, and infuriated Dulles, was the untimely intervention of Britain and France—on the wrong side. Britain looked favorably on Arbenz, primarily because his preoccupation with domestic reform and the opposition of the United States and UFCO had required him to drop Guatemala's long-standing claim to its colony, British Honduras (now the independent country of Belize). And in Paris, the new Mendès-France government sought retribution for the lack of U.S. support for its position at Geneva. What is more, the fear of both European allies becoming caught in the middle of a Soviet-American war drove them to try to endow the UN with the power to mediate and perhaps resolve conflicts. Each broke ranks with the United States and agreed that the UN should call for a cease-fire in Guatemala and send a team to examine the origins of the hostilities.

Dulles fumed that the British and French were willing to undercut the cohesion of the Atlantic alliance even on matters that did not directly concern them. That by doing so they again appeared to be underestimating the severity of the threat of international communism and refusing to follow the United States into battle against it exacerbated his ire. On top of everything, after all the United States—and Dulles personally—had done to establish the UN, France and Britain had the temerity to challenge the U.S. interpretation of the Security Council's jurisdiction and authority. Suffice it to say, Dulles was also concerned that the imposition of a cease-fire while Arbenz was still in power would derail the CIA operation, and an investigation could easily lead to the operation's true headquarters.

Dulles had to move quickly, and as things turned out, the confluence of the interalliance controversies over Guatemala, Indochina, and the EDC worked to his advantage. To address the latter two problems, Churchill and Eden had already scheduled a trip to Washington. Dulles met them at the airport when they arrived on June 25. He went directly to the point. The United States did not want any UN observers in Guatemala, he said, nor did it want a cease-fire. The sole way to guarantee against either was to block further discussion of the Guatemalan complaint in the Security Council. If "we split on this," Dulles warned, turning to Eden, you "had better pack up and go home."[38]

After a meeting at the White House, at which both Eisenhower and Dulles "talked turkey" to the British statesmen, a solution was devised. A majority vote of the Security Council was required if its discussion of Guatemala was to continue. By agreeing simply to abstain, and persuading the French to go along, the British ensured that the United States would have majority support. The plan worked; that evening, with Britain and France abstaining, the Security Council voted 5-4 in favor of excluding Guatemala from its agenda.[39]

Having come up empty in the UN, his nerves shattered, and warned about what the CIA's official historian termed the "horrible truth"—that a "military coup" was imminent—Arbenz resigned two days later and fled the country. Because the Army of Liberation was still camped far from Guatemala City, it took time and complex maneuvering by U.S. Ambassador John Peurifoy to pave the way for Castillo Armas, in contrast to aspirants within the Army, to assume power. But he managed.[40]

Dulles was too impatient "to talk about the biggest success in the last five years against Communism" to await Peurifoy's completing his assignment. An "alien despotism" had tried to "use Guatemala for its own evil ends," he proclaimed over national radio and television after Arbenz's resignation, but "the people of Guatemala have now been heard from." Indeed, the world owed a profound debt of gratitude to the "loyal citizens of Guatemala who, in the face of terrorism and violence and against what seemed insuperable odds, had the courage and the will to eliminate the traitorous tools of foreign despots." They had opened a "new and glorious chapter" in the "great tradition of American States" and the history of freedom everywhere.[41]

In fact, for Guatemalans the chapter opened by the overthrow of Arbenz covered decades of military rule and oppression. For the CIA, the chapter ended much earlier—on the beaches of the Bay of Pigs in 1961. Its effort to apply the same technique to rid Cuba of Fidel Castro produced defeat and embarrassment. For Dulles and the Eisenhower administration, the Guatemala chapter had a happier ending. Nevertheless, there was no time to dwell on it, because other chapters dealing with Indochina and the EDC remained works in progress. And there were more, many more, to write.

Notes

1. Quoted in Richard H. Immerman, "Between the Unattainable and the Unacceptable: Eisenhower and Dien Bien Phu," in *Reevaluating Eisenhower: American Foreign Policy in the 1950s*, eds. Richard A. Melanson and David Mayers (Urbana, IL, 1987), 121.

2. Memorandum of conversation, March 24, 1953, *FR, 1952–54* 13:419.

3. Quoted in Immerman, "Between the Unattainable and the Unacceptable," 127; quoted in George C. Herring and Richard H. Immerman, "Eisenhower, Dulles, and Dien Bien Phu: The 'Day We Didn't Go to War Revisited'," *The Journal of American History* 71 (September 1984): 345.

4. Quoted in Immerman, "Between the Unattainable and the Unacceptable," 130.

5. "The Threat of a Red Asia," *Department of State Bulletin* 30 (12 April 1954): 539–40.

6. Quoted in Herring and Immerman, "Eisenhower, Dulles, and Dien Bien Phu," 353; quoted in Immerman, "Between the Unattainable and the Unacceptable," 135.

7. Quoted in Herring and Immerman, "Eisenhower, Dulles, and Dien Bien Phu," 355.

8. Quoted in Immerman, "Between the Unattainable and the Unacceptable," 140; quoted in Herring and Immerman, "Eisenhower, Dulles, and Dien Bien Phu," 360.

9. Quoted in George C. Herring, " 'A Good Stout Effort': John Foster Dulles and the Indochina Crisis, 1954–1955," in *John Foster Dulles and the Diplomacy of the Cold War*, ed. Richard H. Immerman (Princeton, NJ, 1990), 220.

10. Quoted in Richard H. Immerman, "The United States and the Geneva Conference of 1954: A New Look," *Diplomatic History* 14 (Winter 1990): 60.

11. Quoted in Herring, "Good Stout Effort," 223.

12. Quoted in Immerman, "The United States and the Geneva Conference," 63.

13. Quoted in Gary R. Hess, "Redefining the American Position in Southeast Asia: The United States and the Geneva and Manila Conferences," in *Dien Bien Phu and the Crisis of Franco-American Relations, 1954–55*, ed. Lawrence S. Kaplan, Denise Artaud, and Mark R. Rubin (Lanham, MD, 1990), 140; quoted in Immerman, "Between the Unattainable and the Unacceptable," 145.

14. Quoted in Herring, "Good Stout Effort," 231.
15. Quoted in George C. Herring, Gary R. Hess, and Richard H. Immerman, "Passage of Empire: The U.S., France, and South Vietnam, 1954–55," in *Dien Bien Phu and the Crisis of Franco-American Relations*, ed. Kaplan, Artaud, and Rubin, 173.
16. Quoted in ibid., 186.
17. Dulles to James B. Conant, November 20, 1953, "Germany 1953–54 (2)," Subject Series, DP—Eisenhower.
18. Ibid. (emphasis in original)
19. Dillon and David K. E. Bruce (signed by Dillon) to Department of State, August 5, 1954, *FR, 1952–54* 5:1025.
20. Dulles to Dillon, August 12, 1954, *FR, 1952–54* 5:1029–30.
21. Quoted in Rolf Steininger, "John Foster Dulles, the European Defense Community, and the German Question," in *John Foster Dulles and the Diplomacy of the Cold War*, ed. Immerman, 97.
22. Quoted in ibid., 103; statement by the secretary of state, August 31, 1954, *FR, 1952–54*, 5:1120–22.
23. Quoted in Steininger, "Dulles, the EDC, and the German Question," 104; Charge in the United Kingdom to the assistant secretary of state for European Affairs, September 1, 1954, *FR, 1952–54* 5:1127.
24. Both Eden and Dulles quoted in Steininger, "Dulles, the EDC, and the German Question," 104.
25. Ibid., 105–6.
26. Memorandum of NSC meeting, September 24, 1954, *FR, 1952–54* 5:1263–67.
27. Quoted in Steininger, "Dulles, the EDC, and the German Question," 106.
28. Memorandum of conversation, September 27, 1954, *FR, 1952–54* 5:1286–87.
29. Quoted in Richard H. Immerman, *The CIA in Guatemala: The Foreign Policy of Intervention* (Austin, 1982), 48.
30. Piero Gleijeses, *Shattered Hope: The Guatemalan Revolution and the United States, 1944–1954* (Princeton, NJ, 1991), 144.
31. Quoted in Immerman, *CIA in Guatemala*, 102.
32. Quoted in Richard H. Immerman, "Guatemala as Cold War History," *Political Science Quarterly* 95 (Winter 1980–81): 639.
33. Quoted in Immerman, *CIA in Guatemala*, 161; quoted in Nicholas Cullather, *Operation PBSUCCESS: The United States and Guatemala, 1952–1954* (Central Intelligence Agency, 1994), 67. The CIA's Center for the Study of Intelligence recently released this in-house history of the Guatemalan operation in 1997. It is currently available in Record Group 263 of the National Archives.
34. Quoted in Immerman, *CIA in Guatemala*, 147.
35. Quoted in ibid.
36. Quoted in ibid., 169.
37. Quoted in ibid., 171.
38. Quoted in ibid., 172.
39. Ibid.
40. Cullather, *Operation PBSUCCESS*, 75.
41. Quoted in Immerman, *CIA in Guatemala*, 179.

6

Maximum Bargaining Power

Dulles began September 1954 in Manila, negotiating the establishment of the Southeast Asian Treaty Organization (SEATO). He ended the month in London, negotiating the rearmament of West Germany and its integration into the North Atlantic Treaty Organization (NATO). Despite the vital importance of both efforts for promoting collective security and allied unity, the relentless onslaught of global crises conspired to prevent him from committing his undivided time or attention to either. The purposes of SEATO and NATO were to deter potential Communist aggression. But on September 3, 1954, the People's Republic of China (PRC) initiated artillery attacks on Quemoy (Jinmen), one of the islands held by the Nationalist Chinese in the strait that separated Taiwan (Formosa) from mainland China. The need to respond to immediate Communist aggression hung like a cloud over Dulles at Manila and London. Before the crisis was resolved (temporarily) some eight months later, the free world alliance approached the brink of disintegration, and the United States approached the brink of nuclear war.

For Dulles, formulating a policy toward China, or more accurately toward the two Chinas, was a continual struggle to balance conflicting impulses, interests, and objectives. His emotions and political instincts drove him to identify publicly with the restoration of Nationalist rule on the mainland. In his view, the Nationalists were unquestionably the legitimate heirs to the Chinese government his grandfather had represented when Dulles was a teenager. He perceived the Communist regime, conversely, as an insult to his grandfather's memory. From his point of view, the Communists were alien usurpers who danced to the strings of their Kremlin puppeteers and served the Soviets' expansionist goals. "By the test of conception, birth, nurture, and obedience," Dulles lectured, "the Mao Tse-tung [Mao Zedong] regime is a creature of the Moscow Politburo." Truman's failure to prevent the Soviets' creation from triumphing in 1949 reflected the limitations of the containment strategy, providing reason and justification for pursuing a more aggressive policy of liberation.[1]

Dulles's predisposition received further impetus from the Republican right wing, whose support he considered unreliable yet indispensable. To curry their favor and to make amends for having once written a letter supporting Alger Hiss for the presidency of the Carnegie Endowment, Dulles contributed to the successful effort of McCarthy, Walter Judd, William Jenner, and others in the virulently pro-Nationalist "China Lobby" to expunge the China experts from the State Department. Almost all of these "China hands" maintained that cooperation with the Chinese Communists was not only possible, but because Mao sought to avoid depending on the Soviet Union, it also served U.S. interests.

To most of the Republican Old Guard, this purge was the minimum price for their allegiance to the administration. Especially after California's William Knowland became the GOP leader in the Senate following the sudden death of Robert Taft in July 1953, conservative Republicans demanded that the administration abet the Nationalists' ambition to reconquer the mainland without qualification. Dulles feared the consequences of disappointing them under any circumstances, and his apprehension heightened after the White House irreparably broke with McCarthy, Knowland's close ally.

In truth, Dulles's perspective was far different, and far more restrained, pragmatic, and sophisticated, than that of the China Lobby. He shared its affection for the Chinese Nationalist cause, but not for Chiang Kai-shek (Jiang Jieshi), the leader of the Chinese Nationalist Party, the Kuomintang (KMT) [Guomindang/GMD]. Dulles was not fooled by either Chiang's efforts to portray himself, or the efforts of Henry Luce and others to portray him, as a paragon of democracy, free enterprise, and Christianity. He understood Chiang for what he was: an arrogant, manipulative schemer more interested in self-aggrandizement than in the welfare and security of the Chinese people. What was more, in pursuit of his selfish goals Chiang was determined to implicate the United States directly and appeared willing, almost eager, to provoke a general war in order to do so. Dulles went so far as to write—privately, of course—that Chiang had "a vested interest in World War III."[2]

Dulles's problem, therefore, was how to rid China of the Communist interlopers, or at a minimum to mitigate the threat they posed to the region, without playing into Chiang's hand. What made this problem more vexing was that the Eisenhower administration was under pressure from the Republican right wing to strengthen Chiang's hand and under pressure from the European allies, especially the British, to amputate it. Exacerbating this dilemma, according to U.S. intelligence estimates and Dulles's own State Department staff, the liberation of the Chinese mainland demanded the intervention of U.S. forces. On this issue, NSC 162/2, the administration's initial statement of national security policy, was both explicit and blunt. "The Chinese Communist regime is fully in control," it read, "and is unlikely to be shaken in the foreseeable future by domestic forces or rival regimes, short of the occurrence of a major war." Such a "major war" would require the commitment of large numbers of U.S. troops and atomic bombs; would gravely, perhaps fatally, damage U.S. relations with its NATO partners and Japan; and would entail a very high risk of precipitating a global conflict involving the Soviet Union.[3]

None of this was new to Dulles. He had been grappling with these issues since the Communist victory in 1949 and had already reached the same conclusion. He toyed with the ideas of replacing Chiang with a more effective leader, with transforming Taiwan into a UN trusteeship, and even with officially recognizing the existence of both Chinas. Coupled with Republican Party politics, the entry of the PRC into the Korean War eliminated these options. Dulles came up with a creative solution. He fully appreciated the constraints on U.S. efforts to overthrow Mao's regime. But Washington could encourage the internal decay of the regime while simultaneously driving a wedge between it and its Kremlin patron. From Dulles's perspective, a strategy derived from this premise would ultimately lead to China's liberation; and, in the meantime, it would increasingly impair Sino-Soviet relations, placate the GOP right wing, and keep allied opposition within manageable limits.

Dulles recommended that the United States apply persistent pressure to Mao's government. Although the risk of war and alienating allies precluded using armed forces, there remained many available tactics and instruments. These included continuing to withhold recognition from the Peking (Beijing) regime and opposing its representation in the UN, embargoing its trade, engaging in psychological warfare, and launching covert operations. Forced to respond to this pressure, the Communists would become increasingly less able to satisfy the demands of China's population. The seeds of their destruction would inexorably sprout. "It is not necessary to reconquer China by subsidizing a vast military operation," Dulles explained. "Communism will disintegrate in China, and the Chinese themselves will take care of that because of [the regime's] inability to solve the problems of China."[4]

What was particularly distinctive about his plan, Dulles argued, was that it promised not only the distintegration of Communist rule in China, but also the disintegration of the ties that bound it to the Soviet Union. Dulles believed that the Chinese Communists were creatures of the Kremlin. He believed as well that their partnership was riddled by mutual distrust, competition, and conflicting priorities.

The beauty of Dulles's policy of pressure was that it was consistent with both beliefs. As Peking became increasingly enfeebled and isolated, it would have to swallow its pride and with ever more frequency ask Moscow for help. To relieve the PRC's economic woes, it would request support for domestic programs. To restore the Communist Party's crumbling prestige, it would request support for foreign adventures. But because the Soviets' command economy was inherently weak, Dulles predicted that Moscow would not be able to bail out China. He also predicted that the Kremlin would be loath to provide assistance for Mao's adventurism. Doing so would place the Soviet Union in harm's way and promote the PRC's ambition to rival the Soviets as the Communist leader in Asia. Therefore, the greater the U.S. pressure on the PRC, the greater would become its dependence on the Soviets, and the greater would become the strains on their relations. Although it would take time for Dulles's strategy to produce results, it would both fuel indigenous opposition to Peking and eventually rupture the Sino-Soviet alliance.

Although Eisenhower did not dispute the essence of Dulles's approach, in deference to allied wishes (and against those of the secretary of state), the president relaxed some of the restrictions on trade with the PRC. Nevertheless, so long as the risk of war was assessed as moderate, the policy of pressure was pursued. The outbreak of the offshore island crisis in September 1954 demonstrated, however, that keeping this policy from spinning out of Washington's control and keeping Chiang from seeking to pervert it for his own purposes was much more difficult and dangerous than either Eisenhower or Dulles had imagined.

The crisis reflected the tightrope the administration walked between maintaining pressure on the PRC (and appeasing the Republican right wing) by ardently supporting the Nationalist government on Taiwan and constraining Chiang's irredentism. This precarious balance was jeopardized by the clusters of islands that lay between Taiwan and the PRC. Unlike the Pescadores (Penghus) and Taiwan itself, which had been colonized by the Japanese in 1895, the small islands that composed Quemoy, Matsu (Mazu), and Tachen (Dachen) had always remained Chinese territory. The PRC considered its title to them indisputable.

Even though the islands are hundreds of miles from Taiwan on the opposite side of the Taiwan Strait (the Quemoy group is but two miles from the PRC port of Amoy [Xiamen] and the Matsu group but ten miles from Foochow [Fuzhou]), they remained under the control of the Nationalists. Chiang claimed legal jurisdiction (dubious) and that their possession by Taiwan was essential for its defense (more dubious). He exacerbated the controversy over the status of the island groups by using them for intelligence operations, to harass PRC shipping, and even to conduct coastal raids. To Peking, moreover, the deployment of some 50,000 Nationalist troops to Quemoy alone (another 5,000 were stationed on Matsu) suggested that Chiang intended the islands to serve as stepping-stones for his return to the mainland.

Eisenhower and Dulles worried that this was indeed Chiang's intention. They agreed that the islands were of little value to Taiwan except as a staging ground for an invasion and that their proximity to the mainland made them almost impossible to defend. Nevertheless, in order to signal U.S. commitment to protect the Nationalists, Eisenhower and Dulles deployed the Seventh Fleet menacingly close to PRC positions on the Taiwan Strait. Further, to keep the Republican right wing on board and Peking off balance, they increased U.S. financial and military assistance to Chiang and, using Eisenhower's first State of the Union address, threatened to "unleash" the Nationalists on the mainland.

Dulles actually hoped to keep the leash on Chiang as tight as he could. In the words of the generalissimo's own ambassador to the United States, Wellington Koo, this would be "a hell of a job." By holding up the delivery of F-84 jet bombers to Taiwan, Dulles coerced the generalissmo in April to agree not to undertake offensive military operations against the mainland without prior U.S. approval. But the agreement was reached in secret, and although Chiang privately groused about the restrictions Washington imposed on him, publicly he boasted that his liberation of China was imminent. Peking (and for that matter London and Paris) understandably interpreted literally the threat to unleash him. Wresting control of the offshore islands would serve two mutually reinforcing Communist purposes. The PRC would regain possession of territory it was entitled to and Chiang would be deprived of territory from which to launch an attack. In addition, there is evidence to suggest that Mao was not committed to follow up the shelling with a direct assault on the islands. In his mind, the bombardment alone might be a sufficient—and relatively safe—means to force the United States to think twice before concluding a formal military alliance with the Nationalists and to test the extent of the U.S. resolve to defend Chiang in what was in truth a Chinese civil war. He could then better gauge how Washington would respond to a future invasion of the islands and, ultimately, Taiwan.[5]

Once the situations in Korea and Indochina were relatively stable, Mao made his move in the Taiwan Strait. On the one hand, the PRC could now concentrate its forces in this theater. On the other hand, Mao estimated that the United States, having just finished fighting one war in Korea, would be reluctant to become involved in another. After all, it had not intervened militarily in Indochina.

Mao also undoubtedly reckoned that if the U.S. allies had refused to go along with Dulles's United Action plan for Indochina, they would be downright hostile to any proposals, unilateral or multilateral, to take military measures to defend the offshore islands. No colonies were at stake, both France and Britain recognized the PRC, and London did not want to jeopardize the security of Hong Kong. In addition, to divert forces to protect insignificant real estate in the Taiwan Strait while the question of Germany's contribution to the defense of Western Europe remained unresolved was anathema to the NATO states. Mao may even have calculated that by attacking the offshore islands he could further inflame the divisions between the United States and its European allies, turning Dulles's policy of pressure on its head. At a minimum he hoped to demonstrate the risks of including the Nationalist Chinese in SEATO and thereby generate opposition to any U.S. efforts to do so. Until more Chinese archives become available, Mao's reasoning must remain somewhat obscure. What is clear is that for five hours on September 3, 1954, approximately six thousand PRC artillery shells rained down on Quemoy.

As soon as the SEATO negotiations were completed in Manila, Dulles hastened back to Washington to address the newest crisis. Neither he nor the U.S intelligence community could confidently assess the Communists' intentions. The consensus was that the bombardment was not a prelude to a PRC assault on Taiwan itself, but there was no question that Mao had the military capability to overrun the Nationalist forces garrisoned on the island groups of Quemoy and Matsu. If he choose to do so, the United States would be confronted by, in Dulles's words, a "horrible dilemma."[6]

Dulles explained the dilemma in a carefully prepared memorandum and in remarks made at an NSC meeting on September 12. He stressed that "Quemoy cannot be held *indefinitely* without a general war with Red China in which the Communists are defeated." Only by using atomic weapons could the United States thwart a conventional PRC assault on the islands. Thus, a decision to intervene would "alienate world opinion and gravely strain our alliances." This strategy was risky, Dulles explained, because except for Chiang and Korea's Syngman Rhee, "the rest of the world would condemn us." A U.S. intervention would also run an extremely high risk of escalating beyond the point of no return. Yet a decision not to intervene would be perceived as a repudiation of the U.S. commitment to Chiang, not to mention its pledge to prevent the loss of any additional territory to the Communists. The effect of this perception on the morale of the Nationalist Chinese, or non-Communist nations throughout the periphery, and on vital domestic constituencies would be disastrous.[7]

With the notable exception of Army Chief of Staff Matthew Ridgway, the JCS advocated that United States take whatever steps were necessary to defend the islands, including the use of atomic weapons. Dulles's own assistant secretary for the Far East, Walter Robertson, felt much the same way, as did the U.S. ambassador in Taipei (Taibei), Karl Rankin, and the director of the Office of Chinese Affairs, Walter McConaughy. Most of Eisenhower's advisors, however, counseled caution and restraint. In their view, the strategic value of the islands did not warrant dividing the Western alliance, let alone risking a war with Communist China and possibly the Soviet Union. Secretary of the Treasury George Humphrey went so far as to suggest that Washington demand that the Nationalists completely "pull out" of Quemoy. What the administration should concentrate on, he said, was coming up with the "best possible alibi." Dulles was torn. He hoped that "the Council would never have to make a more difficult decision. An overwhelming case can be made on either side."[8]

Dulles ultimately advised Eisenhower to split the difference by engaging the Communists in a high-stakes game of "chicken." Surely it was the possibility of U.S. intervention that deterred the PRC from a conventional invasion, he said. Accordingly, in contrast to Acheson's public exclusion of Korea from the U.S. defense perimeter in a speech shortly before the Communist invasion, the Eisenhower administration should make clear that it was unequivocally committed to the defense of Taiwan. However, it should leave unclear whether that commitment extended to the offshore islands. That way Eisenhower would retain some flexibility when deciding how to respond if the PRC invaded. But Dulles did not think that Mao would force the president to make the decision. Before the PRC leader ordered a direct assault on the islands, he would have to guess that they were not covered by the U.S. commitment to Taiwan. Based on the experience in Vietnam, Dulles predicted that Mao would be unwilling to guess wrong, and at the least this scheme would buy the United States additional time to try to defuse the immediate crisis caused by the shelling.

The speed and enthusiasm with which Eisenhower embraced Dulles's proposal suggests that the two men collaborated in its formulation. In any event, without additional discussion in or a formal recommendation by the NSC, they undertook its execution. Throughout the final months of 1954, as the PRC continued to flail away at the islands, both the president and secretary of state publicly expressed the U.S. determination to defend Taiwan (and the Pescadores) in the face of the contemptible Communist behavior. Whether that meant defending the island groups under Taiwan's control was anyone's guess.

As Dulles had feared, this uncertainty did not sit well with the European allies. Especially the British suspected that the purpose of the ambiguity was to conceal from them that the administration had already decided to shelter the islands under the U.S. atomic umbrella. Eden particularly distrusted Dulles. The secretary flew to London to assure the foreign minister that the last thing that he or Eisenhower wanted was for the crisis to escalate into an all-out war. Yet he emphasized that if the Communists were allowed to think they could conquer Quemoy and Matsu with impunity, they surely would, and then would probably turn to Taiwan. It was vital, therefore, to nip the aggression in the bud.

Dulles conceded that the Eisenhower administration was still weighing its options but solicited Eden's help on one tactic that he wanted to pursue immediately. He proposed that the British join with the United States in submitting to the UN Security Council a resolution condemning the aggression, calling for a cease-fire based on the status quo, and perhaps even proposing the islands' neutralization. Dulles expressed confidence that with British assistance the West could easily command a majority in favor of such a resolution, which would confront the Soviets with the need to veto a resolution for peace, thereby exposing them to international criticism. It was even possible that the Kremlin, seeking to avoid a repeat of the awkward position that Stalin found himself in during the Korean War, would not exercise its veto. If it did not, Dulles concluded, the resolution might not only contribute to ending the crisis but might also lead to additional steps to stabilize the region. At the same time, another wedge would be driven between Moscow and Peking.

The British much preferred talk about working within the United Nations than talk about war. Eden agreed to cooperate and the other allies quickly followed suit. No doubt, Dulles genuinely hoped something good would result, but his chief priority was to unite the allies behind at least one dimension of the U.S. policy in the Taiwan Strait. Satisfied that he had succeeded, Dulles left it to UN delegate Henry Cabot Lodge, Jr., and others to work out the details. He had more pressing business—with Chiang Kai-shek.

For more than a year prior to the outbreak of the crisis, Chiang had been drawing on his many sympathizers in the U.S. press, Congress, and the State Department to lobby the Eisenhower administration to agree to a mutual defense pact. Such a military alliance, he believed, would ensure against the United States ever retreating from its commitment to preserve an independent Taiwan and would enhance the Nationalists' capability to influence U.S. policy. Dulles kept putting him off. He worried about the potential loss of flexibility and recognized that the European allies would look askance at the United States assuming an additional military obligation in Asia, especially if that obligation was to protect Nationalist China. More important, he suspected that once guaranteed of U.S. protection, the generalissimo would feel no compunction about provoking a PRC attack on Taiwan.

A formal mutual security agreement would remove any doubt in the minds of the Communist Chinese concerning U.S. resolve to safeguard the Nationalist regime. In addition, Dulles calculated that concluding a military alliance was an acceptable, and almost definitely a necessary, price to pay for Chiang's agreement not to veto a cease-fire resolution in the UN Security Council. From Taipei, Ambassador Rankin was already predicting a "violently unfavorable reception" from Chiang to what the generalissimo perceived as "another Yalta" that would all but certainly lead to the Nationalist Chinese being "sold down the river."[9]

Eisenhower agreed, and after a great deal of difficulty, the treaty negotiations were completed in late November. At U.S. insistence, the Nationalists again pledged not to undertake military operations against the mainland without Washington's authorization. In return, they demanded that the administration compromise on the wording of the treaty's scope. The treaty explicitly covered only Taiwan and the Pescadores, but the reference to "such other territories as may be determined by mutual agreement" suggested the possibility that the treaty could be extended to include the Quemoys, Matsus, and Tachens.[10]

Although uncomfortable with this loophole lest the Nationalist Chinese exploit it for the purpose of drawing the United States into hostilities, Dulles rationalized that it could work to the U.S. advantage. The United States was formally no more committed to defend the offshore islands than previously, but the PRC might not think so. When in early January 1955 the Communists intensified their attacks (actually seizing one island in the Tachen group), Dulles developed second thoughts. It appeared that Peking had interpreted the exclusion of the island groups from the Mutual Security Treaty as a sign that the United States was prepared to write them off—that "we were running away when actual danger appeared."[11]

At a meeting with Eisenhower and JCS Chairman Radford on January 19, Dulles advised that the administration "modify" its strategy. Rather than relying on uncertainty about U.S. intentions to deter the PRC, he "felt it important to make our intentions clear and stick to them." Specifically, Dulles proposed that the United States "encourage" the Nationalists to withdraw from the Tachens, which he assumed were militarily indefensible, but publicly announce that the United States was prepared to take whatever measures were necessary to "hold" Quemoy and Matsu. The "time had come for the U.S. to take more positive action and eliminate the fuzziness as to what the U.S. would or would not do."[12]

Save for the part about giving up the Tachens, Dulles's recommendation was music to Radford's ears. Eisenhower was in "general agreement," but he wanted to canvass the opinion of Congress and the NATO allies before reaching a decision. The president became less reserved the next day when confronted by the objections of many NSC members to the U.S. "greatly enhancing the risk of war" in order to "hold these little islands." After Dulles's arguments failed to assuage them, Eisenhower chimed in that "further delay in making up our minds would result in rapid and serious deterioration of the situation." As a matter of fact, he continued, the "chances of general war with Communist China would be less under the course of action now proposed by the Secretary of State than the 'dangerous drift' which we are now in." Both Eisenhower and Dulles reiterated that the objective was to stabilize the region. For this purpose they hoped eventually to persuade Chiang to evacuate all the islands, but he would never, nor should he ever, do so under duress. What was therefore required immediately was to "draw the line" and compel the PRC to respect it.[13]

The continued dissent of NSC members did not alter Eisenhower's determination to follow Dulles's recommendations. Further, even before he had met with the Council, the president received assurance from the European allies (most importantly the British) that although they were "disturbed" by what seemed like a "provisional guarantee" of Taiwan's claim to Quemoy and Matsu, they would mute their complaints so long as Washington remained committed to seeking a cease-fire through the UN. By now the Allies had worked out a plan, code-named Operation ORACLE. New Zealand would submit the resolution condemning the PRC's aggression and calling for a cease-fire based on the status quo to the Security Council, thereby disguising the U.S. role as its author. As a sign of good faith, Dulles agreed that the time had arrived to launch ORACLE.[14]

In between meetings with Eisenhower, his State Department advisors, and ambassadors from Europe and Asia, Dulles found time for an extended discussion with the House and Senate leaders of both parties. Whether constitutionally required or not, and the administration's opinion was divided on this question, the president adamantly insisted that Congress must authorize the commitment of U.S. forces to defend the islands. As he had during the Dien Bien Phu crisis, he instructed the State Department to draft a resolution granting him discretionary authority, and again he delegated to Dulles the responsibility for sounding out Congress on it. This time both Republicans and Democrats indicated their willingness to grant discretionary authority. After a two-hour meeting with them on January 20, Dulles reported that "there is little doubt that the Congress would promptly give the President the powers which he needed."[15]

It did. In the last days of January, both the House and Senate passed what became known as the Formosa (Taiwan) Resolution by overwhelming margins (the Senate also finally ratified the Mutual Security Treaty by a vote of 65 to 6). The resolution granted Eisenhower a blank check to use U.S. force in the Taiwan Strait, but it was so blank that Chiang claimed that he had been betrayed. The reservations expressed by the NSC and European allies had heightened Eisenhower's and Dulles's own concerns about the United States becoming a hostage to the Nationalists' resistance to yielding an iota of control over any of the offshore islands.

The message Eisenhower sent to Congress on January 24 contained some subtle yet highly suggestive last-minute revisions. As "solemn evidence of our determination to stand fast," the president requested and received discretionary authority to defend Taiwan, the Pescadores, and "related positions and territories of that area now in friendly hands." Dropped from the original draft were the explicit references to Quemoy and Matsu. Added was the unambiguous statement that the president would only exercise this authority against Communist actions that were "recognizable" as "definite preliminaries to an attack" on Taiwan itself.[16]

The revised language infuriated Chiang. To calm him, Dulles instructed Ambassador Rankin in Taipei to assure the generalissimo in private that the administration remained committed to defend Quemoy and Matsu. Chiang still seethed. Not only did he want the commitment made public, but in return for even this halfway measure he had had to agree to evacuate the Tachens. Moreover, the resolution clearly expressed the U.S. view that the islands were not integral to Taiwan.

Dulles felt the pressure building on all sides. Chiang was now, if anything, firmer in his belief that any UN agreement on a ceasefire would compromise Taiwan's interests, and Dulles feared giving him and his champions in the United States additional cause to complain. Never sanguine about Operation ORACLE's prospects, he backtracked on his promise to promote it, using as his justification the PRC's intransigence. The British saw through Dulles's excuse and joined with the Nationalist Chinese (although for diametrically opposite reasons) in claiming that they had been betrayed. All the while, there was no evidence that either the Mutual Security Pact with Taiwan or the Formosa Resolution was having any deterrent effect on the Communists. To the contrary, the speed with which they took over the Tachens following the Nationalists' evacuation and their continued buildup of forces on their side of the Taiwan Strait suggested to Dulles that he had severely under-estimated the threat of a direct assault on Taiwan itself.

Although no less reluctant to involve the United States in a war with the PRC, by early March, Dulles had become much less opti-mistic that war could be avoided. At the end of February he went to Taiwan to assess conditions personally, and on his return he stopped in Honolulu for a briefing from the U.S. Pacific Com-mand. Everything he saw and learned, he reported to the NSC on March 10, indicated that the "ultimate objective of the Chinese Com-munists was the liquidation of the Chinese Nationalist Govern-ment." His "emphatic belief" was that toward this end they were preparing "to capture" Taiwan. Because America's reputation, re-solve, and the credibility of its commitments rested on preventing their success, there was "at least an even chance that the United States would have to fight in this area before we were through." Indeed, it seemed to him that the "question of a fight" had all but become "a question of time rather than a question of fact."

To Dulles, the question of time was vitally important. There was no telling how extreme would be the adverse reaction in Eu-rope to an "armed clash" with the Communist Chinese. For this reason, it was crucial that Washington "temporize" until the agree-ments reached at London and Paris on Germany's rearmament and incorporation into NATO had been ratified. Perhaps more impor-tant, the European, Asian, and American publics had to be prepared for what this armed clash would entail: the use of atomic weapons. Dulles had been convinced by the "military people" that only atomic strikes on mainland targets—gun emplacements, airfields, and railroad lines—could effectively neutralize the PRC's conven-tional military superiority. Yet, nowhere in the free world (with the exception of Taiwan, whose population had been urged by Chiang to accept that an atomic attack against their breathren might be-come a "necessity") was public opinion "at all attuned to such a possibility." Thus, within the "next month or two" there was an urgent need to "create a better public climate for the use of atomic weapons by the United States."[17]

Admiral Radford enthusiastically endorsed everything Dulles said. The response of the other NSC participants was silence. Eisenhower hardly uttered a word either. He and Dulles had met in private earlier, and, although less resigned to the likelihood of a war, his position as to what immediately had to be done was identical to that of his secretary of state. In fact, at the president's direction, Dulles initiated the public relations campaign before the NSC convened. Atomic weapons must be considered "interchangeable with the conventional weapons," he announced in a nationally televised speech on March 8. Several days later Vice President Richard Nixon expanded on the theme, emphasizing that "tactical atomic weapons are now conventional and will be used against the targets of any aggressive force."[18]

Reflecting the gravity with which Eisenhower assessed the situation, the president departed from his standard operating procedure and served as his own point man. Asked at a March 16 press conference what his attitude was toward the employment of atomic weapons in the event of a war in the Taiwan Strait, Eisenhower answered that "in any combat where these things can be used on strictly military targets and for strictly military purposes, I see no reason why they shouldn't be used, just exactly as you would use a bullet or anything else."[19]

Eisenhower and Dulles were not bluffing. Both were absolutely certain that if confronted with compelling evidence that a Communist attack on Taiwan was imminent, the United States would have to respond with atomic weapons. In the Pentagon, plans for this contingency were finalized. Nonetheless, there can be no question that the rhetorical barrage was designed to avert having to implement the plans, and that the truculence was intended to impress the Communist audience as much as, if not more than, the free world audience. Throughout the process of formulating the New Look, the president and secretary of state repeatedly drew clear distinctions between atomic and conventional weapons. By conflating them now, they sought to ensure that the Communist Chinese did not miscalculate and that they fully understood that the Eisenhower administration's commitment to counter aggression by relying on the U.S. capability to "retaliate, instantly, by means and at places of our choosing" was not an idle threat.

In addition, the more the United States rattled its atomic saber, the greater would be the strain on the Sino-Soviet alliance and the more likely Moscow would be to restrain Peking. In his public commentary Dulles made a point of depicting the posture of Mao's regime as autonomous from, and even in conflict with, that of the Kremlin. He stressed that the PRC was the "initiator of violence" in the Taiwan Strait and that the Soviet "line" was "less violent than the Chinese Communist line." Indeed, he extrapolated, "one would infer that their disposition is to hold back the Chinese Communists." Dulles's purpose was twofold. In the short term he hoped to encourage the Soviets to rein in Mao's reckless aggression. But by playing upon their divergent priorities, he hoped to further the long-term objective of irreparably damaging the Sino-Soviet relationship.[20]

Nothing Eisenhower or Dulles said or did mitigated the crisis. Through the remainder of March the United States and Communist China edged closer to the brink of war. Desperate to find an escape, in early April Eisenhower wrote Dulles that he could "no longer remain inert awaiting the inevitable moment of decision between two unacceptable choices": to sanction the use of atomic weapons or to cave in to Communist aggression. It might still be possible, he proposed, to induce Chiang to redeploy his forces from Quemoy and Matsu to Taiwan and the Pescadores. Perhaps he could be convinced at long last that their retention was of little significance to the Nationalists' prestige or security, both of which would be enhanced by the augmented power he would be able to project from his home base. Chiang could also be told that in terms of Mao's reputation, gaining control of undefended island "outposts" would be meaningless, and that he would not dare take on the full force of Chiang's military, backed by that of the United States, on Taiwan. Collectively, the United States and the Nationalists would have called Mao's bluff, and it would be the Communist revolutionary's prestige that would suffer.[21]

Dulles sympathized with Eisenhower's objective but did not regard his plan as either realistic or constructive. For years Chiang had rejected U.S. advice concerning the islands—and most everything else. The notion that now, at the eleventh hour, he would listen to U.S. proposals seemed wishful thinking. It was more than likely that Chiang wanted the crisis to erupt into a full-blown war, and he certainly would never willingly agree to evacuate Quemoy and Matsu and surrender them to the PRC. In the present circumstances, it would be disastrous as well as futile to try to make him do so. Chiang had primed his troops to be ready to fight to the death over the islands. To hand them over at this stage would devastate their morale, further whetting the Communists' expansionist appetite.

Eisenhower's position did give Dulles an idea that, with the cooperation of his brother Allen and Admiral Radford, he presented to the president on April 17. In exchange for Nationalist withdrawal from Quemoy and Matsu, the United States would blockade and mine the PRC's entire 500-mile coast along the Taiwan Strait. It would also station nuclear weapons directly on Taiwan. As a result, the PRC's flow of supplies would be intercepted, its reach to Quemoy and Matsu interrupted, and its conquest of Taiwan rendered impossible. The pressure placed on the Sino-Soviet alliance would become excruciating.

Eisenhower hesitated. A blockade was legally an act of war that the PRC could not ignore. Still, Dulles had persuaded him that his own plan was not feasible, and he had run out of other options. He instructed Dulles to send two of Chiang's most ardent sympathizers, Admiral Radford and Assistant Secretary of State Robertson, to propose the plan to the generalissimo in Taipei. .

They had made no headway in convincing Chiang to accept the proposal when on April 23, while attending a conference of the nonaligned nations of Asia and Africa at Bandung, Indonesia, Premier Chou En-lai suddenly announced that the PRC was prepared to halt the shelling and negotiate an end to the tension with the United States. Perhaps the Communist Chinese hoped to demonstrate their interest in peace to their neighbors, whose anxiety had been evident from the start of the Bandung meeting. Perhaps they yielded to pressure by the Soviets. Perhaps they succumbed to fear of war with the United States. In a famous interview published in *Life* magazine several months later, Dulles boasted that it was the latter. But he never knew for certain, and it appears in retrospect that U.S. conduct during the crisis provoked more than deterred the Peking leadership. Regardless, Dulles jumped at the opportunity to avert a war by responding favorably to the PRC initiative. By the end of May the crisis had subsided.

Although America's allies in Europe were relieved, with the exception of West Germany the consensus was that the United States had behaved irresponsibly and even duplicitously. They had held up their end of the bargain by ratifying the agreements sanctioning the restoration of the FRG's sovereignty and its membership in NATO, but Washington had chosen nuclear brinkmanship over an UN cease-fire. Led by the British, the Europeans were more determined than ever to promote negotiations in order to relax tensions between the East and West on a global scale.

Winston Churchill had been campaigning for a summit meeting with the Soviets since 1950. Dulles's rhetoric during the 1952 election gave him added incentive, and Stalin's death in March 1953 provided a golden opportunity. After the new Kremlin leadership proclaimed that the growing danger of nuclear war required East-

West negotiations, Churchill wrote Eisenhower that "we ought to lose no chance of finding out how far the Malenkov regime are [*sic*] prepared to go in easing things up all around." Before the House of Commons the venerable British prime minister was more precise: A "conference on the highest level should take place between the leading Powers without long delay," he announced.[22]

It was at this same time that Eisenhower and Dulles rejected psychological warfare expert C. D. Jackson's proposal to reconvene the Council of Foreign Ministers. For the same reasons, their opposition to a summit meeting was even stronger. Dulles was also influenced by the lesson he drew from President Wilson's decision to participate personally in the Versailles negotiations instead of "remaining in Washington and speaking from the White House," which the secretary believed was a great mistake. During the preparation of his April "Chance for Peace" address, Eisenhower had declared that he was "ready and willing to meet with anyone anywhere from the Soviet Union," but he had added the caveat, "provided the basis for the meeting was honest and practical." Judging from the Soviet response, there appeared to be no such basis. Eisenhower tried to let Churchill down gently. "There is some feeling here also for a meeting between the Heads of States and Governments," he wrote, but "I feel we should not rush things too much." The president explained: "We have so far seen no concrete Soviet actions which would indicate their willingness to perform in connection with larger issues. In the circumstances, we would risk raising hopes of progress toward an accommodation which would be unjustified."[23]

Churchill continued to press his case, and the more urgent were his entreaties, the more intense became the debate within the administration over a summit in particular, and negotiations in general. What emerged were three competing perspectives. Predictably, Eisenhower represented those most willing to negotiate, and equally predictably, the JCS, Radford above all, represented those least willing. The president's view was that, while the Soviets' ultimate goal was world domination, they would not risk their own safety to pursue it. Hence, once the Kremlin recognized that America's allies had the will and capability to resist aggression, and the United States had the will and capability to retaliate massively against such aggression, it might be possible to achieve limited settlements, especially those that mitigated the nuclear predicament. According to the JCS, however, without incontrovertible evidence of a radical change in Soviet objectives and behavior, any settlement would be foolhardy and "self-defeating." The service chiefs argued that rather than try to mitigate the nuclear predicament, the United States should exploit its superiority while it still had it in order to force the Soviets to retract their influence and submit to U.S. demands.[24]

Dulles's position lay between the two. Less confident than Eisenhower in the allies, he was less inclined to negotiate for fear of encouraging their wishful thinking and neutralism. He also did not want significantly to reduce the pressure on either the Soviet economy or the Sino-Soviet alliance, and he always worried about the reaction of the Republican right wing. Yet the posture advocated by Radford would further divide the United States from its allies and "eliminate all hope" of ever arriving at settlements short of a Soviet unconditional surrender. As a compromise, Dulles proposed that the Eisenhower administration commit itself to seeking diplomatic solutions to problems central to the cold war (the status of divided Germany and occupied Austria topped his agenda) but refrain from taking initiatives until more assured that the unity and collective security of the non-Communist world rested on a "firm foundation." If this precondition could be met, he told the NSC during the 1953 deliberations over the first statement of basic national security policy, there "may be a fair chance of some settlement with the Russians."[25]

The language of NSC 162/2 suited both Eisenhower and Dulles (and greatly distressed Radford). Confronted with "the growing strength of the free world and the failure to break its cohesion," the "Soviet leadership might find it desirable and even essential to reach agreements acceptable to the United States and its allies, without necessarily abandoning its basic hostility to the non-Soviet world." NSC 162/2 noted nevertheless that current conditions were "not encouraging," and as events unfolded in 1954, there were few signs of improvement. The Soviets did agree to the Indochina Accords at Geneva, but they were barely acceptable to the United States and hardly reflected the growth of free world strength and cohesion. Worse, the French rejection of the EDC treaty in August underscored how much progress still had to be made in both realms before attaining the "firm foundation" essential to constructive negotiations.[26]

Because of the end-of-the-year agreements to integrate West Germany into NATO and establish SEATO, Eisenhower and Dulles found it increasingly difficult to justify their opposition to a summit even as the escalation of the offshore islands crisis made the

relaxation of East-West tensions appear that much more imperative. By the spring of 1955, Dulles was reporting to Eisenhower
that a "passionate eagerness" for a summit was evident throughout Europe. Churchill's retirement required the Conservatives to
hold new elections in Britain. The central theme of the campaign of
Sir Winston's heir, Anthony Eden, was that the "right moment" for
a summit had arrived. This theme was echoed by Edgar Faure in
France, and even by Konrad Adenauer in West Germany.[27]

Ironically, it was the Soviets who proved decisive in Eisenhower
and Dulles's finally consenting to a summit. For a decade Austrian
leaders had been seeking a treaty that would restore the country's
independence and end its occupation by the World War II victors,
but neither Moscow nor Washington would cooperate. Each tied
resolving the Austrian "problem" to the more intractable problem
of Germany. Following Stalin's death, the new Kremlin leadership
did modify its position by agreeing to withdraw its troops from
Austria in return for a guarantee of Vienna's neutrality. Still, as a
precondition the Soviets insisted on a reunified and disarmed Germany. Eisenhower and Dulles feared that under any circumstances
a neutral Austria would result in a destabilizing power vacuum in
the heart of Europe. More important, they were certain that the
Soviets' proposal was merely another tactic for thwarting West
Germany's rearmament and its integration into Western defense
plans. Negotiations over Austria's future went nowhere.

In early 1955 the Soviets took the initiative to break the dead-
lock. Convinced that there was nothing more they could do to prevent West Germany from joining NATO, they shifted their focus to
preventing Austria from following suit. In behind-the-scenes bilateral talks with Vienna, they dropped their demand that a treaty
with Germany precede one with Austria and made Austrian neutrality the sole prerequisite for the withdrawal of Soviet troops. In
doing so they undercut U.S. arguments against signing an Austrian
State Treaty and against agreeing to a summit meeting. In his 1953
"Chance for Peace" speech, Eisenhower had said that Moscow's
willingness to settle the question of Austria's occupation was a lit-
mus test of its willingness to engage in constructive negotiations
on other issues. It now appeared throughout Europe and in much
of the United States that the Soviets had passed the test. Not "wish-
ing to appear senselessly stubborn in my attitude," Eisenhower announced he would attend a conference of heads of state. At a
meeting in Vienna to sign the Austrian State Treaty in early May,
the United States, Britain, and France formally invited the Soviets

to attend a summit. Shortly thereafter, the four powers decided to convene in Geneva in July.[28]

The administration had no time to lose in formulating its negotiating positions and strategy. Foreign policymakers anticipated that their agenda would encounter opposition from their allies as well as their adversary and that they would have to negotiate with both. They were right. For example, from Washington's perspective any discussion of Germany's reunification at Geneva ran the risk of allowing the Soviets to disrupt the fragile harmony produced by the FRG's recent admission to NATO. Yet the risk of disruption would be even greater if the United States rejected the argument, presented most forcefully by Britain's Eden, that reducing tensions in Europe required addressing Moscow's legitimate security concerns over West Germany's rearmament.

This dilemma emerged at the outset when Eden went beyond arguing. Now prime minister, he proposed that the West, as it had at the Berlin Conference in 1954, put on the table a plan by which a national assembly would be freely elected by both East and West Germany as a first step toward the country's reunification. If the Soviets agreed, Eden was prepared to submit a treaty that limited the force levels and controlled the armaments of both NATO and the Warsaw Pact and established a demilitarized buffer zone between the two.

From Dulles's point of view, Eden's proposal not only threatened to dilute the position of strength in Europe that had finally been achieved, but it also threatened to forfeit the opportunity to exploit that position. Dulles had preached for years that the burden of trying to match the West's military buildup would prove too great for the Soviets, and he interpreted their eagerness for the summit as evidence that he was on the mark. Badly overextended and without an industrial base sufficient to "provide both guns and butter," they had had to "cut out the butter." He testified to the House Committee on Appropriations that their economy was nonetheless "on the point of collapsing."[29]

The result was growing discontent within the Soviet Union and throughout the satellites. This explained what Dulles referred to contemptuously as the Kremlin's attitude of "sweetness and light" that followed Malenkov's recent ouster by Nikolai Bulganin and Nikita Khrushchev. Disregarding his years of criticizing the negotiations at Versailles, the secretary's recommended response was to "press the Soviets hard" and avoid any agreement, such as Eden's initiative, that would "give them the relief they seek." At long last,

Dulles concluded, time had switched to the side of the West. A "policy of pressures can increase the gap between their requirements and their resources," he said confidently.[30]

The crucial question for Dulles was how to keep the allies from breaking ranks at Geneva. His answer was to steer the heads-of-state talks away from concrete proposals such as Eden's plan. The United States could justify its stance by arguing that the complexity of any security structure designed to promote German reunification within the broader context of a security regime for Europe precluded its useful discussion at a brief meeting held in the limelight. Reaching agreement required extended and complicated negotiations, and for these the lower-level and thus lower-key meetings scheduled to take place subsequent to the summit were more appropriate and potentially fruitful. In truth, Dulles did not want fruitful negotiations regardless of the venue in which they occurred. Rather, he wanted the opportunity to derail Eden's scheme without the whole world watching.

If it were up to Dulles, in fact, the Geneva Conference would not be a meeting to launch substantive negotiations on matters of security but an occasion to do battle with the Soviets on matters of principle that the entire West agreed were nonnegotiable. His objective was not merely to score propaganda points. Dulles hoped to lay the foundation for future progress toward the retraction or, in his words, the "rollback" of Soviet power. In pursuit of this goal, Dulles recommended that, early and often, the United States should "raise very affirmatively the issues of freedom for the Soviet satellites and the activities of the international Communist movement."

Doing so, Dulles opined, would unite, energize, and morally uplift the West while at the same time fanning the flames of discontent throughout the East. To defend itself, the beleaguered Kremlin might well feel compelled to extend to its clients "a status not unlike that of Finland"—greater economic and political autonomy and emancipation from direct military control. Under these conditions the prospect for their peaceful liberation would improve dramatically even as the Soviets' military capability was gravely impaired. Dulles realized that this process would take time to unfold. For the present his "big idea" was to plant the seeds necessary "to get the Russians out of the satellite states," which was finally "in the realm of possibility." Manipulating Geneva for this purpose could "lead to [the Soviet Empire's] disintegration."[31]

After uncharacteristically brief discussion the NSC endorsed Dulles's strategy and Eisenhower approved it as policy. At the summit, America's "basic policy on a Germany settlement" would be "to assure that present arrangements based on the Federal Republic's adherence to NATO and its contribution thereto are not prejudiced," either by Soviet or Allied initiatives. Toward this end, the United States would agree only that proposals that combined German reunification with a broader European security treaty were appropriate for future "study." Further, it would "maintain the position that Soviet control of the satellites is one of the principal causes of world tension," indict "the Soviet leaders for their responsibility for this obstacle to international relaxation," and "seek every opportunity to weaken or break the Soviet grip on part or all of the satellite area."[32]

When the administration turned to the question of controlling nuclear weapons, however, Dulles's priorities collided with those of the president. Throughout 1953 and 1954 Eisenhower had received as little cooperation from his own advisors as he had from the Kremlin in his effort to develop ideas to mitigate the nuclear predicament that were consistent with U.S. security interests but still acceptable to the Soviets. In his view, there could be "no final answer to the problem of nuclear warfare if both sides simply went ahead making bigger and better nuclear weapons," and it was "wrong for the U.S. merely to take a negative view of this terrible problem." The administration should at a minimum "determine whether safeguards could be devised entailing less risk for U.S. security than no limitation of armaments." Even for this limited purpose of designing a system for inspection, Eisenhower lamented well into 1954, "more imaginative thinking than was going on at present in this government" was essential.[33]

At the end of the year, despite appointing Harold Stassen as his special assistant for arms control so that he could have one person focus exclusively on the problem, Eisenhower was still complaining. Stassen was ineffective, and the JCS remained unequivocal and unmovable. "Soviet bad faith, evasion, and outright violation would render any disarmament agreement sterile," the service chiefs maintained. They believed that it was "not in the security interests of the United States to have any disarmament for the foreseeable future."[34]

Dulles was only slightly less categorical. The "greater military potential of the United States," he stressed, "gives the United States its maximum bargaining power." He also "doubted that the U.S. could work out any disarmament plan with a powerful nation which we did not trust and which we believed had most ambitious goals." Nevertheless, owing to his concern for allied and world opinion, Dulles's position was less rigid than the JCS's. So great had become the "popular and diplomatic pressure," he argued as the summit approached, that the administration had to "propose or support some plan for the limitations of armaments." But it "had to be extremely careful . . . not to walk into a trap."[35]

Dulles perceived the Geneva Conference as the supreme trap. On the same day the allies invited the Soviets to a four-power meeting of heads of state, the Kremlin's representative to the Subcommittee of the United Nations Disarmament Commission proposed that negotiations begin on a comprehensive treaty. It would provide for the "complete prohibition of the use and production of both nuclear and all other weapons of mass destruction"; a "major reduction in all armed forces"; and the "establishment of a control organ" to oversee compliance. As a consequence, Dulles announced when the NSC first convened to plan for Geneva, it was certain that "the subject of disarmament would be among the most important matters on which the United States must be prepared for discussions at the conference." Because the Soviet proposal "had actually gone a long way to meet the British and French position," he fretted that the discussions would be "hard to handle."[36]

Dulles had little more to contribute—except to point out what a good trap the Soviets had set. In his estimate, the Kremlin had succeeded through its "disarmament propaganda" to generate popular backing for its effort "to relieve itself of the economic burden of the present arms race." This was the last thing Dulles wanted to happen. Yet, if the United States appeared too inflexible, it ran the risk of "forfeiting the goodwill of our allies and the support of a large part of our own people." As a way to square the circle, Dulles suggested that the United States only propose "tentative and exploratory" measures confined to the concept of mutual inspection and contrived to divert attention from the Soviets' comprehensive proposals and to preempt discussion of any alternative that the allies might suggest in order "quickly or radically to alter the present situation."[37]

The JCS's solution was less complicated: "[T]he U.S. approach to the Geneva Conference should be based on the view that the position of the Soviet Union was weakening and that we should accordingly hold its feet to the fire." Regardless of allied opinion, the administration should neither propose, support, nor agree to anything related to arms control until the Soviets had conceded to the West's demands on all fundamental political and territorial issues. The service chiefs' "firm view" remained that without "concrete evidence of a revolutionary change in the ambitions and intentions of the Soviet regime," it would be "better" to continue the "arms race than to enter an agreement with the Soviets."[38]

Eisenhower's patience ran out. How could the JCS "really believe" a continually "mounting spiral" of arms racing and fear best served American and free world security interests? If this was in fact the case, he "wondered why they did not counsel that we go to war at once with the Soviet Union." Eisenhower was only slightly more tolerant of Dulles's prescription. Rather than stonewall, as Dulles advised, he insisted that the United States go "to the Geneva Conference hoping to see if we could penetrate the veil of Soviet intentions." The Kremlin's record of false promises obviously made caution compulsory, Eisenhower said, and he assured the NSC that he would be guided by the motto, "Trust in the Lord but keep your powder dry." Still, he was determined "to find out what these Soviet villains will do [in order] to find out what could be achieved by way of an acceptable inspections system." For this purpose, he needed a plan.[39]

At the last minute Eisenhower received one, but not from Dulles or his other primary advisors. Working independently of the NSC, Nelson Rockefeller, C. D. Jackson's successor as the White House special assistant for cold war strategy, organized a panel of social scientists and former government officials to formulate ideas about how to exploit Soviet vulnerabilities. Among the panel's recommendations was a "proposed agreement for mutual inspection of military installations, forces, and armaments, without limitations provisions" which would be linked to a convention assuring "the right of aircraft of any nationality to fly over the territory of any country for peaceful purposes." It "is highly doubtful" that the Kremlin would accept the proposal, Rockefeller wrote Eisenhower, but if it did, the benefits to U.S. intelligence would far outweigh any costs. Besides, the administration needed a "position at Geneva" that seized the "initiative in disarmament negotiation."[40]

Dulles reacted negatively to the concept. By this time the U-2, a high-altitude reconnaissance plane built as a CIA project, was in the final stages of development. It promised to give the United States a unilateral capability to overfly Soviet territory. Dulles was loath to forfeit this advantage. No less important, he vehemently objected to Rockefeller's trespassing on his turf. The "Secretary of State was supposed to be the principal advisor of the President with relations to foreign affairs," he complained. If Eisenhower "was getting advice on the whole gamut of international issues from Mr. Rockefeller, that would put us into a competitive position."[41]

Normally a stickler for the formal chain of command, in this case Eisenhower had no sympathy for Dulles's protest. The fact of the matter was that on arms control the secretary of state had no advice to offer other than to filibuster. Conversely, and more sincerely than Rockefeller, the president hoped that however remote the possibility, an agreement on reciprocal aerial surveillance might "open a tiny gate in the disarmament fence" by penetrating the Soviets' veil of secrecy. Eisenhower refused to foresake that possibility. Dulles found himself relegated to the sidelines during Geneva's most dramatic episode.[42]

The first three days of the summit produced nothing of substance. As planned, in his opening remarks Eisenhower charged the Soviets with subversion and suppression. After that, the United States concentrated on deferring discussion of such critical issues as German reunification and security agreements to subsequent, low-level meetings. But on July 21, Eisenhower proposed what journalists would soon dub "Open Skies." Speaking in part extemporaneously at the afternoon plenary session, the president pronounced that the "lessons of history teach us that disarmament agreements without adequate reciprocal inspection increase the dangers of war and do not brighten the prospects of peace." Then, turning to face directly Soviet Premier Bulganin, who was presiding, he disclosed the plan for mutual aerial surveillance. "The successful working out of such a system would do much to develop the mutual confidence which will open wide the avenues of progress of all our peoples." Just as Eisenhower concluded, a sudden thunderstorm cut the power lines, plunging the room into darkness.[43]

It did not take long for the lights to come back on, nor for the Soviets summarily to dismiss Open Skies as "but a spy thing." Eisenhower was genuinely disappointed; Dulles was not. Following Geneva, largely due to his participation in NSC deliberations and discussions with the NATO allies, Dulles became more receptive to measures designed to control the nuclear arms race. By the end of his life he fully supported Eisenhower's unsuccessful effort to negotiate a test ban treaty with Khrushchev. Nevertheless, he considered the "false euphoria" that unavoidably accompanied a summit "spectacle" counterproductive. In light of his priorities and concerns in 1955, moreover, Open Skies seemed more likely to cause trouble than to produce something of value.[44]

Still, Dulles conceded that the Geneva initiative did prove valuable. The United States scored a resounding victory in the progaganda war while at the same time diverting discussion of the Soviets' far more comprehensive proposal to the UN, where it quickly stalled. It also won for the administration much-needed support from the British and French, which contributed to its success in keeping German reunification and European security off the summit table. Yet, in this regard the Kremlin was Dulles's most helpful ally. Because Prime Minister Eden insisted on addressing German reunification and European security in tandem, the Soviets refused to discuss either. This blunder united the Western allies more than anything Dulles said or did. On July 23, 1955, the summit adjourned, having accomplished virtually nothing.

Dulles could not have been happier about the outcome. Not only was the West's position enhanced by its display of unity, but diplomatically the Soviets were wounded deeply by their intractability. Over the next months, Dulles met frequently with his French, British, and West German counterparts to discuss ways in which they could "maintain the initiative." This could be achieved, he was sure, by pursuing a diplomatic strategy developed from the convictions that Dulles shared with the FRG's Chancellor Adenauer: namely, that only after Germany had been reunified would it be possible to negotiate a European security system, and that German reunification was an all-or-nothing proposition. Hence, the prerequisite for future negotiations concerning the military balance in Europe had to be Soviet consent to East Germany's participation in free, democratic elections aimed at uniting the country without restrictions, most notably without a prohibition on membership in NATO. This posture would either place the onus for the impasse excusively on the Soviets or, in the unlikely event that they agreed, would require East Germany to participate, as Dulles put it, in "its own funeral."[45]

There is evidence that following Geneva the Kremlin (now dominated by Party Secretary Khrushchev), reeling from its diplomatic rout and beset by economic problems and growing unrest in Eastern Europe, was more willing to seek détente with the West by compromising on both the German question and European security. With Adenauer providing critical input and support, however, at a Conference of Foreign Ministers held from October to November 1955, Dulles persuaded London and Paris (and Eisenhower) that momentum was building so rapidly in favor of the West that nothing should be done to slow it down. He repeated his assessment that allied pressure had forced the Soviets to agree to the Austrian State Treaty, and he thought it "more likely than ever" that "if we are stout," German reunification could be accomplished within a "couple of years."[46]

Dulles was so convincing because he honestly believed in his prediction. He also honestly believed that on the heels of German reunification would come not only Soviet acquiescence to a security system for Western Europe on allied terms, but its pell-mell retreat from Eastern Europe as well. In fact, he told the Senate Foreign Relations Committee in the fall of 1955 that within five years they might well witness the retraction of Soviet military power and political influence throughout the satellites.

If the normally pessimistic secretary of state seemed overly optimistic at the end of 1955, he became all but giddy as 1956 wore on. The U.S. economy was thriving, inflation was under control, and for the first time the administration balanced the budget. Conditions appeared even better in the diplomatic arena. Preoccupied by nationalist upheavals in the vestiges of their empires in the Middle East and North Africa, in which they suspected Soviet involvement, the British and French offered only token resistance to Dulles's program of no concessions. And from his perspective, it did not take long for this program to produce dividends. In February 1956, at the 20th Congress of the Communist Party of the Soviet Union, Khrushchev delivered an astounding speech in which he punctured the myth of Bolshevik infallibility. He denounced Stalin as a mass murderer, repudiated the Marxist-Leninist doctrine of inevitable conflict between the Communist and capitalist worlds, and committed Moscow to tolerating diversity within its bloc by allowing its satellites greater political and economic freedom.

Dulles was confident that the "secret" speech, the text of which the United States quickly acquired through covert channels, indicated that Khrushchev, like him, recognized that the Soviet system and empire was spiralling toward death and was grasping at the straw of reform to resuscitate both. Dulles was just as confident that Khrushchev would fail and, especially after the Poles began to disavow their Stalinist past, that the failure would come sooner rather than later. Meanwhile Eisenhower, having recovered from his late 1955 heart attack, was campaigning at full speed toward almost certain reelection. In light of all they had already accomplished, Dulles mused, in four more years their teamwork might bring the West victory in the cold war.

Notes

1. Quoted in Gordon H. Chang, *Friends and Enemies: The United States, China, and the Soviet Union, 1948–1972* (Stanford, CA, 1990), 83.
2. Ibid.
3. NSC 162/2, October 30, 1953, *FR, 1952–54* 2:580.
4. Quoted in John Lewis Gaddis, "The Unexpected John Foster Dulles: Nuclear Weapons, Communism, and the Russians," in *John Foster Dulles and the Diplomacy of the Cold War* (Princeton, NJ, 1990), ed. Richard H. Immerman, 60.
5. Quoted in Robert Accinelli, *Crisis and Commitment: United States Policy toward Taiwan, 1950–1955* (Chapel Hill, NC, 1996), 112.
6. Quoted in Chang, *Friends and Enemies*, 120.
7. Dulles memorandum, September 12, 1954, *FR, 1952–54* 14:611; Memorandum of NSC meeting, September 12, 1954, ibid., 619 (emphasis in the original).
8. Memorandum of NSC meeting, September 24, 1954, ibid., 660; Memorandum of NSC meeting, September 12, 1954, ibid., 619.
9. Rankin to Department of State, October 5, 1954, ibid., 682.
10. Quoted in Nancy Bernkopf Tucker, "John Foster Dulles and the Taiwan Roots of the 'Two Chinas' Policy," in *John Foster Dulles and the Diplomacy of the Cold War*, ed. Immerman, 242.
11. Memorandum of conversation, January 19, 1955, *FR, 1955–57* 2:42.
12. Ibid.
13. Ibid.; Memorandum of NSC meeting, January 20, 1955, ibid., 69–82.
14. Memorandum of conversation, January 20, 1955, ibid., 86–89.
15. Memorandum of NSC meeting, January 20, 1955, 73.
16. Message from the President to Congress, January 24, 1955, ibid., 115–19; Draft message, January 20, 1955, ibid., 83–85.
17. Memorandum of NSC meeting, March 10, 1955, ibid., 345–50.
18. Quoted in Chang, *Friends and Enemies*, 126, 128.
19. Quoted in Chester J. Pach, Jr., and Elmo Richardson, *The Presidency of Dwight D. Eisenhower* (Lawrence, KS, 1991), 102.
20. Quoted in Chang, *Friends and Enemies*, 129–30.
21. Eisenhower memorandum to Dulles, April 5, 1955, *FR, 1955–57* 2:445–50.
22. Churchill to Eisenhower, April 5, 1953, in Peter G. Boyle, ed., *The Churchill-Eisenhower Correspondence, 1953–1955* (Chapel Hill, NC, 1990), 36; Churchill address to the House of Commons, May 11, 1953, in Robert R. James, ed., *Winston Churchill: His Complete Speeches, 1897–1963*, vol. 8 (New York, 1974), 8484.
23. Quoted in Andrew H. Berding, *Dulles on Diplomacy* (Princeton, NJ, 1965), 22; Memorandum of NSC discussion, March 11, 1953, *FR, 1952–54* 8:1122; Eisenhower to Churchill, April 25, 1953, in Boyle, ed., *Churchill-Eisenhower Correspondence*, 47.
24. JCS memorandum for the Secretary of Defense, "Review of Basic National Security Policy (NSC 162)," October 6, 1953, and Appendix, Records of the Office of the Secretary of Defense, RG 330, National Archives II, College Park, MD.
25. Memorandum of NSC meeting, October 7, 1953, *FR, 1952–54*, 2:529–30.

26. NSC 162/2, ibid., 584–85, 594.

27. Dulles to Department of State, May 9, 1955, *FR, 1955–57* 5:174; Anthony Eden, *Full Circle* (Boston, 1960), 320.

28. Dwight D. Eisenhower, *Mandate for Change* (Garden City, NY, 1963), 506.

29. Memorandum of conversation, February 10, 1955, *FR, 1955–57* 2:253–58; quoted in Coral Bell, *Negotiation from Strength: A Study in the Politics of Power* (London, 1962), 117.

30. Memorandum of conversation, July 5, 1955, *FR, 1955–57* 5:265; Memorandum of conversation, June 13, 1955, ibid., 226–32; Memorandum of conversation, February 10, 1955, ibid., 2:257–58.

31. Memorandum of NSC meeting, May 19, 1955, *FR, 1955–57* 5:184–88.

32. NSC 5524/1, Basic U.S. Policy in Relation to Four-Power Negotiations, July 11, 1955, ibid., 292–96.

33. Memorandum of NSC discussion, May 27, 1954, *FR, 1952–54* 2:1455; Memorandum of NSC discussion, June 24, 1954, ibid., 687–88.

34. Memorandum by the JCS to Secretary of Defense Charles Wilson, June 23, 1954, ibid., 683; Memorandum of conversation, January 4, 1955, *FR, 1955–57*, 20:2.

35. Draft memorandum by Dulles, "Limitation of Armaments," June 29, 1955, *FR, 1955–57* 20:140–41; Memorandum of conversation, January 4, 1955, ibid., 5; Memorandum of conversation, February 9, 1955, ibid., 16.

36. Editorial note, ibid., 76; Memorandum of NSC discussion, May 19, 1955, *FR, 1955–57* 5:183–84.

37. Dulles memorandum to Eisenhower, June 18, 1955, *FR, 1955–57* 5:239; Draft memorandum by Dulles, June 29, 1955, *FR, 1955–57* 20:141–42.

38. Memorandum of NSC meeting, July 7, 1955, *FR, 1955–57* 5:269; Memorandum of NSC discussion, June 30, 1955, *FR, 1955–57* 20:145.

39. Memorandum of NSC discussion, June 30, 1955, 148–49; Memorandum of NSC meeting, July 7, 1955, *FR, 1955–57* 5:272, 269.

40. Summary of recommendations of Quantico Vulnerabilities Panel, attachment to Walt W. Rostow to Nelson A. Rockefeller, June 10, 1955, *FR, 1955–57* 5:218; Rockefeller memorandum to Eisenhower, July 6, 1955, reproduced in Walt W. Rostow, *Open Skies: Eisenhower's Proposal of July 21, 1955* (Austin, TX, 1982), 134.

41. Memorandum of conversation, July 12, 1955, *FR, 1955–57* 5:305.

42. Quoted in Rostow, *Open Skies*, 46.

43. U.S. Delegation at the Geneva Conference to Department of State, July 21, 1955, *FR, 1955–57* 5:451–53.

44. Dwight D. Eisenhower Oral History, Columbia Oral History Project, Columbia University, New York, NY; quoted in Berding, *Dulles on Diplomacy*, 24.

45. Memorandum of conversation, August 1, 1955, *FR, 1955–57* 5:542; Memorandum of conversation, September 28, 1955, ibid., 601.

46. Dulles to Adenauer, August 15, 1955, ibid., 550.

7

Walking a Tightrope

The approach of the 1956 election brought an abrupt end to Dulles's cheerfulness. Even as his prognosis for Europe was improving dramatically, conditions were deteriorating seriously in the Middle East. In addition, U.S. and allied positions were rapidly converging in the former region, but they were just as rapidly diverging in the latter. Dulles believed that because the Western alliance was in such good shape and the Eastern bloc in such disarray, that any trade-offs between U.S. policy toward the competing fronts in Europe and the Middle East were unnecessary. But by the end of 1956, he had suffered grave defeats in both cold war arenas. The British and French believed that so long as they remained faithful to the policy of pressure toward the Soviets, Eisenhower and Dulles would grant them greater latitude on the periphery. They were proved very wrong by U.S. behavior during the Suez crisis that erupted in October 1956.

The impetus for the crisis, which had been brewing for years, came from the 1952 overthrow of Egypt's corrupt but pro-Western King Farouk by young army officers led by Gamal Abdul Nasser. An ardent nationalist, Pan Arabist, and neutralist, Nasser demanded that the British evacuate their military bases surrounding the Suez Canal. Following contentious negotiations, in 1954 Churchill and Eden reluctantly agreed to a phased withdrawal to be completed by mid-1956.

Both Eisenhower and Dulles had encouraged the British to relent, and, despite their wariness of Nasser, saw the 1954 agreement as a vital step toward overcoming the bitter legacy of British imperialism and toward harnessing Middle Eastern nationalism to the West. To further this objective while simultaneously deterring a Soviet effort to fill the defense vacuum created by Britain's departure, in 1955 they orchestrated the Baghdad Pact, a military alliance that included Turkey, Iran, Iraq, and Pakistan as well as Great Britain (the United States was not formally a member). Moreover, as a means to promote regional stability, Washington launched in concert with London a program intended to resolve the Arab-Israeli dispute. Through "Project Alpha" the United States offered to bear most of the cost for resettling in the Arab countries the Palestinian refugees trapped in Israel and to guarantee boundary adjustments, such as Israel's giving up some territory that it had won in 1948–49.

Egypt's geopolitical importance to the Middle East as well as Nasser's influence and ideological appeal dictated that Dulles seek the Egyptian president's cooperation. Neither diplomacy nor bribery, however, mitigated Nasser's suspicions that the United States was hostile to his ambitious goals for both Egypt and the region. He interpreted the Baghdad Pact as a more sophisticated form of Western imperialism, and the effort to reconcile Arabs and Jews as a Zionist conspiracy. The Israelis' unprovoked attack on Egyptian camps in the Gaza Strip in February 1955 further convinced Nasser that his agenda and the U.S. agendas were intrinsically incompatible. To punctuate his refusal to abide by Washington's guidelines as much as to strengthen Egypt's defenses, in September Nasser struck a deal to purchase arms from behind the Iron Curtain.

Dulles was irate. Nevertheless, encouraged by his recent string of successes, he still thought it possible to do business with Nasser. "We have a lot of cards to play," he told Undersecretary of State Herbert Hoover, Jr., by which he meant a lot of money. As a boon to Egyptian development and a monument to his rule, Nasser dreamed of constructing a massive dam at Aswan on the Nile River. Not only would the dam turn the river into a much-needed source of electrical power, but it would also control the Nile's endemic floods and provide the year-round irrigation essential to increase crop yields. Nasser's engineers had drafted plans to build the Aswan Dam. What he needed was the money to implement the plans. To get it he appealed to the United States.[1]

The Eisenhower administration responded positively. Funding such a humanitarian project would go a long way toward offsetting Third World criticism that the administration spent billions of dollars abroad to purchase arms or to assist its allies, especially in Europe, but pinched pennies in areas populated by the truly needy and led by independent-minded regimes. In the case of the Aswan

Dam, the United States would demonstrate to Nasser its eagerness to promote Egypt's welfare and modernization notwithstanding their differences. As a result, Washington hoped that Nasser would be wooed toward the West even as his preoccupation with the dam's construction constrained his inclination to stir up trouble.

Dulles repressed his anger over Nasser's arms deal and in December 1955 informed Nasser that the administration would finance building the Aswan Dam by putting together a $400-million package that combined U.S. grants and low-interest loans with supplemental contributions from Britain and the World Bank. Stiff congressional opposition to approving the necessary appropriations surfaced immediately. Anti-Communist zealots objected to spending millions of taxpayers' dollars on a government that refused to align with the United States in the global struggle for freedom, and fiscal conservatives complained that the United States could not afford such largesse. Representatives from southern states chorused in unison that the administration appeared bent on subsidizing a competitor to their cotton-growing constituents, while Jewish Americans lobbied furiously to head off assistance to an avowed enemy of Israel's very existence. Nasser sought to provide Washington with more incentive to overcome domestic resistance by raising the international stakes. First, he extended diplomatic recognition to the People's Republic of China. Then he threatened that if the United States would not honor its financial commitment, he would secure funding from the Soviet Union.

Having already developed serious doubts about the wisdom of expending tremendous amounts of financial and political capital on Nasser, Eisenhower and Dulles deemed this blatant attempt at diplomatic blackmail the final straw. "Do nations which play both sides get better treatment than nations which are stalwart and work with us?" Dulles roared. The question was rhetorical; Dulles delivered the answer personally to the Egyptian ambassador on July 19 by rescinding the U.S. offer to contribute money for the Aswan Dam. The secretary of state could not predict what would be Nasser's next move, but he confided to Senate Republican leader William Knowland that it would be instructive to find out. It was. A week later Nasser nationalized the Suez Canal Company, the largely British-controlled company that owned and operated the Canal. He intended to use the tolls he collected to finance the Aswan Dam.[2]

Dulles's fury was nothing compared to that of the British, Prime Minister Eden above all. The Canal was a vital source of British revenue, and it was the primary passageway for Britain's supply of oil from the East. It was also a vital transit route to London's remaining colonies and Commonwealth underlings. But Eden had even more fundamental concerns. The Suez Canal was the most prominent symbol of Britain's past imperial glory, and to lose it would underscore how low the nation had sunk in the ranks of global powers. Eden considered this personal and national humiliation to be intolerable. After Britain's feeble showing in the 1930s, it would also be equally intolerable to appease a leader whom Eden had repeatedly and publicly compared to Hitler.

There were limits to Eisenhower and Dulles's empathy with their beleaguered ally. They agreed that by seizing control of the Suez Canal, Nasser jeopardized Western security and economic interests. Yet they had no sympathy with Eden's obsession with retaining Suez as the final outpost of the British empire. Consistent with Dulles's decades-long warnings about the consequences of static powers resisting dynamic change, the president and the secretary of state firmly believed that British colonialism was as much to blame for the crisis as was Nasser's arrogance and belligerence.

Eisenhower and Dulles believed even more firmly that Eden's recommended solution—"to use force to bring Nasser to his senses"—would make a bad situation exponentially worse. As Dulles said privately to the president, U.S. efforts to disassociate the free world alliance from the history of European imperialism would suffer immeasurable damage from such strong-arm tactics. As a result the "influence of the West in the Middle East and most of Africa [would be] lost for a generation, if not a century." Dulles predicted that the Soviet Union would "reap the benefit." In addition to fueling Moscow's propaganda machine, British intervention might lead Nasser to invite the Red Army to intervene on Egypt's behalf. The U.S. choice would then be to acquiesce to the Soviets' "position of predominant influence in the Middle East and Africa" or retaliate, perhaps massively. Dulles's conclusion was "that, regrettable as it might be to see Nasser's prestige enhanced even temporarily, I did not believe the situation was one which should be resolved by force." Eisenhower "entirely agreed" with this "basic analysis."[3]

With the president's enthusiastic support, Dulles summoned all his legal and diplomatic acumen in an effort to resolve the crisis peacefully. Selecting his words with utmost care, he attempted to convince the British that "there was no basis for military action." Thus far, Nasser was guilty of neither territorial aggression, endangering the lives of foreign nationals in Egypt, nor violating the 1888 Suez Canal Convention that prohibited interfering with the navigation of the Canal. Rather, he had exercised his sovereign right to nationalize the Suez Canal Company's concession, which, unlike the convention, was not granted in perpetuity. The legally appropriate and diplomatically most constructive course of action, Dulles maintained, had to be confined to the question of the Canal's management. He devised a scheme to establish a Suez Canal Users Association (SCUA), comprised of some two dozen maritime nations, and entrust it with the authority to ensure that the Canal remained open to international traffic, to schedule pilots to provide safe passage, to collect tolls, and to guarantee the Egyptian government fair compensation.[4]

Dulles's proposal was acceptable to neither Nasser nor Eden. To Britain's prime minister, the issue was Nasser's having placed his "thumb on our windpipe," not international law. Dulles convened a conference to set up the SCUA. Eden made plans to seize the Canal and, he hoped, to topple Nasser in the process.[5]

From summer to fall of 1956, Eden drew Britain's natural allies into his secret plot. France also owned stock in the Suez Canal Company. More important, it blamed Nasser for encouraging the Algerian rebellion against French rule. Israel held Nasser responsible for guerrilla attacks from bases in the Gaza Strip and feared that his recent purchase of weapons from the Soviet bloc presented an immediate threat to the Jewish homeland.

Both nations rapidly signed onto Eden's plan, Operation MUSKETEER, the specifics of which were proposed by the French. They agreed that Israel would invade first, striking across the Sinai Peninsula and heading directly toward the Suez Canal. Posing as innocents interested only in safeguarding the Canal from damage and preventing the disruption of traffic, Britain and France would demand that all forces withdraw from the area. The Israelis would comply; Nasser would not. Under no circumstances would he permit the European powers to tell him where or where not to deploy his troops on Egyptian soil, let alone inhibit him from responding to an external attack. His rejection of the ultimatum would justify the intervention of France and Britain, which would result in their occupying the Canal and, with any luck, in Nasser's political downfall. If he happened to be killed in the fighting, so much the better.

Eden later charged that Dulles had deliberately led him to think that the United States would at a minimum look the other way in the event of a military operation. This charge, driven by the prime minister's personal animus toward Dulles as well as by his attempt to exonerate his own behavior, is spurious. Eden went to great lengths to keep the United States in the dark, and he succeeded. The CIA, based on intelligence produced by U-2 surveillance, did speculate that something might be in the air, but it estimated an Israeli invasion of Lebanon as the most likely scenario. It did not suspect collusion between Israel, France, and Britain.

Although Eisenhower and Dulles discussed in private the possibility of initiating a covert operation to oust Nasser once there was less international attention focused on Egypt, both repeatedly warned London against using force. Eden simply would not allow himself to believe that they meant it. Indeed, he had gone along with what he considered Dulles's "cock-eyed idea" for a SCUA on the assumption that after the proposed association's fate was sealed the United States would support forceful measures. Eden also assumed that Washington would applaud the restoration of control of the Canal to the West. Besides, when push came to shove, the United States would never turn its back on an ally with whom it had a "special relationship."[6]

Eden could not have been farther off the mark. On October 29 the Israelis struck across the Sinai and advanced rapidly toward the Canal. On cue, London and Paris jointly issued an ultimatum giving both sides twelve hours to withdraw, which Nasser promptly dismissed. A French and British armada set sail for Port Said and their bombers attacked Egyptian airfields, but before the fleet arrived to take control of the Canal, Nasser blocked all transit through it by scuttling some fifty Egyptian ships. The ostensible rationale for the Anglo-French invasion—to secure the Canal's continued operation—produced the opposite result.

Eisenhower and Dulles were outraged that, ignoring their advice, three key allies in the struggle for global freedom collaborated to go behind their backs and play "the part of a bully" in a manner reminiscent of nineteenth-century gunboat diplomacy. Further, the collusion was so blatant and the plan took so long to unfold that avoiding international condemnation became impossible. Making matters worse, what Dulles described as a "crude and brutal" use of force in Egypt prevented the United States from capitalizing on the Soviets' even more crude and brutal use of force in Hungary.[7]

It was no coincidence that in the midst of the Suez crisis, Khrushchev determined the time had come to put an end to the challenge to Soviet hegemony spawned by his earlier speech that denounced Stalin and indicated a willingness to tolerate diversity within the Eastern bloc. Khrushchev had actually developed second thoughts about the speech shortly after delivering it, and he had been seriously tempted to crush the Polish movement for reform after the anti-Stalinist Wladyslaw Gomulka took power. But Gomulka stressed his intention to remain loyally within the Soviet orbit and made clear that he would arm Polish workers and peasants if Moscow intervened. On October 24 (the day before Britain, France, and Israel made the final decision to invade Egypt), Khrushchev informed the Soviet party presidium that he preferred compromise to confrontation with the Poles.

Hungary posed a more severe problem than did Poland, and the Suez crisis provided Khrushchev with the opportunity to remedy it. Evidently Soviet restraint toward Gomulka encouraged the Hungarians to think they could push the envelope of liberalization open farther still. They were also encouraged by America's Radio Free Europe, which in the heady days following Khrushchev's speech turned up the volume on its broadcasts promoting liberation. The Hungarians expected the United States to assist them, and East European émigrés who trained to engage in covert operations under the CIA's RED SOX/RED CAP program were in Hungary helping to organize demonstrations.

By the last week of October the rioting in Hungary had become so widespread that Khrushchev, after much hesitation, felt that he had no alternative but to restore order by sending the Red Army into Budapest. The army encountered throngs of angry residents throwing stones and homemade Molotov cocktails. With the capital city in a state of virtual anarchy and fearing a full-scale insurrection, on October 28 Khrushchev negotiated an agreement with Hungarian Communist Party head Imre Nagy for the withdrawal of the Soviet troops. Emboldened, Nagy declared that Hungary would leave the Warsaw Pact. The West's preoccupation with the Suez crisis made Khrushchev's response easier. Rather than withdraw, 200,000 Soviet troops and 4,000 tanks swept through the streets of Budapest, crushing the rebellion. Twenty thousand Hungarians were killed; Nagy was deposed and executed.

Despite the rebel's hopes and CIA entreaties, neither Eisenhower nor Dulles seriously considered extending aid to the Hungarians. The objective of their campaign of psychological warfare, buttressed by covert operatives, was to fan the flames of discontent, strengthen the morale of the discontented, place an ever-increasing burden on the Kremlin's instruments of control, and, not incidentally, appeal to America's East European voters. Irresponsibly, they never expected a quixotic revolution, and they recognized from the start that the United States could not provide the underarmed and undermanned insurrection with the assistance necessary to resist a Soviet force of this magnitude without running an unacceptable risk of general war. The administration did, of course, denounce the Soviets' behavior in the strongest words, but owing to the concurrent behavior of the British, French, and Israelis, their words lost a lot of their bite.

Washington would have repudiated the intervention in Suez even had the Soviets not intervened in Hungary at the same time. The congruence of events made it more urgent to stop the fighting in Suez and more imperative to make a ringing declaration of U.S. opposition to imperialism, regardless of its form or agent. When the British and French vetoed a cease-fire resolution that the United States sponsored in the UN Security Council, Eisenhower instructed Dulles to present the U.S. case directly to the UN General Assembly on November 1.

The secretary of state prefaced his remarks with the assertion, "I doubt that any delegate ever spoke from this forum with as heavy a heart as I have brought here." The United States, Dulles declared, "finds itself unable to agree with three nations with whom it has ties, deep friendship, admiration and respect, and two of whom constitute our oldest, most trusted, and reliable allies." Still, "that disagreement involves principles which far transcend the immediate issue"; and therefore, "we feel impelled to make our point of view known to you and through you to the world." Dulles then juxtaposed another resolution urging a cease-fire, a ban on all military aid to the combatants, and the withdrawal of all belligerent forces, with an impassioned, atypically eloquent expression of Wilsonian idealism. Serious as they were, Egypt's "provocations," he said, "cannot justify the resort to armed force which has occurred." If the aggression was allowed to stand, "we would have, I fear, torn this [UN] charter into shreds and the world would again be in a world of anarchy."[8]

Dulles spoke from the heart; his speech reiterated themes he had been propounding for decades. He subsequently commented to his associates that "if that [speech] had been my very last act on earth, it would have been exactly as I would have wished it. I would have liked it for my epitaph." Nevertheless, it was in speaking to the NSC that morning that Dulles revealed in full the motives and beliefs that influenced his thinking.[9]

"For many years now the United States has been walking a tightrope between the effort to maintain our old and valued relations with our British and French allies on the one hand, and on the other trying to assure ourselves of the friendship and understanding of the newly independent countries who have escaped from colonialism," Dulles began. "Unless we now assert and maintain" U.S. leadership, we "will be looked upon as forever tied to British and French colonialist policies," and "all of these newly independent countries will turn from us to the USSR." Referring to the events in Hungary, Dulles then lamented that the present situation was all the more "tragic" because "at this very time, when we are on the point of winning an immense and long-hoped-for victory over Soviet colonialism in Eastern Europe, we should be forced to choose between following in the footsteps of Anglo-French colonialism in Asia and Africa, or splitting our course away from their course."[10]

As Dulles's analysis makes clear, it was more the dictates of the cold war than anticolonialist principles, genuine as the latter were, that drove him to disavow publicly the conduct of America's allies in Suez. It was also the dictates of the cold war that drove U.S. conduct after Dulles's speech. Even as the UN General Assembly voted overwhelming to adopt the U.S. cease-fire resolution (only Britain, France, Israel, Australia, and New Zealand dissented), the Soviets warned that they were prepared to intervene with force on Nasser's behalf. Despite barely surviving a vote of confidence in Parliament and the resignations of several members of his Cabinet, Eden refused to terminate the operation. The invasion sparked a precipitate decline in the value of the pound, and Britain did not have nearly the gold reserves to halt the free fall. Its economy would collapse without U.S. assistance, which Eisenhower promised to provide only in exchange for Eden's agreement to a cease-fire.

Shattered, Eden gave in, which left the French no choice but to follow suit. On November 6, despite the fact that the Democrats increased their majority by one seat in the Senate and two in the House, Eisenhower won reelection, again over Stevenson, by an even greater landslide than in 1952. The cease-fire went into effect on the same day. The administration withheld economic assistance until the British and French troops actually began their withdrawal several weeks later, and in secret communications with members of Eden's cabinet hinted very strongly that in the future a British government headed by someone other than Anthony Eden would have far fewer financial worries. Among those Washington contacted was the chancellor of the exchequer and Eisenhower's close World War II associate, Harold Macmillan. When Eden, politically and psychologically broken, resigned on January 9, 1957, Macmillan succeeded him as prime minister.

The withdrawal of the British and French forces from Suez (Israel did not evacuate the Sinai and Gaza Strip until March 1957), the anticipation of improved Anglo-American relations, and even the resounding reelection of Eisenhower were of small consolation to Dulles. For four years he had struggled mightily against the centrifugal forces within the free world and the expansionist forces of global communism. After the Geneva summit, he had become progressively more confident that this struggle was on the verge of bearing fruit. The combination of the Suez and Hungarian crises appeared to have reversed the momentum.

Although Dulles's will and determination remained indomitable, he could no longer be sure that he could trust his body. On the night of November 2, while the world was still digesting his speech to the UN General Assembly, Dulles had awakened with a sharp pain in his abdomen. He had long suffered from chronic gout. Whenever possible he retreated to the quiet of his Washington home or the rustic seclusion of his primitive cabin on Lake Ontario's Duck Island. In these sanctuaries he received succor and seeming sustenance from his devoted wife Janet, and he endured incredible discomfort without complaining. This pain, however, was too much for him to bear. Suspecting that something was seriously wrong, Janet called for an ambulance.

Her suspicions proved correct. At Walter Reed Hospital the next day, Dulles was operated on for a cancerous tumor. The doctors hoped that they had removed all the malignancy, and the secretary of state was back at his desk in a month. Still, approaching his 69th birthday, Dulles had to wonder how much time he had left even as the events of the last months forced him to accept the fact that there was still so much for him to do.

After recovering from his operation, Dulles immmediately set to work to prevent the Soviet Union from taking advantage of the residue from the Suez crisis to extend its tentacles deep into the Middle East. Averse to adding to the list of U.S. global commitments, the administration's security policy for this region until this point had relied largely on the continued presence of the British; pro-Western countries such as the Baghdad Pact members, Jordan, and Lebanon; the U.S. nuclear deterrent; and when necessary, the CIA. The fiasco at Suez, however, demonstrated that the British were as ineffectual as they were imperious. Exacerbating the problem, Nasser emerged as the peerless and fearless champion of Arab nationalism and, because of Israel's participation in the invasion, Muslim irredentism.

Having thought long and hard about the problem while bedridden, Dulles met on January 2, 1957, in closed session with the Senate Committee on Foreign Relations to discuss the corrosive consequences of the Suez crisis for Western interests and to generate congressional support for expanding the U.S. role in the region. Already back at full strength, the secretary of state, as he so often did, began by reciting a lesson in history. For more than a century, he lectured, the British and Russian empires had collided in the Middle East. Britain had always prevailed, but as a result of the "very improvident and unwise action of the British in the attack upon Egypt," that "bulwark" against Russia's historic ambitions had been "swept away." Unless the United States provided the "free nations of the area" with a more concrete security guarantee than its existential strategic deterrent, Dulles warned in typically alarmist fashion that they "will almost certainly be taken over by Soviet communism." These "people with exposed positions . . . have got to have in addition to an invisible protection outside of their own border which they cannot see, something within their border which they can see." Dulles identified that "something" as direct U.S. military and economic assistance.[11]

Prior to the meeting the administration had drafted a resolution requesting congressional sanction for a more assertive policy to deter "Communist aggression in the Middle East area." After Dulles reported a positive response to his presentation, Eisenhower hastened to submit it. Appearing before a joint session of Congress on January 5, the president enunciated what journalists, noting the parallels with Truman's similar rhetoric and purposes when confronted with the Greek-Turkish crisis a decade earlier, soon began to call the Eisenhower Doctrine. The danger posed by international communism's quest for world domination, the president declared, had "abruptly" brought the Middle East to a "new and critical stage in its long and important history." Should the Soviets achieve their goal of hegemony in the region, they would "gravely endanger all the free world" by blocking sea lanes vital to its defense and oil supplies vital to its economy. Fortunately, the leaders of most Middle Eastern nations were wise to Moscow's treachery, but they required U.S. help in countering the popular appeal of the Kremlin's "superficially attractive offers" of assistance. Accordingly,

Eisenhower asked Congress to appropriate and authorize his discretionary use of $200 million in economic and military aid over the next two fiscal years.

In requesting this small amount of money (in 1947 Truman had requested twice as much just for Greece and Turkey), Eisenhower betrayed the administration's woeful neglect of the root causes of Middle Eastern turmoil and of nationalist resentment of the West: the widespread poverty and hunger produced by decades of colonial pillage. Despite their sensitivity to these internal forces, Eisenhower and Dulles subordinated them to the external threat presented by Soviet communism. In their view the president needed discretionary authority to employ U.S. armed forces, not merely to spend its money. The Middle East Resolution ended up closely resembling the Formosa Resolution. What defined the Eisenhower Doctrine was the president's request for another blank check to engage U.S. forces whenever and wherever an unspecified Middle Eastern country encountered "overt armed aggression from any nation controlled by International Communism."[12]

Reaction in both Houses was rapid and, confounding Dulles's prediction, hostile. Some legislators were disturbed over the potential further erosion of Congress's constitutional prerogatives, while others objected to the vague reference to "any nation controlled by International Communism." Several senators, led by Arkansas Democrat William Fulbright, expressed concern that the administration might apply the label Communist to someone like Nasser, which could lead to an intervention no less misconceived and counterproductive than that of the British, French, and Israelis. Eisenhower's failure to stipulate what form of military action he had in mind provoked additional anxiety. With but one battalion of Marines attached to the Sixth Fleet in the Mediterranean, would he consider a nuclear strike a viable response? The memories of the recent crisis in the Taiwan Strait remained too fresh to rule out this possibility. The administration "asks for a blank grant of power," Fulbright cautioned, "to be used in a blank way, for a blank length of time, under blank conditions with respect to blank nations in a blank area."[13]

As was the case in 1965 when Lyndon Johnson proposed the Gulf of Tonkin Resolution concerning Vietnam, few in Congress challenged the administration's fixation with containing Communist expansion. Fewer still were willing to go on record as refusing to grant the president the power he publicly declared was necessary in order to do so, especially in the wake of his smashing reelection. As soon as tensions in the Middle East subsided following Israel's withdrawal from the Sinai and Gaza Strip, the Senate approved Eisenhower's resolution. Eisenhower signed it into law on March 9. It was put to the test almost immediately, and it turned out to be a lengthy and onerous examination.

Elections in Jordan in April 1957 brought to power a decidedly pro-Nasserite National Socialist party headed by Sulayman al-Nabulsi, who had strong ties with the anti-Western commander of Jordan's army, Ali Abu Nuwar. Within days the new prime minister demonstrated his determination to break all ties with the West. He preemptorily terminated Jordan's alliance with Britain and simultaneously announced his government's intention to establish diplomatic relations with Moscow. Interpreting Nabulsi's radical nationalism as a slap to his royal face and a threat to his reign, Jordan's King Hussein dismissed the prime minister, cobbled together a more conservative government, and declared martial law. Nabulsi's supporters rioted in the streets of Amman, and from neighboring Syria, where along with a faction of the Jordanian Army he had established a government in exile, the deposed prime minister vowed to return. Hussein pushed the right buttons. Claiming that he was besieged by "international Communist subversion," he appealed to the United States for help.[14]

In Dulles's judgment Nabulsi's "extremist nationalist views" were "to some extent at least, Communist inspired." Based on this premise, the secretary intuitively concluded that the danger to Hussein's Hashemite dynasty represented a "challenge under the Middle East Doctrine." Dulles consulted in person with both the British and the Israelis and by phone with Eisenhower, who was in Georgia at his favorite vacation spot, the Augusta National Golf Club. The president issued a public statement that "both the Secretary of State and I regard the independence and integrity of Jordan as vital," thus implying that Hussein's problem was foreign—hence Communist—in origin. Then the White House annnounced that Eisenhower would use the discretionary authority Congress had just given him to grant the king $20 million in aid and that the Sixth Fleet, with its two aircraft carriers and battalion of Marines, would deploy to the Eastern Mediterranean and prepare to intervene on Hussein's behalf should Nabulsi attack. When the ex-prime minister did not attack, Dulles declared a victory for the Eisenhower Doctrine.[15]

Dulles spoke prematurely. A modicum of stability returned to Jordan, but Nabulsi had many kindred spirits in what was now his

Syrian home base. Washington had been long concerned with the growth of Nasserite and Soviet influences in Syria. The country, Eisenhower opined, was "far more vulnerable to Communist penetration" even than Egypt, and hence was "ripe to be plucked at any time."[16]

The administration's concerns escalated when Damascus sided against Nabulsi in Jordan and reached a $500 million grain-for-weapons agreement with Moscow. As a quick fix, Eisenhower authorized Operation WAPPEN, a CIA plan hatched in the immediate aftermath of the Jordanian crisis to return to power former president and military strong man, Colonel Adib al-Shishakli. The conspiracy, however, required the support of Syria's military officers, and U.S. operatives were too indiscriminate in recruiting accomplices. Several whom they approached quickly informed Syrian intelligence. On August 12 the Syrian government trumpeted that it had uncovered an American plot to overthrow it. The next day the secretary general of the Ministry of Foreign Affairs notified the U.S. embassy that in order to "preserve good relations between Syria and the United States it was necessary" to declare three U.S. diplomats persona non grata. Syria's army chief of staff resigned two days later. Washington considered his successor, Afif al-Bizri, to be a Communist sympathizer.[17]

Beyond declaring the Syrian ambassador persona non grata in a tit-for-tat rejoinder, the Eisenhower administration was undecided about what to do. The United States "could not afford to have exist a Soviet satellite not contiguous to the Soviet border and in the midst of the already delicate Middle East situation," said Dulles at a State Department meeting. After conferring with Eisenhower, he called Air Force General Nathan Twining, Radford's successor as JCS chairman. Dulles reported that "we are thinking of the possibility of fairly drastic action" but that the administration had not reached a decision. Since Syria had broken diplomatic relations with Britain and France following the Suez invasion, Eisenhower worried that if the Syrian government now severed ties with the United States as well, the Soviets would be handed a "fairly open field." Dulles was anxious not to provide Israel with any excuse to "stimulate an incident with Syria" that could unite all the Arab nations behind Damascus. The secretary of state recommended keeping "the Syrian Government uncertain as to our intentions." Eisenhower concurred, in no small measure because he was uncertain as to what the United States should intend to do.[18]

Eisenhower and Dulles resisted the urge to invoke the Middle East Resolution. Nevertheless, even as the president stated publicly that he had not yet determined whether Syria was controlled by international communism, he ordered the Sixth Fleet back to the Eastern Mediterranean. Concurrently, in an effort to line up an anti-Syrian coalition, Dulles dispatched State Department emissaries to Lebanon, Jordan, Turkey, Saudi Arabia, and Iraq, and the Pentagon shipped them arms and munitions. If some kind of military action proved necessary, the administration hoped these countries would initiate it, and the U.S. presence would be needed only to deter Soviet intervention and possibly provide subsequent support.

The problem was that although each Arab country Washington contacted felt threatened by the developments in Syria, none was willing to take the initiative. This resulted in part from Washington's inability to make up its mind as to what initiative it should recommend they take, and in part from their great distrust of one another. Each also realized that a military move against Syria, which was second only to Egypt in the hearts of Arab nationalists, would inevitably precipitate a domestic backlash. Dulles was stumped. "There is nothing that looks particularly attractive and the choice of policy will be hard," he wrote Britain's Prime Minister Macmillan on September 5. "We are not completely satisfied with any of the alternatives which have thus far been suggested. There are risks involved in and objections found to all of them."[19]

Two days later Dulles met at the White House with Eisenhower, Twining, Assistant Secretary of State for Near Eastern Affairs William Rountree, and several other key security advisors to explore the options. By setting the tone of the meeting at the outset, Dulles foreshadowed his conclusion. The "crude and impulsive" Kremlin leader, Nikita Khrushchev, he said, was "more like Hitler than any Russian leader we have previously seen." Then, explicitly dredging up the memories of the horrific repercussions that followed in the wake of Britain's and France's effort to appease Germany at Munich, Dulles asserted that "if the Soviets pulled this operation [in Syria] off successfully . . . the success would go to Khrushchev's head and we might find ourselves with a series of incidents like the experience with Hitler." The implication was that Moscow was using Syria as its proxy, and if a resolute stand was not taken against it, Syria's Middle Eastern neighbors in the 1950s would go the way of Czechoslovakia in the 1930s.[20]

Eisenhower agreed with Dulles's diagnosis, but he found unsettling its lack of a precise prescription. Dulles had not indicated "specifically what we [should] aim to do," nor had he suggested how to do it. Chastened, Dulles went directly from the White House to Foggy Bottom, where he and his staff drafted a policy paper. The "United States judges that Syria has become, or is about to become, a base for military and subversive activities in the Near East designed to destroy the independence of those countries and to subject them to Soviet Communist domination," read its premise. "If the aggressive spirit which is being inculcated into Syria by means of Soviet arms, propaganda, etc., should, as it seems likely, manifest itself in actual deeds," it followed, "the United States would hold that a case existed for individual or collective self-defense under Article 51 of the United Nations Charter." Pursuant to the Middle East Resolution, moreover, "If Syria's Moslem neighbors should consider their security endangered by the threat of Syrian aggression and should request from the United States economic assistance and military supplies in connection with a concrete plan effectively to meet such aggression, the U.S. would give prompt and sympathetic consideration to such a request." Finally, if "any of Syria's Arab neighbors were physically attacked by the Sino-Soviet Bloc, the United States, upon request, would be prepared to use its own armed forces to assist any such nation or nations against such armed aggression."[21]

Dulles's paper addressed some, but not all, of Eisenhower's reservations. The statement reiterated that increased U.S. economic assistance and military supplies remained contingent on the formulation of a "concrete plan." Thus far no such plan had even been proposed. The use of U.S. armed forces remained contingent on any of Syria's neighbors being "physically attacked by the Sino-Soviet bloc," leaving up in the air whether Syrian aggression—and more ambiguously, Syrian subversion—satisfied this criterion. Eisenhower approved the policy nevertheless.

For his part, Dulles began immediately to fill in the holes. He explicitly implicated Syria in the international Communist conspiracy by issuing a public statement that, in order to "carry out the national policy expressed in the Congressional Middle East Resolution," the administration was accelerating arms deliveries to the Middle East. Then, with Eisenhower's approval, he contacted Prime Minister Adnan Menderes of Turkey, who had expressed a willingness to spearhead a regional anti-Syrian coalition. Previously, Washington had urged Turkey to keep a low profile. It was too closely associated with the West because of its membership in NATO, and many of Syria's Moslem neighbors would feel compelled to rally to its defense against a non-Arab foe. Having concluded that there was no alternative, Dulles now encouraged Menderes to augment the Turkish forces on the Syrian border and, if possible, to provoke a military engagement. At the same time, he called JCS chairman Twining to be sure that the U.S. Strategic Air Command had been placed on alert. In light of the belligerent tone of recent Soviet statements, Dulles emphasized that the situation in Syria had "a considerable amount of danger in it."[22]

Dulles's maneuvering backfired. As tensions escalated, Damascus went out of its way not only to profess its independence of Moscow, but, more effectively, to draw parallels between its position and that of Cairo in 1956. As the number of Turkish troops on its border grew from 32,000 to 50,000, so grew the number of Syria's Arab neighbors who agreed. Almost overnight the governments of Saudi Arabia, Lebanon, Jordan, and Iraq shifted their rhetoric about Syria from criticism to support. As a consequence, the United States found itself in the awkward and isolated position of claiming that Syria seriously threatened the region while its own regional allies proclaimed their solidarity with Damascus against outside—specifically Turkish—aggression. It "is hard for us to say it's dangerous when they [the Arabs] say the opposite," bemoaned a frustrated Dulles at the beginning of October.[23]

By the middle of the month Dulles was expressing apprehension more than frustration. On October 16, Syria's foreign minister formally asked the UN to establish an impartial commission to investigate the "threats to the security of Syria and to international peace" posed by the concentration of Turkish troops on its border. Dulles shivered. Such an investigation would undoubtedly turn up evidence that the United States had conspired with Turkey against Syria much like Britain and France had conspired with Israel against Egypt. The diplomatic ramifications would be catastrophic. It was imperative, he told UN delegate Henry Cabot Lodge, Jr., to find a way "to get out." Four days later Saudi Arabia's King Saud provided a way by offering to mediate. Given the king's rivalry with Nasser for leadership of the Arab world and his participation in the initial U.S. effort to assemble an anti-Syrian coalition, his mediation effort would surely, Dulles calculated, avoid discussing any areas of the "most highly sensitive character" which would be "disastrous" if "exposed."[24]

On Dulles's instructions Lodge proposed that the UN suspend a decision on the Syrian request for an investigation until Saud had time to mediate. On October 22 the General Assembly voted to adopt the U.S. recommendation. Within a month Ankara agreed to withdraw most of the Turkish forces from the Syrian border, and Damascus agreed to withdraw its request for an investigatory commission. Under the circumstances Eisenhower and Dulles considered this outcome satisfactory, but they were far from pleased. Their attempt to apply the Eisenhower Doctrine to Syria had increased Soviet influence in the region and alienated previous U.S. allies. It had also provided the Syrians with additional incentive to look to Nasser for protection.

In February 1958, Egypt and Syria agreed to merge, forming the United Arab Republic. As a consequence the Eisenhower administration, although still licking its wounds, plunged right back into the Middle East morass. Two months after the Egyptian-Syrian merger, Lebanon erupted into a crisis that verged on civil war. The catalyst was exclusively domestic. The president, Camille Chamoun, was the one Middle Eastern leader who, in concert with his Harvard-educated ambassador to the United States, Charles Malik, had endorsed the Eisenhower Doctrine, as Chamoun boasted, "one hundred percent." He was also a Maronite Christian who presided over a regime that included representatives of Lebanon's Muslim (divided between Sunni and Shi'ite Muslims) majority. The more vocal Chamoun became in supporting Washington's hostile posture toward Nasser and his Syrian cohorts, the less cooperative the Muslims became. When in May 1958 a Christian member of the Chamber of Deputies proclaimed his intention to propose an amendment to the constitution that would circumvent the prohibition on a president from serving two consecutive terms in office, Lebanon's facade of political and religious unity fractured. Two Shi'ite ministers resigned, and violent strikes and riots shook the capital city of Beirut. Doubting the loyalty of his armed forces, on May 11 Chamoun sent U.S. Ambassador Robert McClintock a handwritten note asking for "twenty tanks by airlift with the ammunition." At a meeting two days later, Chamoun requested that McClintock deliver an "oral message" to the White House that, in accordance with the Eisenhower Doctrine, the president "consider [the] possibility of landing armed forces in Lebanon within 24 hours after an appeal for such intervention by President of Lebanon."[25]

That afternoon (coincidentally this was the same day anti-American protesters attacked Vice President Richard Nixon in Venezuela), Eisenhower and Dulles met with CIA Director Allen Dulles and JCS chairman Twining. The president was prepared to send in the Marines if Chamoun asked for help. He "felt that resolute action should be taken as necessary to preserve the situation." This time it was the secretary of state who advised restraint. He "did not see how we could invoke the provisions of the Middle East Doctrine," Dulles cautioned, "since that would entail a finding that the United Arab Republic had attacked Lebanon and that the United Arab Republic was under the control of international communism." Despite his strong suspicions that the Egyptians and Syrians were to blame for the unrest, Dulles had learned over the past year how difficult it was to make such a "finding" credible. The introduction of U.S. troops, he warned, "might create a wave of anti-Western feeling in the Arab world comparable to that associated with the British and French military operation in Egypt." Nasser would ride the crest to even greater prominence and influence in the region, and those governments that supported the United States, especially Jordan and Iraq, might "collapse." The U.S. position would thus deteriorate regardless of the outcome in Lebanon. Dulles concluded presciently, "once our forces were in, it would not be easy to establish a basis upon which they could retire and leave behind an acceptable situation."[26]

Allen Dulles confirmed his brother's assessment. Eisenhower backed off, but he did approve the delivery of eighteen tanks and once again returned the Sixth Fleet to the Eastern Mediterranean. He also authorized Ambassador McClintock to inform Chamoun that he would consider, upon request, sending "certain combat forces to Lebanon." Eisenhower wanted Lebanon's president put on notice, nevertheless, that the introduction of U.S. forces would be "a grave step which could have the most far-reaching consequences and one which should not be lightly requested or other than under the most compelling necessity." Such a compelling necessity, he specified, would have to include "protecting American life and property" as well as preserving the "independence and integrity of Lebanon." Eisenhower directed McClintock to tell Chamoun that the "request should be couched" accordingly. What is more, Lebanon's president should seek the support of other Arab leaders and renounce any intention to remain in office after his term expired in September.[27]

McClintock did as instructed, and reported to Dulles that Chamoun "understood every word." On May 27, Chamoun pledged to abide by Lebanon's constitution and step down from office; the violence subsided, and he did not request U.S. intervention. In July, however, conditions took a decided turn for the worse. In neighboring Iraq, a linchpin of the Baghdad Pact, Egypt's archenemy in the Middle East and Chamoun's closest Arab ally, King Faisal, the Crown Prince, and Prime Minister Nuri as-Said were brutally murdered during a successful coup led by the pro-Nasser general, Abdel Karim Kassem. Fearing he was next on the hit list, Chamoun, after accusing Washington of "consistently" underestimating the threat his government faced, appealed for military help. "Well, you see what is happening," he said. The "fury of Nasserism and Communism was utterly unleashed," and "Lebanon is in real danger."[28]

Six minutes after receiving the request for aid from Chamoun on the morning of July 14, Dulles called Eisenhower to urge the president to convene an emergency meeting at the White House. At the moment, he conceded, he had "no ideas" because the coup in Iraq had "happened so fast." By the time the president's principal advisors had assembled two hours later, the secretary had collected his thoughts. On the one hand, he predicted that if "we do not respond to the call from Chamoun, we will suffer the decline and indeed the elimination of our influence"—from Indonesia (where a CIA operation to oust the nationalist President Sukarno had just collapsed) all the way to Morocco. "If, on the other hand, we do respond to the request, we must expect a very bad reaction through most of the Arab countries," which would probably include the interruption of the oil pipeline to the West and transit through the Suez Canal. Dulles also raised the possibility of Soviet intervention, but he estimated that risk to be acceptable. "What the Russians will do depends upon what they judge to be the balance of power for a general war," he explained, and he had been assured by the JCS that at least for now that balance favored the United States. ("The Russians aren't going to jump us," Twining put it, "because we've got them over the whing whang and they know it.") Besides, Dulles stressed, if "we do not accept the risk now, they will probably decide that we will never accept risk and will push harder than ever, and the border countries will submit to them."[29]

Dulles concluded "on balance" that "the losses from doing nothing would be worse than the losses from action." He recommended the introduction of U.S. forces. Eisenhower concurred without hesitating. It was "clear in his mind" that "we must act or get out of the Middle East entirely." This "is probably our last chance to do something in the area," and "to lose this area by inaction would be far worse than the loss in China, because of the strategic position and resources of the Middle East." As always, the president postponed a final decision until Dulles had the opportunity (that afternoon) to consult the congressional leaders. Unlike times when he had sought congressional endorsement during comparable past crises, however, this time the president accompanied the secretary of state. Further, he unambiguously expressed his determination to demonstrate "American fortitude and readiness to take risks to defend the values of the free world" regardless of congressional opposition. What opposition there was (for example, Montana's Senator Mike Mansfield objected to the United States "getting into a civil war") rapidly melted away.[30]

Eisenhower, the two Dulles brothers, and Twining remained in the Oval Office after the congressional leaders left "to fix firmly upon specific action steps" to execute Operation BLUE BAT, the largest amphibious invasion since MacArthur's invasion at Inchon during the Korean War. "Land Marines at 1500 Bravo [Beirut] time 15 July," Chief of Naval Operations Arleigh Burke cabled the commmander in chief of U.S. naval forces in the Eastern Atlantic and Mediterranean almost immediately afterward. "Do not notify Lebanese" until three hours before, he added. At nine o'clock Washington time the next morning, just as the Marines came ashore, the president issued a public statement explaining that he had committed U.S. forces at Chamoun's request in order to "protect American lives and by their presence there to encourage the Lebanese government in defense of Lebanese sovereignty and integrity." Several hours later Lodge declared to the UN Security Council that the U.S. intervened for "the sole purpose of helping the Government of Lebanon at its request in its efforts to stabilize the situation, brought on by threats from outside." Eisenhower amplified the U.S. position that evening in a televised address. He described Lebanon as the "victim" of Communist-inspired aggression, and as Dulles had during the crisis in Syria, drew an explicit parallel between its circumstance and that of Czechoslovakia two decades earlier. Appeasement in the 1930s had "made World War II inevitable," Eisenhower proclaimed. The United States was determined that "history shall not now be repeated."[31]

There was no danger of that. Despite the fears of Eisenhower and Dulles, the primary cause of Lebanon's turmoil was its endemic religious strife, which Chamoun's ambition exacerbated. Nasser's direct role was minimal; Khrushchev's less ("slight" was the adjective used later by the CIA to describe Communist influence).

Neither played a part in the coup in Iraq. The more than 14,000 U.S. troops (Army and Marines) that stormed the beaches of Lebanon encountered surprised sunbathers, not armed soldiers. U.S. Ambassador McClintock and Lebanon's Army Chief of Staff Fuad Chehab, whom U.S. intelligence had feared would oppose the intervention, personally escorted U.S. commander Admiral James Holloway back to Beirut. Not a single U.S. soldier was killed.[32]

Indeed, the problem confronting Washington was not resistance to the invasion, but, as Dulles had foreseen, how to terminate the intervention while weathering the storm of criticism it provoked from the Arabs and that Moscow sought to exploit. As a first step, Dulles dispatched Robert Murphy, his deputy undersecretary for political affairs and Eisenhower's political advisor during World War II, to talk with Chamoun. By the end of July, Murphy had convinced Lebanon's president to arrange a special election that assured that Chehab would succeed him (the same formula which Nasser had proposed but which the United States had rejected a month before). From Lebanon, Murphy went on to Iraq, and on August 2 the United States extended recognition to Kassim's government.

Extricating the U.S. troops from Lebanon proved more complicated. In his presentation to the Security Council, Lodge had emphasized that a U.S. military presence would be required "until such time as the United Nations can take the steps necessary to protect the independence and political integrity of Lebanon." Even though it was now clear that Lebanon needed no such protection, Dulles believed that it would undermine the U.S. justification for intervening if the United States withdrew its forces without the UN agreeing to some form of peace-keeping mission. Hence, he developed a proposal for a "standby United Nations Peace Force" that would be mandated to respond to aggression, direct or indirect, anywhere in the Middle East. Eisenhower personally presented the proposal to the UN General Assembly on August 13.[33]

It went nowhere. Nasser insisted that the United States withdraw immediately and unconditionally, and no Arab nation objected. For six weeks the resolution languished as the United States deferred a vote lest its proposal be rejected by the nations that the administration alleged required protection. The Sudanese broke the impasse by submitting an alternative resolution empowering UN Secretary-General Dag Hammarskjöld to make "practical arrangements" in order to "facilitate the early withdrawal" of the U.S. troops. When Nasser expressed his support and thereby implicitly dropped his demand for an immediate withdrawal, Washington eagerly followed suit. On September 20 the General Assembly voted unanimously to adopt Sudan's motion. The next month, after the new Chehab government accepted Hammarskjöld's offer to send an observation team to Lebanon, the United States evacuated its forces.[34]

Shortly after the last U.S. Marine left Lebanon, the president, with Dulles's enthusiastic second, approved a new statement of policy toward the Near East (NSC 5820/1) that effectively placed the Eisenhower Doctrine in mothballs. The intervention—and the previous threats to intervene—had cost the United States the good- will earned by its stance during the Suez crisis. The lesson was clear, albeit painful. Because of the U.S. support of "conservative regimes opposed to radical nationalism," the statement acknowledged, the "Soviets have established themselves as its [the Middle East] friends and defenders." More specifically, by allowing itself to be "cast in the role of Nasser's opponent," Washington had forfeited to Mos- cow the role of "his champion." In the future, the United States should seek "to work more closely with Arab nationalism," to "as- sociate itself" with the "aims and aspirations of the Arab people," and to "normalize our relations" with Nasser and the UAR. In short, the Eisenhower administration admitted that it had blundered.[35]

Notes

1. Quoted in Donald Neff, *Warriors at Suez: Eisenhower Takes America into the Middle East* (New York, 1981), 92–93.
2. Quoted in Townsend Hoopes, *The Devil and John Foster Dulles* (Boston, 1973), 337.
3. Quoted in Dwight D. Eisenhower, *Waging Peace, 1956–1961* (Garden City, NY, 1965), 36; Memorandum of conversation, August 30, 1956, *FR, 1955–57* 16:334–35.
4. Quoted in William Roger Louis, "Dulles, Suez, and the British," in *John Foster Dulles and the Diplomacy of the Cold War*, ed. Richard H. Immerman (Princeton, NJ, 1990), 147.
5. Quoted in Chester J. Pach and Elmo Richardson, *The Presidency of Dwight D. Eisenhower* (Lawrence, KS, 1991), 129.
6. Quoted in Louis, "Dulles, Suez, and the British," 148.
7. Quoted in Pach and Richardson, *Eisenhower*, 133; quoted in Neff, *Warriors at Suez*, 375.
8. Dulles statement in the UN General Assembly, November 1, 1956, *Department of State Bulletin* 35 (July–December 1956), 751–55.
9. Quoted in Hoopes, *Devil and Dulles*, 379.
10. Quoted in Louis, "Dulles, Suez, and the British," 153.
11. Quoted in Pach and Richardson, *Eisenhower*, 160.

12. *Public Papers of the Presidents of the United States: Dwight D. Eisenhower, 1957* (Washington, DC, 1958), 6–17.

13. Quoted in Thomas G. Paterson and J. Garry Clifford, *America Ascendant: U.S. Foreign Relations Since 1939* (Lexington, MA, 1995), 130–31.

14. Quoted in Pach and Richardson, *Eisenhower*, 164.

15. Memoranda of conversation, April 24, 1957, *FR, 1955–57* 13: 104–7; quoted in Hoopes, *The Devil and Dulles*, 412.

16. Quoted in Douglas Little, "Cold War and Covert Action: The United States and Syria, 1945–1958," *Middle East Journal* 44 (Winter 1990): 69–70.

17. Quoted in David W. Lesch, *Syria and the United States: Eisenhower's Cold War in the Middle East* (Boulder, CO, 1992), 138.

18. Memorandum of conversation, August 19, 1957, *FR, 1955–57* 13:641; Eisenhower quoted in Lesch, *Syria and the United States*, 139–41; Memorandum from Dulles to Eisenhower, August 20, 1957, *FR, 1955–57* 13:641.

19. Dulles to Macmillan, September 5, 1957, *FR, 1955–57* 13:681.

20. Memorandum of conversation, September 7, 1957, *FR, 1955–57*, 13:685–89.

21. Ibid.; Dulles incorporated the paper into a telegram to the U.S. embassy in Turkey on September 10. Ibid., 691–93.

22. Quoted in Lesch, *Syria and the United States*, 156–60.

23. Quoted in ibid., 194.

24. Quoted in ibid., 196–98.

25. Quoted in Douglas Little, "His Finest Hour? Eisenhower, Lebanon, and the 1958 Middle East Crisis," *Diplomatic History* 20 (Winter 1996): 34; U.S. Embassy in Lebanon to Department of State, May 11, 1958, *FR, 1958–60* 11:37; U.S. Embassy in Lebanon to Department of State, May 13, 1958, ibid., 41–2.

26. Memorandum of conversation, May 13, 1958, *FR, 1958–60* 11:45–8.

27. Department of State to the U.S. Embassy in Lebanon, May 13, 1958, ibid., 49–50.

28. U.S. Embassy in Lebanon to Department of State, May 14, 1958, ibid., 51; U.S. embassy to Department of State, July 14, 1958, ibid., 207–8; quoted in Hoopes, *Devil and Dulles*, 434.

29. Memorandum of Dulles telephone conversation with Eisenhower, July 14, 1958, *FR, 1958–60* 11:209; Memorandum of a conference with the president, July 14, 1958, ibid., 211–15; quoted in Pach and Richardson, *Eisenhower*, 192.

30. Memorandum of a conference with the president, July 14, 1958, 211–15, 218–26.

31. Ibid., 226; Burke to Admiral James Holloway, Jr., July 14, 1958, *FR, 1958–60 11:* 231; editorial note, ibid., 242–43; quoted in Pach and Richardson, *Eisenhower*, 192.

32. Quoted in Little, "His Finest Hour?" 51.

33. Editorial note, *FR, 1958–60* 11:243.

34. Quoted in Hoopes, *Devil and Dulles*, 438.

35. NSC 5820/1, "U.S. Policy toward the Near East," November 4, 1958, *FR, 1958–60* 12:187–99.

8

The Final Crises

U.S. meddling in the Middle East did help to repair relations with the British. Both Eisenhower and Dulles consulted regularly with London throughout their travails in Jordan, Syria, and Lebanon, and Macmillan gave them his blessing and allegiance. While U.S. troops landed in Lebanon, British paratroopers dropped into Jordan. On occasion, Macmillan and Foreign Minister Selwyn Lloyd grumbled about Washington's insistence that Britain, so vilified by the Arabs, play a subordinate role in the region in which it had historically called the shots. Nevertheless, they consistently swallowed their objections—and their pride. Only when asked did Macmillan offer advice and troops. He consistently offered deference.

Concurrent developments among the NATO partners on the European continent were similarly positive. The implications of the Suez crisis for their economies and access to Middle Eastern oil provided European governments with additional impetus to build upon the European Coal and Steel Community. Western Europe's twin goals were to establish a common market through lower tariffs to facilitate commerce among the states (thereby lessening the impact of an international disruption of trade) and to improve their capacity to exploit atomic energy as an alternative to oil.

Eisenhower and Dulles encouraged these initiatives. Both considered them intrinsically beneficial. They were also promising steps toward greater cooperation between France and West Germany, further integration of the economies of continental Europe (Great Britain, again stressing its geopolitical distinctiveness, refused to participate), and eventual political unity. With Washington cheering in the background and lending a hand whenever asked, negotiations progressed rapidly. On March 25, 1957, representatives of France, the Federal Republic of Germany, Italy, Belgium, Luxembourg, and Italy met in Rome to sign a treaty creating a European Economic Community (EEC) and European Atomic Energy Community (EURATOM). In contrast to the European experience with the EDC, by the end of the summer the Treaty of Rome had been ratified by each country, including France.

The juxtaposition of the increasingly unilateral and pugnacious U.S. military posture toward the Middle East and the improvement of its relations with the NATO partners—and their relations with each other—provides the framework critical to understanding one of the most remarkable yet least-remarked-upon features of Dulles's tenure as secretary of state: his challenge to the New Look policy that gave pride of place to America's nuclear capacity. More than any other dimension of Eisenhower's foreign and security policy, it is with the New Look that Dulles is most intimately identified and for which he has continued to be criticized.

As U.S. intervention under the Eisenhower Doctrine became more likely (and a reality in Lebanon), Dulles's doubts grew about a military strategy that relied so heavily on extended nuclear deterrence. Heightening these doubts, the Europeans reiterated their anxiety about getting caught in the middle of an atomic exchange provoked by a conflict on the periphery, an anxiety fueled by Soviet threats to come to the aid of outgunned Arab nationalists. Over time, Dulles concluded that in order both to afford the United States more flexibility in military planning and to sustain the improvement in allied relations, it was essential to augment America's conventional capabilities. To Dulles's chagrin, Eisenhower vigorously disagreed.

Dulles actually began to rethink his position on nuclear weapons in the aftermath of the Taiwan Strait crisis and then, more seriously, as tensions rose over the Suez Canal. On several occasions during the course of the NSC's reviews of basic national security policy in 1956, he commented that both America's friends and enemies tended to interpret U.S. military policy as either saber rattling or passing the buck. As a result, the allies were more inclined to appease than to resolutely oppose Communist aggression. Furthermore, because the Soviets were developing long-range bombers and intercontinental ballistic missiles (ICBMs) aimed at the United States, the Europeans had less confidence that Washington would live up to its pledge to come to their defense were they to be attacked.

Concomitantly, the Soviets appeared more willing to commit aggression because they assumed that Eisenhower would never risk a nuclear confrontation over a local "incident." The antidote, Dulles advised (with a hearty endorsement from Maxwell Taylor, now Army chief of staff), was for the administration to signal by increasing its conventional force levels that it had available options other than nuclear retaliation or backing down. Eisenhower appeared to halfway concede the point. Still convinced that the best deterrent against the Soviets was the virtual guarantee that the United States would respond "massively," he left conventional force strength essentially unchanged. He approved a statement of national security policy, however, that provided ambiguously for the United States to maintain a "flexible and selective nuclear capability" so that it could respond to local aggression without "applying force in a way which our own people or our allies would consider entails undue risks of nuclear devastation."[1]

Dulles was not satisfied, but in light of his preoccupation with the Suez Canal (and subsequent developments in the Middle East), the presidential campaign, and his hospitalization for cancer, he postponed pushing the matter in the NSC. When in Europe, however, he used all his verbal skills to assure the NATO powers that the United States was not locked into a defense plan that would invariably cross the nuclear threshold. He sought simultaneously to dispel rumors (accurate rumors) that JCS chairman Arthur Radford had proposed for reasons of both strategy and economy to substantially reduce the number of U.S. troops deployed abroad.

In October 1957, Dulles published "Challenge and Response in United States Policy," an article in the special volume of *Foreign Affairs* commemorating the 35th anniversary of its founding. Dulles intended the article to be read as a sequel to his more famous 1954 exposition on U.S. strategy in the same journal. His purpose was to influence uneasy domestic constituents and international allies. Perhaps more important, he hoped to influence Eisenhower.

Dulles could not, needless to say, go public with his differences with the president over the size and mission of conventional forces, about which he wrote not a word. Yet he could rededicate the United States to a "strategy of collective defense." More significant, Dulles applauded technological developments in the "field of science and weapon engineering." These developments, he predicted, would "alter the character of nuclear weapons" so that it would no longer be necessary "to rely upon a peace which could be preserved only by a capacity to destroy vast segments of the human race." Dulles claimed that recent tests "point to the possibility of possessing nuclear weapons the destructiveness and radiation effects of which can be confined substantially to predetermined targets."

Dulles was leading up to the promise of a strategic posture premised on finite deterrence that gave meaning to the NSC policy statement phrase, "flexible and selective nuclear capability." The United States, he wrote, was not "wedded to doctrinaire concepts," and he forecast a future when the "resourcefulness" of U.S. scientists would provide an escape from the "Red or dead" dilemma of massive retaliation. Mobile, "cleaner" tactical nuclear weapons would allow for "an effective defense against full-scale conventional attack" by "decisively" dominating the invasion routes. These weapons could stop an enemy force in its tracks regardless of its numerical superiority, with little danger to surrounding states and populations.

This capability would not only improve the means to fight and keep limited wars on the periphery, but it would also permit "technically qualified" allies to "participate more directly" in their defense and afford them "greater assurance that this defensive power will in fact be used." It would also, even more than the U.S. strategic arsenal, deter the Soviets from initiating a conflict, particularly through proxies. As Dulles explained, the "tables may be turned, in the sense that instead of those who are non-aggressive having to rely upon all-out nuclear retaliatory power for their protection, would-be aggressors will be unable to count on a successful conventional aggression, but must themselves weigh the consequences of invoking nuclear [i.e., general] war." He did not need to spell out the consequences.

Dulles was arguing that because of U.S. technological advances, it was developing the capacity for flexible response despite Eisenhower's refusal to accept his advice to build up U.S. conventional forces. He believed that this argument would comfort friends, warn foes, and persuade the president "to adjust our policies to the demands of the hour." Even as the article was published, however, the Soviets appeared to blow a hole in its foundation—the confidence in the supremacy of U.S. science and technology and the accompanying security of the Western Alliance. On August 3, 1957, the Soviets conducted the first successful test of an intercontinental ballistic missile. On October 4, a Soviet ICBM blasted off from Kazakhstan in Central Asia, placing for the first time in history an artificial satellite, the 184-pound Sputnik, into orbit around the world. Sputnik II followed the next month. It weighed more than a thousand pounds and carried a live dog as a passenger.[2]

Overnight, popular perceptions of the East-West balance of power were reversed. Unlike the development of the atom and hydrogen bombs, Russian scientists had beaten the Americans into space, and without having stolen any secrets. The implications of this victory far transcended national pride or the competition between ideologies. If a Soviet ICBM could launch a satellite that large into space, could it not launch a nuclear warhead at any earthly target? Americans' sense of vulnerability took a quantum leap.

Further, just as the Sputnik satellites seemed to indicate that the Communists had gained a decided technological advantage, the press printed leaked portions from a top-secret report of a panel (headed by Ford Foundation president H. Rowan Gaither) that included Paul Nitze, the force behind Truman's NSC 68. The Gaither Report estimated that due to the inadequacy of U.S. defenses, a surprise Soviet ICBM strike would devastate the continental United States. The combination of the Sputniks and the Gaither Report provoked dread throughout the United States. The reaction among the allies verged on panic. They assumed that no U.S. president, his pledges to collective security notwithstanding, would put his own citizens at risk of annihilation by coming to their defense. The free world nations of both Europe and beyond would be left unprotected, regardless of the form a Soviet attack might take.

Eisenhower remained calm and confident. Because of photographs taken by U-2 overflights, he had for months been aware that the Russians were close to rocketing a satellite into space. He refused, nevertheless, to accelerate America's own program. He was not going to abandon his fiscal restraint in order to be the first to put "one small ball in the air." Nor would he allow partisan sniping about a bomber and the "missile gap" to break the budget by implementing the Gaither Report's recommended crash program to build more nuclear-configured bombers, missiles, and fallout shelters. The Soviets' ICBMs were more powerful and greater in number than America's but that did not compensate for their lack of accuracy. Indeed, because of his access to overflight and other intelligence that he obviously could not disclose, the president knew that the United States retained the lead not only in the design of nuclear warheads, but also in the development of solid fuels for long-range missiles and the guidance systems necessary to direct them to their targets.[3]

Eisenhower remained positive that the best deterrent against a Soviet attack was not the number of U.S. missiles (let alone fallout shelters), but the security of the capability to retaliate. Accordingly, he enhanced programs already under way to secure this second strike capability. These included improving radar warning networks, dispersing Strategic Air Command bombers, and hardening missile silos. More important, Eisenhower moved up the timetable for bringing on line the strategic "triad" comprised of ICBMs (Atlas, Titan, and Minuteman); bombers (primarily B-52s); and SLBMS (submarine-launched ballistic missiles—Polaris). The president recognized that this systemic redundancy would make the U.S. capacity for a retaliatory strike virtually invulnerable. The Soviets would be mad to launch a surprise attack. And Eisenhower was certain that they were not mad.

Although Dulles completely agreed with the president's analysis of the strategic balance and his perspective on strategic deterrence, he was more concerned than ever about the analyses and perspectives of the allies, America's NATO partners above all. A secure second strike capability might deter a Soviet nuclear attack on the United States, but what about a conventional attack on Western Europe? The Europeans could not count on the Americans endangering themselves by retaliating, and a response with tactical nuclear weapons of the sort Dulles wrote about in his *Foreign Affairs* article would likely provoke the Soviets to react in kind. There was no question about their capability to hit targets in Europe and Asia. Even if the war remained limited to a particular area, as Dulles projected it might, that would be small consolation to its inhabitants.

Convinced that the events of late 1957 accentuated the allies' lack of confidence in the U.S. nuclear umbrella and greatly increased their susceptibility to Soviet nuclear blackmail, Dulles renewed his effort to persuade Eisenhower to enhance U.S. conventional capabilities. "New conditions are emerging," he argued in April 1958 when the NSC undertook its annual review of basic national security policy. They "do not invalidate the massive retaliation concept, but put limitations on it and require it to be supplemented by other measures." After explaining that "our allies are beginning to doubt as to whether we would in fact use our H-weapons if we are not ourselves attacked," Dulles all but returned to his pessimistic prediction of 1953 that NATO was "losing its grip." His "considered opinion" was that "although we can hold our alliance together for another year or so, we cannot expect to do so beyond that time on the basis of our present concept."[4]

When the NSC met on May 1 to discuss the draft of NSC 5810, Dulles threw down the gauntlet. According to the record of the meeting, he turned directly to face Eisenhower and "expressed the hope that our basic security policy, when we finally adopt it, won't compel us to allocate so much of our resources to maintenance of the nuclear deterrent that we will weaken our capability for limited war." The "massive nuclear deterrent was running its course as the principal element in our military arsenal" because the allies "demand that they be provided with a capability for local defense." They believed "either we do not intend to resort to nuclear war to defend them against the Soviets, or, if they think that we will resort to such warfare, they will disassociate themselves from us." The antidote was to strengthen America's conventional forces. "The allies must at least have the illusion," Dulles concluded, "that they have some kind of defensive capability against the Soviets other than the United States using a pushbutton to start a global nuclear war."

Eisenhower held firm by reiterating, in some cases virtually verbatim, the arguments he had used during the formulation of the initial New Look strategy in 1953. He was all for the allies developing what Dulles said was necessary. After all, "what else" had the administration been "trying to do these last years but to try to induce our allies to provide themselves with just such a local defensive capability"? It must continue, but the United States simply could not afford to make up for their shortfall. The administration's budgetary planning had been hit hard by the 1957–58 recession, which resulted in the largest peacetime deficit in U.S. history. Eisenhower was as embarrassed as he was frustrated, and he vowed to respond aggressively. His political philosophy also precluded spending more on defense. The methods required to "maintain very much larger military forces than we have previously done," the president declared, would "almost certainly involve what is euphemistically called a controlled economy, but which in effect would amount to a garrison state."

Indicating that fiscal restraint was not the primary determinant of his thinking on defense strategy, Eisenhower characterized the very concept of a limited war with the Soviets as more "unrealistic" than ever. There are some, he acknowledged, who maintained that "mutual deterrence was an umbrella under which small wars could be fought without starting a global war." To them he would respond that "the umbrella would be a lightning rod. Each small war makes a global war the more likely," and global war would inevitably go nuclear. In short, the era of "a nice, sweet, World War II type of war" was passed. The name of the game had to be, therefore, to deter the Soviets from ever starting a war. That could be done only by confronting them with an unambiguous choice between peace and destruction. In this regard, an improved capacity for flexible response might actually undermine the strategic deterrent and invite Soviet aggression by suggesting that the regime could survive a failure.[5]

Eisenhower, therefore, rejected the inclusion in NSC 5810 of any references to limited war or the means to fight one. He did agree to revisit the issue in the future, which gave Dulles some hope that the president might eventually change his mind. "We must recognize," the secretary commented at an NSC meeting on July 24, "that the military paragraphs which we write into Basic Policy at the moment may not remain valid very long, and certainly will not be fixed for all time." But a month was much too short a time to "unfix" them. On August 23, the Communist Chinese embargoed and resumed their shelling of Quemoy and Matsu.[6]

It had been more than three years since Chou En-lai's announcement of the PRC's willingness to negotiate a reduction of the tension in the Taiwan Strait had brought to an abrupt end the initial offshore islands crisis. The causes of the crisis remained unabated in the interim. The United States did hold ambassadorial-level talks with the Communist Chinese, at Geneva and then Warsaw, that led to an agreement to return citizens held captive in each other's countries. But discussions about the future status of Taiwan went nowhere, nor did PRC demands for U.S. recognition and UN representation. Meanwhile, Chiang Kai-shek continued, as Eisenhower euphemistically put it, to "complicate the problem" by continuing to build up the Nationalist Chinese forces on Quemoy and Matsu and to harass PRC traffic in the strait. Washington consistently objected that merely the "presence of such large numbers of Nationalist forces" was "itself a kind of 'provocation,'" but it also consistently extended more economic and military aid to the Nationalist Chinese. The United States installed nuclear-capable Matador missiles on Taiwan and constructed an airport with a runway long enough to accommodate B-52 bombers.[7]

When the United States broke off the Sino-American talks in late 1957 because the PRC refused to renounce the use of force against Taiwan, Mao concluded that no peaceful resolution to Communist China's predicament over the renegade Nationalists was possible. He also evidently predicted, as did so many in the United States and throughout the world, that the implications of the launchings of the Sputnik satellites would deter the Eisenhower administration from using nuclear weapons to defend Taiwan, let alone Quemoy and Matsu. The best way to assess U.S. resolve in the new strategic environment was to test it. The "main purpose of our bombardment," Mao explained to the Standing Committee of the Politburo, was to "probe the attitude of the Americans in Washington." What is more, with the Americans' attention still focused on the intervention in Lebanon (in reaction to which Mao believed the PRC had to "teach the Americans a lesson" and signal its support for "the Arabs' anti-imperialist struggle"), the opportunity to strike a blow for pride, security, and revolution appeared at hand. Mao hoped that Washington would refuse to back Taipei's insistence on retaining control of the islands and ultimately recognize the futility of propping up the Nationalist regime on Taiwan.[8]

Mao's measure of success did not require achieving this goal, at least for the time being. In the near term, it would be enough to confirm the PRC's resolve to "fight the imperialists to the end." Doing so would provide a necessary shot in the arm for his campaign to mobilize the domestic population to support the Great Leap Forward, the recently inaugurated radical program of economic collectivization and industrialization, military modernization, and political indoctrination. It would simultaneously reinforce Mao's personal claim to leadership over the Third World.[9]

Mao was deeply troubled by what he perceived as the conservative, indeed counterrevolutionary, thrust of Soviet policy under Khrushchev. He took "very seriously" Dulles's speeches about liberation, particularly those that stressed U.S. moral superiority, which he had translated "word for word with the help of an English dictionary." Mao judged Dulles a "very thoughtful" man of "many schemes" who "controlled the helm in the United States." Resuming the shelling of Quemoy and Matsu was Mao's way of showing up Dulles and demonstrating that Peking would not be intimidated by either words or weapons. The "proof of the superiority of our people's democratic dictatorship," Mao said, is that our soldiers "are brave and dare to look death in the face."[10]

Unlike the situation in 1954, the increased volume of the Communist Chinese denunciations of both the United States and the Nationalist Chinese alerted the administration to the prospect of a renewed attack on the offshore islands in 1958. Dulles and Eisenhower discussed the possibility in the middle of August, but they could not agree on how the United States should respond. Based on the position he took during the earlier crisis, Dulles recommended that the administration assume that an attack on Quemoy and Matsu was a prelude to an attack on Taiwan. The Mutual Security Treaty committed the United States to Taiwan's defense; the Formosa Resolution authorized Eisenhower to take whatever he deemed necessary to do so. Dulles argued that the administration should prepare for the contingency by deciding immediately that an attack would warrant U.S. retaliation against the PRC. That retaliation would entail nuclear weapons. Dulles hoped that tactical bombs would be sufficient and produce "no more than small air bursts without fallout."[11]

Eisenhower agreed only to consider Dulles's advice. He had hardly begun when, on the first day alone, some 50,000 PRC shells fell on Quemoy. Dulles issued a pointedly ambiguous statement. He said that the United States would not tolerate an actual Chinese invasion, leaving vague the definition or site of the invasion. When a disappointed Chiang asked for "a more explicit statement," Eisenhower demurred. Because the generalissimo would like nothing better than to "drag us into attacking Peiping and the whole of China," he explained, "he did not want to put ourselves on the line with a full commitment." Warning his advisors that the "Orientals can be very devious," Eisenhower instructed them to "avoid making statements from which we might later back off."[12]

The president's actions, nevertheless, spoke loudly and clearly. Placing the military on full alert, he orchestrated a massive display of U.S. force in the region. The Seventh Fleet was buttressed by the addition of two air carrier groups, which translated into the assemblage of the most powerful armada in history. It included almost one hundred nuclear-capable planes. What is more, although the president, as he had during the 1954–55 crisis, refused to grant Chiang all the firepower he asked for, he delivered to the Nationalists aircraft, artillery, and even missiles. If the Communist Chinese shelling was intended to test U.S. resolve before deciding on an invasion, Eisenhower was determined to allow no doubt that it would pass.

Yet unlike the secretary of state, the president thought it prudent to commit the United States only to defend Taiwan proper and leave the Communists once again guessing as to U.S. intentions regarding the offshore islands. He also remained convinced that Chiang would do everything he could to entrap the United States into fighting his war to recapture the mainland. When after a few days the intensity of the Communist bombardment subsided (it did not cease) and the U.S. military completed its initial measures, Eisenhower made a series of public comments reaffirming that the United States would safeguard the security of Taiwan. But he rejected the military's request that he predelegate to local commanders the authority to use atomic weapons against mainland China should an invasion occur. And to signal that he did not deem credible a broadcast from Radio Peking stating the government's intention "to liberate Taiwan" and threatening that a "landing on Quemoy is imminent," Eisenhower had Dulles take a vacation.[13]

Eisenhower did not discount the potential for a war, nor would he have shied away from using nuclear weapons if the Communist Chinese had attacked Taiwan. He had not ruled out using them to defend Quemoy and Matsu. He remained sanguine, however, that given enough time his strategy of deterrence would work. He was confident that so long as the Kremlin (in contrast to Dulles and the JCS) never questioned what he considered axiomatic—that a conflict precipitated by Communist aggression in the Taiwan Strait would not be limited to the region and that the United States had the will and the capacity to obliterate the Soviet Union—Moscow would put the brakes on Peking's recklessness. Despite U.S. intelligence estimates of a growing Sino-Soviet split (in fact, evidence not available at the time indicates that Mao did not inform Khrushchev of this plan to renew the shelling), to Eisenhower it was inconceivable that the PRC would behave independently of the Soviet Union.

For the president the key to preventing the crisis from escalating was to ensure against Khrushchev's underestimating the danger confronting the Soviet Union, while concurrently resisting the advice of Dulles and the military, and the pleas from Chiang Kai-shek, to initiate hostilities against the PRC. (Eisenhower later reflected that throughout the crisis "I was continually hounded—almost pressured—by Chiang on one side and our own military [he could have included Dulles] requesting the authority for immediate action.") At the end of August, Eisenhower ordered the deployment of additional U.S. nuclear-equipped forces to the Taiwan area and instructed the Defense Department to leak "a few revealing words" to the press that would ensure that the moves "would not escape the notice of the Communists." He also directed a U.S. naval squadron to escort Nationalist Chinese supply ships from Taiwan to Quemoy and Matsu (albeit commanding them to stay in international waters), virtually daring the Communist Chinese to try to interdict them. However, when after returning from vacation at the beginning of September Dulles advised that the United States should knock out Communist Chinese airfields and artillery emplacements, Eisenhower said no. But he did invite Dulles to join him in Newport, Rhode Island, where the president had retreated to relax and think.[14]

Dulles met with the JCS prior to meeting with Eisenhower on September 4, which reinforced his opinion that an assault "can be expected" and that the United States could delay a strike against the mainland no longer. It had to raise the ante before the Communist Chinese completely changed the stakes. In addition, Dulles tried to convince Eisenhower that especially at this stage, the crisis afforded the administration the opportunity to prove the thesis of his *Foreign Affairs* article: tactical nuclear weapons could effectively defeat aggression without precipitating a general, thermonuclear war. (In presenting their "case for U.S. intervention" on September 2 the JCS estimated that "small" [10–80 kiloton] atomic weapons would be sufficient.) Dulles doubted that the Soviets would come to the aid of the PRC "merely because of a treaty obligation," and he considered it vital to demonstrate that the perceived increase in Soviet nuclear capabilities would not deter the United States from using its own nuclear weapons. To refrain from using these weapons when it appeared that "the chips are down" would cause irreparable damage to the credibility of the United States and its entire "defense setup."[15]

Eisenhower would not be persuaded. If the United States used atomic weapons against Communist Chinese, he countered, the Soviets would undoubtedly retaliate in kind against Taiwan. In that case, there would be no Nationalist Chinese left for the United States to protect. Further, this would compel the United States to retaliate in greater kind against the Soviet Union, and so it would go up the escalatory ladder. In short, Eisenhower was still certain that Dulles's notion of a limited war was fatally flawed. Unless and until the Communists forced his hand, he was determined not to be proven right.

Rather than continue the discussion of when and how best to use U.S. atomic weapons, Eisenhower drafted Dulles into helping him write a statement targeted at Peking, Moscow, and Taipei. The "President has not yet made any finding," it began, as to whether "the employment of the Armed Forces of the United States is required or appropriate in ensuring the defense of Formosa [Taiwan]." But he would not "hesitate to make such a finding if he judged that the circumstances" made it "necessary," and, albeit in wording that left room to maneuver, categorized an assault on Quemoy and Matsu as such a circumstance. This warning was buttressed by the reminder that military "dispositions" had already been undertaken "so that a Presidential determination, if made, would be followed by action both timely and effective." Having thus put the Communists on notice to expect the U.S. stick if the aggression intensified or perhaps did not cease, the statement then extended a carrot. Communist China need not "abandon its claims, however ill founded," to Taiwan and the offshore islands. It need only declare that it would pursue them by "peaceful means" and agree to resume the Sino-American talks (which the United States had broken off).[16]

Only at Eisenhower's insistence did Dulles write and read publicly the statement, and he would have preferred something closer to an ultimatum: Stop the shelling now or else. From Eisenhower's perspective, however, the statement appeared to produce dividends rapidly. On September 6, Khruschchev's Foreign Minister Andrei Gromyko went to Peking for two days of talks with Mao. The result was, on the one hand, a series of expressions of solidarity by the Soviets with their comrades and warnings to the United States. On the other hand, largely because Gromyko "pressed on all pedals to deter Mao," Foreign Minister Chou En-lai announced Communist China's acceptance of Eisenhower's offer to return to the bargaining table at Warsaw.[17]

Having no way to know what transpired between the Soviets and Chinese, Dulles suspected a ruse. Chou said nothing about ending the bombardment. There was a good chance that Peking hoped that in combination with the Soviets' apparent support, the agreement to negotiate would be sufficient to keep the United States from intervening while continued shelling further eroded Nationalist Chinese morale and Taiwan's defenses against an invasion. Dulles advised the president to refuse to negotiate until the Communists stopped the shelling and unequivocally renounced any intention to invade. Eisenhower described his views as "somewhat at variance with the Secretary of State's." He saw nothing to lose and much to gain by agreeing to talk.[18]

Eisenhower agreed with Dulles that for the talks to be effective both the Communist Chinese and the Soviets needed to believe that the U.S. resolve to defend the Nationalists was undiminished. It was equally important to rebut the avalanche of Republican right-wing criticism that the administration appeared poised to sell out the Nationalists by appeasing the Communists. Consequently, on September 11, four days before the talks were scheduled to resume in Warsaw, Eisenhower delivered over television a scathing indictment of the PRC and Soviets' "hand in hand" efforts since the Korean War to "liquidate all of the free world positions in the Western Pacific area and bring them under captive governments." His agreement to negotiate proved his desire to settle the current crisis through diplomacy, the president said. Yet if the price of avoiding war endangered Nationalist China's independence or regional security, he would not pay it. There is "not going to be any appeasement," Eisenhower promised.[19]

To Eisenhower and Dulles's consternation, all the speech accomplished was to revive allied concerns over U.S. truculence and inflexibility. Even Britain's Prime Minister Macmillan, who, unlike Churchill and Eden in 1954–55, had endorsed Washington's position, protested its belligerent tone. Conversely, the speech did not allay the trepidation of Chiang Kai-shek and his Republican confederates, who complained that in contrast to the statement read by Dulles on September 4, Eisenhower said explicitly that the United States would not engage its forces merely for the sake of Quemoy and Matsu. Profoundly suspicious of the impending Sino-American talks in Warsaw, the Nationalist Chinese Assembly issued what Eisenhower called an "extraordinary statement." The statement advised its "American ally that [the] government of the Republic of China, as [the] duly constituted government of [the] Chinese people in accordance with [the] constitution, will not tolerate any commitments reached which are detrimental to [the] legal interests and status of [the] Chinese Republic." Lest there be any question whether those interests and status included the offshore islands, it added: "We also wish [to] sound [a] solemn warning to any countries which attempt to trade our vested interests to appease Reds." Chiang's concurrent statement was more blunt. "Taiwan will not be coerced into changing its position because of the allied nations' attitude," he vowed. "If necessary, Taiwan will fight alone."[20]

Eisenhower's speech did not appear to have made much of an impact on the enemy either. The start of the talks on September 15 brought neither an end to the shelling nor evidence of Mao's willingness to bargain. Further, Dulles's acquiescence, if only to mollify Macmillan, to a British suggestion that London's ambassador in Moscow "approach the Soviets in a manner calculated to have them urge restraint on the Chinese Communists" seemed to backfire. On September 19, Khrushchev wrote Eisenhower emphasizing that "the other side too has atomic and hydrogen weapons." Should the United States use its own nuclear weapons, he threatened, it "would spark off a conflagration of a world war" and thus "doom to certain death sons of the American people." The letter was so intemperate that the president returned it to Moscow without comment.[21]

For the next several weeks, even as Eisenhower authorized paratroopers from the 101st Airborne Division to enforce the court-mandated integration of Central High School in Little Rock, Arkansas, the administration weighed its options. While deciding among them, it made a mockery of the PRC's embargo by convoying supplies of military matériel from Taiwan to Quemoy, including nuclear-capable 8-inch howitzers. Apparently concluding that because the Soviets offered only bluster there was nothing more he could do at the present time to alter the status quo, that he had succeeded in aggravating the friction between Taipei and Washington, and that he had already manifested that Communist China was the vanguard of the anti-imperialist struggle, Mao unilaterally announced on October 6 that the Chinese would cease their fire for a week in return for the U.S. agreement to terminate its convoys.

The announcement convinced Dulles as much as Eisenhower that the danger of a Communist invasion had passed. After accepting the offer, Eisenhower decided to send Dulles to Taipei "to have a serious talk with the Generalissimo." The secretary had "to convert Chiang to flexibility," the president said. Try as he might, Dulles could not persuade Chiang that there would be less likelihood of future flare-ups over the islands if he finally agreed to demilitarize them. Chiang would not renounce his intention to reunify China under his leadership, but he did all but promise not to do so by military means. It remained Nationalist China's "sacred mission" to restore "freedom to its people on the mainland," read his and Dulles's October 23 joint communiqué of the talks. Nevertheless,

as the "principal means" for fulfilling this mission, the Nationalists would implement "Dr. Sun Yat-sen's three people's principles
[nationalism, democracy, and social well-being] and not the use of
force." To signal that he was neither satisfied nor was he backing
down, Mao resumed the shelling—but restricted it only to odd-
numbered days of the calendar. Shortly thereafter he discontinued
it completely.[22]

Dulles was left relieved and confused. He was pleased that the
crisis had ended peacefully, and essentially on U.S. terms. Still,
while he obviously would not have preferred that Eisenhower had
accepted his advice and ordered tactical nuclear strikes against
mainland China, he worried that the successful outcome of the crisis would make the president less inclined to compromise on his
inflexible reliance on the strategic deterrent. In this regard, Dulles
could not "even guess intelligently" as to what had gone on between Moscow and Peking during the crisis from beginning to end,
and hence was more conflicted than ever about the future of the
Sino-Soviet relationship.[23]

Dulles rarely had much time for reflection; in this case, he had
virtually none at all. While speaking at a Soviet-Polish Friendship
Meeting in Moscow on November 10, Nikita Khrushchev declared
that the Soviet Union intended to sign a new treaty with East Germany. The treaty, he explained, would supersede the World War II
agreements calling for joint occupation of Berlin and stipulate that
the East German government had unilateral authority for controlling access to and travel within it. In a formal note later that month
Khrushchev both elaborated and threatened. Berlin would be transformed into a demilitarized "free city," he clarified, and he gave
the West six months (until May 27, 1959) to negotiate a congruent
arrangement directly with the GDR. If no settlement was achieved,
the Soviet-East German treaty would be signed regardless, and
Western rights of transit to and presence in Berlin would be terminated by fiat. Should the NATO powers seek by force to retain privileges that were rendered "null and void," the Soviets would "rise
in defense" of their loyal Warsaw Pact ally. Put another way, Western failure to accept the Soviet ultimatum would probably result in
war.[24]

Although Khrushchev's announcement came suddenly and
without warning, it was the consequence of years of mounting pressure. Berlin had been a thorn in the Soviets' side since their failed
effort to blockade the divided city's Western sectors in 1948–49.
Their need to suppress forcibly the 1953 uprising attested to the

precarious state of their client regime in the GDR. Thereafter, the steady stream of East German defectors who escaped to the West through West Berlin provided vivid testimony of the Communist system's ills. Khrushchev sought to enhance security and stability behind the Iron Curtain and simultaneously end the humiliating exodus of refugees who poured through it.

Additional considerations had exacerbated Khrushchev's anxieties by 1958. The FRG's rapid economic development, coupled with Chancellor Adenauer's confident predictions of German reunification on Western terms, raised the specter of a more aggressive effort to devour and then digest the GDR, an effort that could include military measures. In this context, the Kremlin, convinced that Dulles, not Eisenhower, was the architect of U.S. policy, interpreted the secretary's emphasis on tactical nuclear weapons in his 1957 *Foreign Affairs* article as substantiation of rumors that Washington was considering making warheads available to its NATO allies. Ironically, at the same time the always nervous Adenauer worried that in the wake of the Sputnik flights the United States might either extend recognition to the GDR, or worse, agree to some formula for Germany's neutralization as a means to avert the risks inherent in its commitment to the FRG's defense. He let slip to the Soviet ambassador that, faced with U.S. opposition to providing the German Bundeswehr with a nuclear capability, he was close to deciding to develop an independent program (a decision Charles de Gaulle, who came to power in France in the spring of 1958, did make shortly afterward).

These developments brought Khrushchev to the verge of taking a dramatic step to demonstrate that the Soviets stood resolutely behind the GDR (at least until the United States agreed to a neutral reunified Germany) and, if possible, to provoke dissension between Washington and Bonn. It was the Taiwan Strait crisis, however, that was the immediate catalyst. Having urged Mao to exercise restraint, Khrushchev believed that in order to preserve Soviet leadership over the Communist world and his own leadership in the Kremlin, he had to show that he was tough and bold, not "soft" and "naive," toward the Western imperialists.[25]

Khrushchev designed the ultimatum he delivered, which was "ninety percent improvisation," to achieve all these objectives in a single stroke. The assessment in Washington was much less complex. The consensus was that the Soviets, emboldened by their Sputnik coup, confident that America's NATO partners would appease rather than countenance brinkmanship, and perhaps even believing that the correlation of forces had shifted in their favor, had concluded that the moment had arrived to execute Stalin's original policy expelling the West from Berlin.[26]

Dulles subscribed to this assessment. Even more important, he believed that because the United States lacked the capability to defend Berlin by means short of nuclear weapons, the Kremlin assumed that the risk of general war would compel the West to accommodate a Soviet ultimatum concerning real estate that was more than 100 miles removed from a vital Western ally. A note from Khrushchev hand-delivered by Gromyko appeared to say just this: only "madmen," it read, "can go the length of unleashing another world war over the preservation of privileges of occupiers in West Berlin." To mitigate this strategic dilemma Dulles had for some two years promoted a diversified military posture permitting a more flexible response. Khrushchev seemed to be rubbing his nose in his failure to persuade Eisenhower to adopt this strategy.[27]

Dulles was not a madman, but he was willing to conform to Khrushchev's definition of one to protect the West's rights in Berlin and to prove that the United States, neither alone nor in concert with NATO, was vulnerable to nuclear blackmail. Believing that U.S. credibility and the sanctity of its security guarantees were on the line, Eisenhower agreed. "[W]e were where we were," he said to Dulles on November 18, "and had to stand firm." And firmness was what the secretary of state told the European allies was required. The Soviets would back down if the NATO powers stated unequivocally that they "would shoot" rather than relinquish their rights to Berlin. The Kremlin would not have encouraged negotiations with the GDR and proposed a deadline as long as six months for their completion if the leadership really sought a military showdown.[28]

As Dulles had feared and Khrushchev had predicted, the NATO allies, Britain above all, balked at accepting such a dangerous risk and refused to commit themselves in advance. Macmillan told Eisenhower point-blank that the British "were not prepared to face obliteration for the sake of two million Berlin Germans, their former enemies." In order to maintain a united Western front, the administration ruled against recommendations by the Pentagon and NATO Supreme Commander General Lauris Norstad that forces be readied to respond to any Communist provocation. After the Soviets briefly detained several U.S. trucks en route from West Berlin to the FRG, Norstad proposed that the United States quickly send another convoy to show its resolve. Dulles took the lead in arguing against this "extreme" measure. For the time being the United States would have to appear moderate in both word and deed. Further, to lessen the chances of an incident and to signal the illegitimacy of East Germany's status in Berlin, it would have to minimize all contact with GDR officials or military personnel.[29]

While the Eisenhower administration struggled to arrive at a policy that would satisfy U.S. allies yet make clear to the Soviets that it would not be intimidated, Adenauer grew increasingly concerned. He was particularly distraught over a British suggestion that to mitigate the tension it might help to "work out a set of rules" by which the West could deal with authorities from the GDR as well as authorities from the Soviet Union. London insisted that this could be done without in any way compromising the West's stance in Berlin or its nonrecognition of East Germany. Adenauer responded that even limited, nonofficial relations with the GDR would undermine his government's position that Bonn exclusively represented the German people, and would cause irreparable damage to his reunification strategy. He protested that by accepting the British proposal, NATO would "sell him down the river."[30]

Although Dulles felt closer to Adenauer than to any other European leader and consistently bent over backwards to placate him, he considered the chancellor's anxieties "unjustified." In fact, at a press conference at the end of November, he raised the possibility of dealing with the East Germans "as agents of the Soviet Union." Adenauer's reaction was swift and "little short of violent." Dulles dropped the idea and persuaded the British to do likewise.[31]

Because the NSC's statement of policy toward Berlin was almost a year old, at the beginning of December a working group composed of representatives of the State and Defense Departments drafted a position paper on contacts with the GDR and on military policy for Dulles's use at the NATO Council meeting scheduled for the middle of the month. The paper's recommendations addressed Adenauer's concerns about a potential sellout. If the Soviets turned over to GDR personnel the responsibility for inspecting Western traffic at check points in Berlin or at the border of West Germany, the West should refuse to acknowledge them. If this resulted in Westerners being denied the right of passage, local military commanders would be authorized to use limited force to push their way through. This would impress upon the Soviets that the West would fight before it relinquished its rights of access or consented to the GDR's monitoring, thereby compelling Khrushchev to choose between provoking a war that he knew he could not survive or backing down from his ultimatum. The authors of the paper were confident that once warned that NATO was united behind this policy, Khrushchev would find a way to avoid being confronted with this choice. Dulles's task at Paris was to forge that unity.

Dulles agreed with the paper in principle, but he could not review it with his characteristic attention to detail or discuss it fully with Eisenhower before the NATO meeting. He told no one except the president and members of his immediate family that he was again experiencing acute abdominal distress. Dulles's discomfort did not prevent him from flying to Mexico to attend the inauguration of its new president. The trip did, however, make the pain worse. On Saturday, December 6, Dulles went for a checkup at Walter Reed Hospital. After six days of testing, the diagnosis was that he had a hernia that required an operation without delay. Dulles was sure that his cancer had recurred, but he had time neither for further tests nor for the operation. On December 12 he signed himself out and drove directly to the airport. To make the secretary as comfortable as possible during the flight to Paris, Eisenhower lent him the presidential plane, the *Columbine III*. Even Dulles's critics must admire, read a *New York Times* editorial, "the energy and courage which make a man more than 70 years of age get up from a hospital bed and tear off on one of the most difficult diplomatic errands in all our history."[32]

Difficult it was. For the duration of the meetings, Dulles could scarcely eat or sleep. Still, he presented the U.S. case with a vigor that belied his condition. The Soviet threat "is an empty one which ought not to frighten anyone," he said. The history of the last decade demonstrated that so long as the Allies stood together and stood firmly, the Soviets would back down from a direct military confrontation. They would never "risk war about Berlin." The British especially were not altogether convinced. They would not sanction authorizing local commanders to use force, however limited, until they had the opportunity to discuss the matter further, and with Eisenhower. Dulles invited the British to come to Washington for this purpose. The NATO Council agreed only to reconfirm its decade-long position by declaring "that the Berlin question can only be settled in the framework of an agreement with the USSR on Germany as a whole."[33]

The council hoped that the renewed offer to negotiate would offer the Soviets a face-saving way to resolve the crisis, even if the framework for the negotiations was broader than Khrushchev intended. The allies did follow Dulles's advice by insisting that they would not talk under the pressure of a six-month deadline. Furthermore, Adenauer remained adamantly opposed to placing German reunification on the table for fear of a deal on some form of East-West German confederation. "Reunification could only be achieved through free elections," he said. Merely the suggestion that another formula might be possible was "inadmissable" and "totally unacceptable."[34]

Suffering from excruciating pain and sleep deprivation, Dulles flew from Paris to Jamaica. He met his wife, Janet, at the estate of Clarence Dillon for a brief respite. By the beginning of 1959 he was back in Washington shuttling between the State Department, White House, Pentagon, and foreign embassies in an effort to design an effective response to the Soviet ultimatum that bridged the chasm dividing the British at one extreme, and the West Germans at the other. Adenauer rigidly held to his view that while a nuclear war would be devastating (the FRG would face certain annihilation), coercion was preferable to diplomacy, at least if diplomacy meant opening the Pandora's box of German reunification. But he left it to Washington to devise a way to square the circle. Macmillan appeared more flexible. He stuck to his position that getting negotiations started was the top priority and that authorizing the use of limited force was premature. But he accepted a French proposal that, so long as each nation concurred that implementation would require "common accord at the appropriate time, taking into account all the circumstances," NATO would undertake contingency planning to ensure that the West retained "free access to Berlin whether by land or air."[35]

The administration acceded to the compromise, although Dulles was unhappy with it. He was persuaded by a meeting with Deputy Prime Minister Anastas Mikoyan on January 16 that Khrushchev recognized that he had overplayed his hand and was eager for a diplomatic resolution. Similar to his thinking about United Action prior to the 1954 Geneva Conference, Dulles believed that a prior agreement by NATO to use force would bolster the West's bargaining position. Still, he could make do with an agreement limited to contingency planning by making clear to the Kremlin that the West was united in its resolve to reject the Soviet ultimatum and possessed the "moral courage" to take whatever military measures were necessary to resist an attempt to deny its rights to and in Berlin.[36]

Eisenhower concurred. Yet, as always, he disputed Dulles's judgment that should military measures become necessary a general war with the Soviets could be avoided. He insisted that in his discussions with the allies, Dulles (who was scheduled for another trip to Europe at the end of January) not seek to convince them otherwise. For deterrence to be effective, Eisenhower reiterated, there must be no question that "when we decide to act, our whole stack will be in the pot." Dulles put up little protest. In fact, he joined with Eisenhower in dismissing JCS plans based on the premise that with or without allies, the United States could defend Berlin by fighting a limited war.[37]

Following a contentious NSC meeting on January 29, Dulles met with the president to review policy once more before he departed for Europe the next day. To buy time, generate public support, and ensure against the British (and possibly the French) breaking ranks, they affirmed that Dulles would promote negotiations with the Soviets. These negotiations should be conducted at the foreign ministerial level, should encompass all the dimensions of the German question, and should begin prior to the ultimatum's deadline of May 27 (thereby providing the Kremlin with an excuse to extend, if not drop, the deadline). Dulles would make it clear that the United States would under no circumstances recognize East German authority in Berlin. In addition, he would propose that as a means to signal that NATO would fight before it abandoned West Berlin, the allies would agree to measures that the Soviets could neither fail to detect nor appreciate the implications, but were unlikely to appear provocative. These included expanding patrols on the autobahns and evacuating military dependents from the city. This "double-barrelled" effort, Dulles told Macmillan, "was the most moderate program that the United States would find acceptable."[38]

Fighting through his pain and exhaustion, and accompanied by Janet, Dulles set off for London, Paris, and Bonn on January 30. His physicians still believed that the problem was only a hernia, for which he was now scheduled to have an operation immediately upon his return. Dulles, however, was more convinced than ever that his cancer had recurred. He had already established a record for U.S. secretaries of state by traveling more than 550,000 miles during his tenure, and he suspected that these miles would be his last. He also suspected that they might prove to be the most important. Never were the stakes higher.

Dulles achieved something approaching an accord with Macmillan and de Gaulle. Both agreed to the general strategy he and Eisenhower had decided upon at their final meeting. Macmillan, however, threw a monkey wrench into the program by informing Dulles that Khrushchev had invited him to Moscow the next month for bilateral talks on Berlin and possibly to begin planning for another summit, and he had accepted. To Dulles, a meeting between Macmillan and Khrushchev without the United States being present, especially before the allies had reached agreement on what precisely was open to negotiation, was fraught with danger. He could not keep out of his mind memories of Neville Chamberlain appeasing Hitler at Munich in 1938. Further, in proposing a summit earlier, the Kremlin recommended the FRG's exclusion because of Adenauer's obstructionist attitude. Dulles feared that Khrushchev would make the same proposal to Macmillan, who might not be able to resist the temptation to agree. But 1958 was an election year in Britain, and Dulles could say nothing to dissuade Macmillan from going.

The press quickly made public Macmillan's plans to visit Moscow, and Dulles flew to Bonn expecting to encounter a raging Konrad Adenauer. Although visibly distraught, the chancellor was uncharacteristically accommodating, probably in part because of his sympathy for Dulles's condition and his admiration for his stoic perseverance. By this leg of the journey Dulles could barely tolerate solid foods, and the evident delight with which he devoured a gruel that Adenauer prepared from his private recipe seems to have had a salutary effect on their relationship. Adenauer's belief that Dulles was a Christian warrior like himself was apparently renewed, as was his confidence that the secretary would not let him down.

In any event, Adenauer accepted Dulles's assurance that regardless of what transpired between Macmillan and Khrushchev, and regardless of what militant measures might become necessary to maintain access to Berlin (Dulles disingenuously disclosed some of the Pentagon's plans despite his and Eisenhower's rejection of them), the United States would never recognize a GDR "substitute" for the Soviet presence. What is more, just as had been its position at the Berlin Conference in 1954 and the Geneva summit the next year, Dulles emphasized, the Eisenhower administration would insist that Germany could not be reunified on any basis other than free elections. Under these conditions Adenauer acquiesced to negotiations.

Dulles arrived back in Washington the morning of February 9. He went straight to bed. A chauffeur drove him to the White House to brief Eisenhower late that afternoon and to Walter Reed

Hospital the next day. On February 13 he underwent the long-delayed hernia operation. It took longer than expected; the doctors decided to take a biopsy at the same time. As Dulles suspected, the biopsy indicated the presence of cancer cells throughout his abdominal cavity. Deep radiation treatments were begun at once. Told that he would have to remain in the hospital for a minimum of a month and fearful that the radiation would sap his energy and cloud his mind, Dulles offered to resign. Eisenhower summarily refused.

Dulles settled into the routine of working from bed. He met with Eisenhower, his assistants, and foreign envoys; he incessantly dictated memoranda or spoke on the phone. With tensions over Berlin still running high and just before Dulles turned 71 on February 25, Macmillan went to Moscow. Khrushchev did his best to browbeat him into conceding at least to East Germany's taking over the responsibility for monitoring traffic in and out of West Berlin. Confounding U.S. and West German predictions, Macmillan held firm, even on the principle of "no substitution." Khrushchev perceived Britain's prime minister as his best hope to divide the allies. Macmillan's refusal to compromise evidently convinced him that his effort to gain concessions through intimidation was at a dead end. Khrushchev was left with a choice between allowing his ultimatum to lapse or facing the consequences of making good on it. Dulles and Eisenhower had intended to confront him with that precise choice, and what he chose conformed to their expectations. On March 2, the day his talks with Macmillan concluded, Khrushchev notified Washington that he would agree to a meeting of foreign ministers to prepare for a subsequent summit, and that the agenda need not be restricted to Berlin. He thus tacitly acknowledged that the expiration of his ultimatum on May 27 was no longer a factor.

Two weeks later Macmillan came to the United States to tell Eisenhower personally what had transpired in Moscow and to ensure that the United States agreed that all contingency plans for a military showdown over Berlin should be shelved pending the outcome of negotiations. Eisenhower emphasized that with Khrushchev buckling under the pressure of allied unity and resolve, it was no time to relax the pressure. Nevertheless, he assured his World War II colleague that no one wanted to avoid a confrontation more than he. To underscore the point, Eisenhower reviewed the current estimates of casualties from a nuclear war (67 million Americans alone). More substantively, he reversed his previous opposition to attending a summit and promised Macmillan he would go if the foreign minister's meeting produced any progress at all. (Shortly thereafter Eisenhower confided to his advisors that he was thinking of "startl[ing] Macmillan a little bit" by inviting Khrushchev for a tête-à-tête at Camp David, which he did later in 1959 when the foreign minister's meeting proved unproductive.)[39]

When Macmillan visited Dulles in his hospital room, the secretary seized what he undoubtedly realized would be his last opportunity to chastise the prime minister for, and vent his frustration over, what he considered Britain's chronic pathology: the weak-kneed attitude that had plagued him throughout his tenure as secretary of state. Why spend $40 million each year on defense and then pay whatever price the Soviets demand for peace, Dulles fumed. "If appeasement and partial surrender are to be our allies," he continued, "we had better save our money." Macmillan was taken aback. In light of his steadfast performance in Moscow, he could not imagine what Dulles was complaining about. He attributed the secretary's harangue to his cancer and its treatments.[40]

There may have been some truth to this diagnosis. Dulles's condition had deteriorated rapidly. On March 30, the day Khrushchev officially announced that Foreign Minister Andrei Gromyko would attend a meeting with his Western counterparts in Geneva, the secretary of state, unable to write legibly, dictated a letter of resignation and asked his brother Allen to hand-deliver it to the president. Eisenhower solicited a medical evaluation. The prognosis was unequivocal: Dulles had but weeks to live. On April 15, Eisenhower accepted the letter of resignation. He named Christian Herter secretary of state but insisted that Dulles continue to serve as his special advisor with full cabinet rank.

The Geneva Conference of Foreign Ministers convened on May 11 but was in recess when Khrushchev's Berlin ultimatum expired without incident on May 27. That day Roswell Barnes, the Federal Council of Churches' secretary, presided at a funeral service at the National Cathedral's Bethlehem Chapel for John Foster Dulles, who had died three days before. Afterward, by presidential proclamation, Dulles was buried with full military honors at Arlington National Cemetery. The Geneva Conference had recessed to allow the foreign ministers, including Gromyko, to attend. They were joined by kings and prime ministers, the secretaries-general of NATO and the UN, and a who's who of past and current U.S. and allied officials. Eisenhower marched at the head of the procession.

The tribute befitted a man who had for a half-century played such a vital role in the evolution of what history may yet record as the American century. It was likewise befitting that the leaders of America's allies and adversaries alike took time out from the cold war to pay their respects to its most notorious practitioner, although they soon went right back to waging it. In 1961 the Soviets began constructing the Berlin Wall, and the Berlin crisis that Dulles had tried to manage to his dying day but had left simmering returned to a turbulent boil. East and West once again approached the brink of nuclear war; once again they did not cross it. Thirty years after Dulles's death the Berlin Wall came tumbling down without a shot being fired, signalling that the cold war was finally over. Dulles was responsible for neither how it was fought nor how it ended. Yet his very large imprint was manifest on both.

Dulles left an impressive yet contradictory legacy. He has been legitimately criticized for exaggerating the Communist threat, particularly the extent to which the Soviet Union influenced indigenous peoples and regimes. From the Versailles conference through World War II, Dulles demonstrated a sophisticated and enlightened understanding of the problems inherent in an international system that did not accommodate nationalist aspirations. As secretary of state, however, he promoted policies antithetical to those he had previously advocated.

By overestimating the reach of communism, Dulles underestimated the power of nationalism. He thereby aligned the United States with the status quo, producing the very alienation, unrest, and instability that he predicted would result from opposing dynamic elements within the globe's less developed regions. His responses to the ensuing crises were often quick-fix solutions ranging from covert operations to hollow alliances, and he displayed his greatest shortcomings when negotiating with both friends and foes. Dulles thought strategically but too often behaved tactically.

Dulles was nonetheless not the inflexible moralist immortalized in Herblock cartoons. His ability to repress his pessimistic view of West European leaders and to compromise contributed to achieving his primary goal: strengthening the North Atlantic Alliance. He was more of a pragmatist than a crusader; his religious beliefs were values, not dogmas. Dulles also demonstrated the capacity to learn and change, a rare attribute inside the Beltway. The most dramatic example was his persistent reexamination of the question of how most effectively to exploit U.S. nuclear superiority even as it was eroding in order to deter, reassure, but not provoke. Although Dulles was no more able than contemporary or subsequent U.S. policymakers to resolve this riddle, the effort he expended in trying and his willingness to revise his earlier judgments warrant kudos and emulation.

Also worthy of praise is the relationship Dulles cultivated with his advisors, his colleagues on the NSC, and, most important, the president. His relationship with Eisenhower reflected mutual respect, the long-standing dedication of each man to public service, and a shared conviction that personal or political interests must not interfere with affairs of state. It was a model relationship, with few precedents and, unfortunately, fewer descendants. As an architect of U.S. foreign policy, Dulles made many mistakes, but he also did a lot of things right. There is much to be learned from studying both.

Notes

1. NSC 5602/1, "Basic National Security Policy," March 1, 1956, *FR, 1955–57* 19: 246–47.
2. Dulles, "Challenge and Response in United States Policy," *Foreign Affairs* 36 (October 1957): 25–43.
3. Quoted in Chester J. Pach, Jr., and Elmo Richardson, *The Presidency of Dwight D. Eisenhower* (Lawrence, KS, 1991), 171.
4. Memorandum for the record, April 7, 1958, *FR, 1958–1960* 3:62–64.
5. Memorandum of discussion of NSC meeting, May 1, 1958, ibid., 85–97.
6. Memorandum of discussion of NSC meeting, July 24, 1958, ibid., 130.
7. Dwight D. Eisenhower, *Waging Peace, 1956–1961* (Garden City, NY, 1965) 293; Campbell Craig, *Destroying the Village: Eisenhower and Thermonuclear War* (New York, 1998), 87.
8. Wu Lengzi, "Inside Story of the Decision Making during the Shelling of Jinmen," translated in *Cold War International History Project Bulletin* 6–7 (Winter 1995/1996): 209–10.
9. Ibid., 209.
10. Bo Yibo, "To Prevent 'Peaceful Evolution' and Train Successors to the Revolutionary Cause," translated in ibid., 229–30; quoted in Shu Guang Shang, *Mao's Military Romanticism: China and the Korean War, 1950–1953* (Lawrence, KS, 1995), 12.
11. Quoted in Gordon H. Chang, *Friends and Enemies: The United States, China, and the Soviet Union, 1948–1972* (Stanford, CA, 1990), 186.
12. Memorandum of conference [August 25, 1958], August 29, 1958, *FR, 1958–60 (Microfiche Supplement)* 19:document #44.
13. Quoted in Eisenhower, *Waging Peace*, 694.
14. Ibid., 299; quoted in Chang, *Friends and Enemies*, 188.
15. Quoted in Eisenhower, *Waging Peace*, 691; "Taiwan Straits: Issues Developed in Discussion with the JCS: The Case for Intervention," September 2, 1958, *FR, 1958–60 (Microfiche Supplement)* 19:document #73; quoted in Rosemary Foot, *The Practice of Power: U.S. Relations with China since 1949* (New York, 1995), 126; quoted in Stephen E. Ambrose, *Eisenhower: The President* (New York, 1984), 483.

16. *Public Papers of the President: Eisenhower, 1958* (Washington, DC, 1959), 688.

17. Quoted in Vladislav M. Zubok, "Khrushchev and the Berlin Crisis (1958–1962)," *Cold War International History Project Working Paper* 6 (May 1993): 7.

18. Quoted in Ambrose, *Eisenhower*, 483.

19. *Personal Papers of the President, 1958*, 694–700.

20. Eisenhower, *Waging Peace*, 302; quoted in He Di, "The Evolution of the People's Republic of China's Policy toward the Offshore Islands," in *The Great Powers in East Asia, 1953–1960*, ed. Warren I. Cohen and Akira Iriye (New York, 1990), 239.

21. Dulles to Macmillan, September 12, 1958, "September 1958 (2)," Chronological Series, DP-Eisenhower; Quoted in Townsend Hoopes, *The Devil and John Foster Dulles* (Boston, 1973), 451.

22. Eisenhower, *Waging Peace*, 303; Dulles telephone call to the president, September 22, 1958, *FR, 1958–60 (Microfiche Supplement)* 19:document #141; Quoted in Hoopes, *Devil and Dulles*, 456.

23. Quoted in Chang, *Friends and Enemies*, 195.

24. Quoted in Marc Trachtenberg, *History and Strategy* (Princeton, NJ, 1991), 169.

25. Quoted in Vladislav Zubok and Constantine Pleshakov, *Inside the Kremlin's Cold War: From Stalin to Khrushchev* (Cambridge, MA, 1996), 199.

26. Zubok, "Khrushchev and the Berlin Crisis," 8.

27. Soviet note, November 27, 1958, *FR, 1958–60* 8:88.

28. Memorandum of conversation, November 18, 1958, *FR, 1958–60* 8:84–88; quoted in William Burr, "Avoiding the Slippery Slope: The Eisenhower Administration and the Berlin Crisis, November 1958–January 1959," *Diplomatic History* 18 (Spring 1994): 178.

29. Quoted in Pach and Richardson, *Eisenhower*, 203; Memorandum of conversation, November 18, 1958, *FR, 1958–60* 8:84–85.

30. Burr, "The Eisenhower Administration and Berlin," 187.

31. Quoted in ibid., 191; quoted in Trachtenberg, *History and Strategy*, 196–97.

32. Quoted in Eleanor Lansing Dulles, *John Foster Dulles: The Last Year* (New York, 1963), 222.

33. U.S. delegation to the North Atlantic Council meeting, December 17, 1958, *FR, 1958–60* 8:212; quoted in Jack M. Schick, *The Berlin Crisis, 1958–1962* (Philadelphia, 1971), 20.

34. Quoted in Trachtenberg, *History and Strategy*, 197.

35. Quoted in Burr, "The Eisenhower Administration and Berlin," 197.

36. Dulles, "Thinking Out Loud," n.d., *FR, 1958–60* 8:293.

37. Quoted in Thomas A. Schwartz, "Eisenhower and the Germans," in *Eisenhower: A Centenary Assessment*, ed. Gunter Bischof and Stephen E. Ambrose (Baton Rouge, LA, 1995), 220.

38. Quoted in Burr, "The Eisenhower Administration and Berlin," 202.

39. Quoted in John Lewis Gaddis, *We Now Know: Rethinking Cold War History* (New York, 1997), 142.

40. Quoted in Pach and Richardson, *Eisenhower*, 203–4.

Bibliographical Essay

Archival documentation of John Foster Dulles's life and work is fertile and voluminous. His personal papers, along with those of his brother Allen, are located at the Seeley G. Mudd Manuscript Library at Princeton University. Also at Princeton are the large and useful John Foster Dulles Oral History Collection and the papers of many individuals pivotal to the history of U.S. foreign relations throughout Dulles's lengthy career and with whom he corresponded frequently. An even richer locus of archives is the Dwight D. Eisenhower Library in Abilene, Kansas. On deposit there (copies are available at Princeton) are Dulles's official papers as secretary of state. They complement the Eisenhower Library's records of other administration officials, executive offices, and, of course, Eisenhower's own papers as President of the United States. Known as the Ann Whitman File, Eisenhower's papers are perhaps the most extensive and well-organized archive of any U.S. president.

Equally essential are the U.S. government records, primarily but not exclusively those of the Departments of State and Defense and the National Security Council, that were recently moved to National Archives II in College Park, Maryland. While scholars and journalists have had some success in using the Freedom of Information Act (FOIA) to penetrate the veil of secrecy surrounding the U.S. intelligence community, and the release of some archives has attended the end of the cold war, the vast majority of the records of the Central Intelligence Agency remain classified.

Printed primary sources are also abundant. The most vital is the official documentary record of U.S. foreign policy—U.S. Department of State, *Foreign Relations of the United States*—published by the Government Printing Office. The first volume for the Eisenhower years appeared in 1979, and with most of the triennial volumes now available (many with microfiche supplements), the series comprises more than sixty volumes. While it suffers from lacunae created by still-classified records, especially those concerning covert operations, the *Foreign Relations* series is indispensable.

Research on Dulles, of course, requires consulting the volumes on earlier administrations also.

Also important are U.S. Congress, Senate, Committee on Foreign Relations, *Executive Sessions of the Senate Foreign Relations Committee (Historical Series), 1953–1961*, (Washington, DC, 1977–84); and U.S. Congress, House, Committee on Foreign Affairs, *Selected Executive Session Hearings of the Committee, 1951–1956* (Washington, DC, 1980). For many of Dulles's speeches, public statements, and press conferences, see the *Department of State Bulletin*; for Eisenhower's, see *Public Papers of the Presidents of the United States, Dwight D. Eisenhower*, 8 vols. (Washington, DC, 1958–61). The excellent *Papers of Dwight D. Eisenhower* (Baltimore, 1970–), currently edited by Louis Galambos, provide much insight on Dulles and now extend to the presidential years. See as well the president's personal diary, most of which is published in Robert H. Ferrell, ed., *The Eisenhower Diaries* (New York, 1981); and the diary of Eisenhower's press secretary, idem, ed., *The Diary of James C. Hagerty: Eisenhower in Mid-Course, 1954–1955* (Bloomington, IN, 1983).

There are a number of useful memoirs, starting with Eisenhower's two-volume account of his White House years: *Mandate for Change, 1953–1956* (Garden City, NY, 1963); and *Waging Peace, 1956–1961* (Garden City, NY, 1965). Other Eisenhower administration memoirs include Emmet John Hughes, *The Ordeal of Power: A Political Memoir of the Eisenhower Years* (New York, 1963); Robert Cutler, *No Time for Rest* (Boston, 1966); Steven Jurika, Jr., *From Pearl Harbor to Vietnam: The Memoirs of Admiral Arthur W. Radford* (Stanford, CA, 1980); and more episodic, Richard M. Nixon, *Six Crises* (Garden City, NY, 1962) and *The Memoirs of Richard Nixon* (New York, 1978). All should be read with caution. With the exception of Dean Acheson, *Present at the Creation: My Years in the State Department* (New York, 1969), there are no comparable memoirs for the previous administrations. Harry S. Truman's *Year of Decisions* (Garden City, NY, 1955), and *Years of Trial and Hope* (Garden City, NY, 1956), are disappointing. Eleanor Lansing Dulles, *John Foster Dulles: The Last Year* (New York, 1963), is an engaging and touching account by his sister, an academic and a State Department veteran herself. Andrew H. Berding, *Dulles on Diplomacy* (Princeton, NJ, 1965), part memoir and part scholarly analysis, is often overlooked.

Although Dulles did not produce a memoir, he was a prolific writer. His two books: *War, Peace, and Change* (New York, 1939), and *War or Peace* (New York, 1950), are musts. Of his many articles, the most important are the two-part "Thoughts on Soviet Foreign

Policy," *Life*, June 3, 1946, and June 10, 1946; "A Policy of Boldness," *Life*, May 19, 1952; "Policy for Security and Peace," *Foreign Affairs* 32 (April 1954); and "Challenge and Response in United States Policy," *Foreign Affairs* 36 (October 1956). Of critical significance also is James Shepley, "How Dulles Averted War," *Life*, January 16, 1956, which is in essence a lengthy interview with Dulles about Korea, Vietnam, and the Offshore Islands and gave rise to the term "brinkmanship." Many of Dulles's writings with religious themes are collected in Henry P. Van Dusen, ed., *The Spiritual Legacy of John Foster Dulles* (Philadelphia, 1960).

There are few good biographies of Dulles. The best, Ronald W. Pruessen, *John Foster Dulles: The Road to Power* (New York, 1982) ends before his tenure as secretary of state. Further, the majority of Dulles's biographers wrote prior to the opening of critical personal papers and government records, and reflect the preconceptions of the authors. Representative of this first wave, which is generally favorable, are John Robinson Beal, *John Foster Dulles: A Biography* (New York, 1957); Mildred H. Comfort, *John Foster Dulles: Peacemaker* (Minneapolis, MN, 1960); Roscoe Drummond and Gaston Coblentz, *Duel at the Brink: John Foster Dulles's Command of American Power* (Garden City, NY, 1960); and most important, Louis L. Gerson, *John Foster Dulles* (New York, 1967). The climax of the first wave came with the almost concurrent publication of Michael A. Guhin, *John Foster Dulles: A Statesman and His Times* (New York, 1972); and Townsend Hoopes, *The Devil and John Foster Dulles* (Boston, 1973), which capture the contrasting interpretations. Guhin's Dulles is a consummate realist; Hoopes's, a crusading idealogue. For perspective on this early historiography, see Hans Morgenthau, "John Foster Dulles (1953–1959)," in *An Uncertain Tradition: American Secretaries of State in the Twentieth Century*, ed. Norman A. Graebner (New York, 1961); Gordon A. Craig, "John Foster Dulles and American Statecraft," in Craig, *War, Politics, and Diplomacy: Selected Essays* (New York, 1966); and two articles by Ole R. Holsti: "The 'Operational Code' Approach to the Study of Political Leaders: John Foster Dulles's Philosophical and Instrumental Beliefs," *Canadian Journal of Political Science* 3 (March 1970); and "Will the Real Dulles Please Stand Up," *International Journal* 30 (Winter 1974–75).

As is stressed in Richard H. Immerman, "Eisenhower and Dulles: Who Made the Decisions?" *Political Psychology* 1 (Autumn 1979) and "Diplomatic Dialings: The John Foster Dulles Telephone Transcripts," *Society for Historians of American Foreign Relations Newsletter* 14 (March 1983), the release of a mountain of archives beginning in the mid-1970s shed new light on Dulles, the Eisenhower administration, and U.S. foreign policy. The journalist Leonard Mosley used hardly any of this material in his *Dulles: A Biography of Eleanor, Allen, and John Foster Dulles and their Family Network* (New York, 1978), which contains fascinating insights on all the Dulleses but tends toward the sensational. Mark G. Toulouse, *The Transformation of John Foster Dulles: From Prophet of Realism to Priest of Nationalism* (Macon, GA, 1985), is much more scholarly, but its purpose is to analyze Dulles's religious beliefs. Although extensively researched, Frederick W. Marks III, *Power and Peace: The Diplomacy of John Foster Dulles* (Westport, CT, 1993), is uncritical, idiosyncratic, and iconoclastic. The essays in Richard H. Immerman, ed., *John Foster Dulles and the Diplomacy of the Cold War* (Princeton, NJ, 1990), offer a more balanced and credible archive-based reassessment.

The opening of new archives led to an explosion of literature on Eisenhower, much of which is revisionist and indispensable for studying Dulles. The most prominent examples are Fred I. Greenstein's pathbreaking *The Hidden-Hand Presidency: Eisenhower as Leader* (New York, 1982); and Stephen E. Ambrose's mammoth two-volume biography, *Eisenhower: General of the Army, President-Elect, 1890–1952* (New York, 1982); and, with more material on Dulles, *Eisenhower: The President* (New York, 1984). The best one-volume biography is Chester J. Pach, Jr., and Elmo Richardson, *The Presidency of Dwight D. Eisenhower* (Lawrence, KS, 1991). Eisenhower is commended in Herbert S. Parmet, *Eisenhower and the American Crusades* (New York, 1972); R. Alton Lee, *Dwight D. Eisenhower: Soldier and Statesman* (Chicago, 1981); William Bragg Ewald, Jr., *Eisenhower the President: Crucial Days, 1951* (Englewood Cliffs, NJ, 1981); Robert A. Divine, *Eisenhower and the Cold War* (New York, 1981); and William B. Pickett, *Dwight D. Eisenhower and American Power* (Wheeling, IL, 1995). For more negative assessments, see Peter Lyon, *Eisenhower: Portrait of the Hero* (Boston, 1974); and Piers Brendon, *Ike: His Life and Times* (New York, 1986).

The essays in Richard A. Melanson and David Mayers, eds., *Reevaluating Eisenhower: American Foreign Policy in the Fifties* (Urbana and Chicago, 1987); and Günter Bischof and Stephen E. Ambrose, eds., *Eisenhower: A Centenary Assessment* (Baton Rouge, LA, 1995) are explicit exercises in Eisenhower revisionism. Many articles also evaluate the recent literature. Very useful are Arthur M. Schlesinger, Jr., "The Ike Age Revisited," *Reviews in American History* 11 (March 1983); Anthony James Joes, "Eisenhower Revisionism and American Politics," in *Dwight D. Eisenhower: Soldier, President, Statesman,* ed. Joann P. Krieg (Westport, CT, 1987); and Stephen G. Rabe, "Eisenhower Revisionism: The Scholarly Debate," in *America in the World: The Historiography of American Foreign Relations since 1941,* ed. Michael J. Hogan (New York, 1995). More narrowly framed are Robert J. McMahon, "Eisenhower and the Third World: A Critique of the Revisionists," *Political Science Quarterly* 101 (Centennial Year 1886–1986); and Richard H. Immerman, "Confessions of an Eisenhower Revisionist: An Agonizing Reappraisal," *Diplomatic History* 14 (Summer 1990).

For understanding the environment in which Dulles matured, begin with Robert H. Wiebe, *The Search for Order, 1877–1920* (New York, 1967), and then move on to Walter LaFeber, *The New Empire: An Interpretation of American Expansion, 1860–1898* (Ithaca, NY, 1964); and Robert L. Beisner, *From the Old Diplomacy to the New, 1865–1900* (New York, 1975). The two-volume memoir by Dulles's grandfather, John W. Foster, *Diplomatic Memoirs* (Boston, 1909), must be correlated to Michael J. Devine, *John W. Foster: Politics and Diplomacy in the Imperial Era* (Athens, OH, 1981). For assessments of Foster's role in the Hawaiian revolution and its significance as a way station in the growth of U.S. global power and influence, see Merze Tate, *The United States and the Hawaiian Kingdom: A Political History* (New Haven, CT, 1965), followed by Thomas J. Osborne, *"Empire Can Wait": American Opposition to Hawaiian Annexation, 1893–1898* (Kent, OH, 1981).

On Dulles's religious education and outlook, Toulouse's *Transformation of Dulles* should be compared to Avery Dulles, S.J., "John Foster Dulles: His Religious and Political Heritage," The Flora Levy Lecture in the Humanities, University of Southwestern Louisiana, 1994 (available through the University of Southwestern Louisiana). For the more general context, read William R. Hutchinson, ed., *Between the Times: The Travail of the Protestant Establishment in America, 1900–1960* (Cambridge, MA, and New York, 1989).

Daniel M. Smith, *Robert Lansing and American Neutrality, 1914–1917* (Berkeley, 1958), is an astute study of Dulles's "Uncle Bert," but it does not extend to the Versailles negotiations. Lansing's *The Peace Negotiations, a Personal Narrative* (Boston, 1921) is helpful but self-serving. Highlights of the immense secondary literature on the conflicts at Versailles are Arno N. Mayer, *Politics and Diplomacy of Peacemaking: Containment and Counterrevolution at Versailles, 1918–1919* (New York, 1967); N. Gordon Levin, *Woodrow Wilson and World Politics: America's Response to War and Revolution* (New York, 1968);

Lloyd E. Ambrosius, *Woodrow Wilson and the American Diplomatic Tradition: The Treaty Fight in Retrospective* (New York, 1987); and Thomas J. Knock, *To End All Wars: Woodrow Wilson and the Quest for a New World Order* (New York, 1992). On Germany and the reparations issue specifically, see Klaus Schwabe, *Woodrow Wilson, Revolutionary Germany, and Peacemaking, 1918–1919: Missionary Diplomacy and the Realities of Power*, trans. by Rita and Robert Kimber (Chapel Hill, NC, 1985); and Stephen Schuker, *The End of French Predominance in Europe: The Financial Crisis and the Adoption of the Dawes Plan* (Chapel Hill, NC, 1976).

Warren I. Cohen, *Empire Without Tears: American Foreign Policy, 1921–1933* (New York, 1987) is a brief but exemplary survey of foreign policy in the interwar years that privileges the role of private individuals and includes a comprehensive bibliographic essay. An unflattering account of Dulles's legal career is Nancy Lisagor and Frank Lipsius, *A Law Unto Itself: The Untold Story of the Law Firm Sullivan & Cromwell* (New York, 1988). On the Council on Foreign Relations, see Robert D. Schulzinger, *The Wise Men of Foreign Affairs: The History of the Council on Foreign Relations* (New York, 1984); and Peter Grose, *Continuing the Inquiry: The Council on Foreign Relations from 1921 to 1966* (New York, 1996).

Robert Dallek, *Franklin D. Roosevelt and American Foreign Policy, 1932–1945* (New York, 1979); and Warren F. Kimball, *The Juggler: Franklin Roosevelt as Wartime Statesman* (Princeton, NJ, 1991) place Dulles's activities before and during World War II in context. Toulouse, *Transformation of John Foster Dulles* deals in depth with his work with the Federal Council of Churches, but see also William McGuire King, "The Reform Establishment and the Ambiguities of Influence," in Hutchinson, ed., *Between the Times*, which relates this work to the social gospel tradition. On Dulles's growing involvement in Republican politics, see Richard Norton Smith, *Thomas E. Dewey and His Times* (New York, 1982); Arthur H. Vandenberg, Jr., *The Private Papers of Senator Vandenberg* (Boston, 1952); and James T. Patterson, *Mr. Republican: A Biography of Robert A. Taft* (Boston, 1972). Because Dulles played a seminal role in establishing the UN, see Robert Hilderbrand, *Dumbarton Oaks: The Origins of the United Nations and the Search for Postwar Security* (Chapel Hill, NC, 1990); and Townsend Hoopes and Douglas Brinkley, *FDR and the Creation of the U.N.* (New Haven, CT, 1997). Howard B. Schonberger, *Aftermath of War: Americans and the Remaking of Japan, 1945–1952* (Kent, OH, 1989) includes a chapter on Dulles. See also Seigen Miyasato, "John Foster Dulles and the Peace Settlement in Japan," in Immerman, ed., *Dulles and the Cold War.* More generally, see Michael Schaller, *The American Occupation of Japan: The Origins of the Cold War in Asia* (New York, 1985); and Walter LaFeber, *The Clash: U.S.-Japanese Relations throughout History* (New York, 1997).

Gary W. Reichard, *Politics as Usual: The Age of Truman and Eisenhower* (New York, 1988) is a fine introduction to the postwar era. James T. Patterson, *Grand Expectations: The United States, 1945–1974* (New York, 1996), is an exquisite one. On Truman, see David McCullough, *Truman* (New York, 1992); and the more scholarly Alonzo L. Hamby, *Man of the People: A Life of Harry S. Truman* (New York, 1996). Melvyn P. Leffler, *A Preponderance of Power: National Security, the Truman Administration, and the Cold War* (Stanford, CA, 1991) is unparalleled on Truman's foreign policies. Nevertheless, John Lewis Gaddis, *The United States and the Origins of the Cold War, 1941–1947* (New York, 1972); and *Strategies of Containment: A Critical Appraisal of Postwar United States National Policy* (New York, 1982) remain essential. Gaddis's *We Now Know: Rethinking Cold War History* (New York, 1997), is a thought-provoking but perhaps premature attempt at a post-cold war history of the period. For a more traditional revisionist perspective, see Walter LaFeber, *America, Russia, and the Cold War, 1945–1996* (8th ed., New York, 1997). America's special and, to Dulles, tortured relationship with Britain is covered in Wm. Roger Louis and Hedley Bull, eds., *The Special Relationship: Anglo-American Relations Since 1945* (New York, 1986). For relations with France, see Frank Costigliola, *France and the United States: The Cold War Alliance Since World War II* (New York, 1992).

On the bitter 1952 presidential campaign, see Robert A. Divine, *Foreign Policy and Presidential Elections, 1952–1960* (New York, 1974); and John R. Greene, *The Crusade: The Presidential Election of 1952* (Lanham, MD, 1985). David M. Oshinsky, *A Conspiracy So Immense: The World of Joe McCarthy* (New York, 1983); Gary W. Reichard, *The Reaffirmation of Republicanism: Eisenhower and the Eighty-Third Congress* (Knoxville, TN, 1975); Duane A. Tananbaum, *The Bricker Amendment Controversy: A Test of Eisenhower's Political Leadership* (Ithaca, NY, 1988); and Jeff Broadwater, *Eisenhower and the Anti-Communist Crusade* (Chapel Hill, NC, 1992) take different approaches to the problem Dulles and Eisenhower confronted with a divided Republican Party. On fiscal policy, see Iwan W. Morgan, *Eisenhower versus "The Spenders": The Eisenhower Administration, the Democrats, and the Budget, 1953–1960* (New York, 1990); and John W. Sloan, *Eisenhower and the Management of Prosperity* (Lawrence, KS, 1991).

Phillip G. Henderson, *Managing the Presidency: The Eisenhower Legacy—from Kennedy to Reagan* (Boulder, CO, 1988) analyzes the administration's reorganization of national security operations from the perspective of a political scientist. For a historian's perspective, see Anna Kasten Nelson, "The 'Top of Policy Hill': President Eisenhower and the National Security Council," *Diplomatic History* 7 (Fall 1983). Robert R. Bowie and Richard H. Immerman, *Waging Peace: How Eisenhower Shaped an Enduring Cold War Strategy* (New York, 1998), traces the evolution and multiple dimensions of the initial New Look security policy, stressing change and continuity from the Truman legacy and dealing in depth with such critical watersheds as Stalin's death and the Solarium exercise. See also Robert J. Watson, *History of the Joint Chiefs of Staff*, vol. 5, *The Joint Chiefs of Staff and National Policy, 1953–1954* (Washington, DC, 1986); and Saki Dockrill, *Eisenhower's New-Look National Security Policy, 1953–61* (New York, 1996). A more disapproving assessment that highlights the influence of C. D. Jackson is Blanche Wiesen Cook, *The Declassified Eisenhower: A Divided Legacy of Peace and Political Warfare* (Garden City, NY, 1981). Jackson is also pivotal in Walter L. Hixson's study of psychological warfare efforts in Eastern Europe and the Soviet Union, *Parting the Curtain: Propaganda, Culture, and the Cold War, 1945–1961* (New York, 1997). On other key security advisors, see H. W. Brands, Jr., *Cold Warriors: Eisenhower's Generation and American Foreign Policy* (New York, 1988).

The most important examination of nuclear strategy in particular is David Alan Rosenberg, "The Origins of Overkill: Nuclear Weapons and American Strategy, 1945–1960," *International Security* 7 (Spring 1983). It should be read along with Marc Trachtenberg, "A 'Wasting Asset': American Strategy and the Shifting Nuclear Balance," *International Security* 13 (Winter 1988/89); Tami Davis Biddle, "Handling the Soviet Threat: Project Control and the Debate on American Strategy in the Early Cold War Years," *Journal of Strategic Studies* (September 1989); MacGeorge Bundy, *Danger and Survival: Choices About the Bomb in the First Fifty Years* (New York, 1988); and Samuel R. Williamson, Jr., and Steven L. Rearden, *The Origins of U.S. Nuclear Strategy, 1945–1953* (New York, 1993). For the conventional critique, see Henry A. Kissinger, *Nuclear Weapons and Foreign Policy* (New York, 1957); and Maxwell Taylor, *The Uncertain Trumpet* (New York, 1959).

Before and after his appointment as secretary of state, Dulles was preoccupied with the Korean War. Burton I. Kaufman, *The Korean War: Challenges in Crisis, Credibility, and Command* (New York,

1986) is an excellent synthesis with an extensive bibliographic essay. Two works by Rosemary Foot warrant special mention: *The Wrong War: American Policy and the Dimensions of the Korean Conflict, 1950–1953* (Ithaca, NY, 1985); and *A Substitute for Victory: The Politics of Peacemaking at the Korean Armistice Talks* (Ithaca, NY, 1990). So, too, do Edward C. Keefer, "President Dwight D. Eisenhower and the End of the Korean War," *Diplomatic History* 10 (Summer 1986); and Roger Dingman, "Atomic Diplomacy during the Korean War," *International Security* 13 (Winter 1988/89). On the war's origins, see the interpretation of Bruce Cumings, *The Origins of the Korean War*, vol. 1, *Liberation and the Emergence of Separate Regimes, 1945–1947* (Princeton, NJ, 1981), and vol. 2, *The Roaring of the Cataract, 1947–1950* (Princeton, NJ, 1990), corrected by the new evidence presented in Kathryn Weathersby, "Soviet Aims in Korea and the Origins of the Korean War, 1945–1950," *Cold War International History Project Working Paper* 8 (November 1993). For a challenging interpretation of Mao's behavior, see Shu Guang Zhang, *Mao's Military Romanticism: China and the Korean War, 1950–1953* (Lawrence, KS, 1995). William Stueck, *The Korean War: An International History* (Princeton, NJ, 1995) is a monumental study based on prodigious multinational research.

The U.S. response to the 1953 East German uprising is examined in Klaus Larres, "Preserving Law and Order: Britain, the United States, and the East German Uprising of 1953," *Twentieth Century British History* 5 (1994); Valur Ingimundarson, "The Eisenhower Administration, the Adenauer Government, and the Political Uses of the East German Uprising in 1953," *Diplomatic History* 20 (Summer 1996); and Christian F. Ostermann, " 'Keeping the Pot Simmering': The United States and the East German Uprising of 1953," *German Studies Review* 19 (February 1996). The best biography of Allen Dulles, Peter Grose, *Gentleman Spy: The Life of Allen Dulles* (Boston, 1994), also surveys Eisenhower's covert operations. Other informed surveys are John Ranelagh, *The Agency: The Rise and Decline of the CIA from Wild Bill Donovan to Bill Casey* (New York, 1986); John Prados, *Presidents' Secret Wars: CIA and Pentagon Covert Operations Since World War II* (New York, 1986); and Christopher Andrew, *For the President's Eyes Only: Secret Intelligence and the American Presidency from Washington to Bush* (New York, 1995).

Kermit Roosevelt, *Countercoup: The Struggle for Control of Iran* (New York, 1979) is a candid and controversial memoir by the CIA's chief operative during the overthrow of Muhammad Mossadegh. More scholarly but written without access to CIA archives are Barry

Rubin, *Paved with Good Intentions: The American Experience in Iran* (New York, 1980); James Bill, *The Eagle and the Lion: The Tragedy of American-Iranian Relations* (New Haven, CT, 1988); Richard Cottom, *Iran and the United States: A Cold War Case Study* (Pittsburgh, PA, 1988); and Mark Gasiorowski, *U.S. Foreign Policy and the Shah: Building a Client State in Iran* (Ithaca, NY, 1991). Scholars have had more success exploiting the FOIA when examining the Guatemalan operation. For conflicting interpretations, see Stephen Schlesinger and Stephen Kinzer, *Bitter Fruit: The Untold Story of the American Coup in Guatemala* (Garden City, NY, 1982); Richard H. Immerman, *The CIA in Guatemala: The Foreign Policy of Intervention* (Austin, TX, 1982); and Piero Gleijeses, *Shattered Hope: The Guatemalan Revolution and the United States, 1944–1955* (Princeton, NJ, 1991). On the dissension among NATO allies, see Sharon I. Meers, "The British Connection: How the United States Covered Its Tracks in the 1954 Coup in Guatemala," *Diplomatic History* 16 (Summer 1992). The CIA's recently released in-house history, Nicholas Cullather, *Operation PBSUCCESS: The United States and Guatemala, 1952–1954*, is available in Record Group 263 at National Archives II. Stephen G. Rabe, *Eisenhower and Latin America: The Foreign Policy of Anticommunism* (Chapel Hill, NC, 1988) places U.S. hostility to the Arbenz regime in an inter-American framework.

A comprehensive examination of Eisenhower and Dulles's efforts in Indochina (Vietnam) is David L. Anderson, *Trapped by Success: The Eisenhower Administration and Vietnam, 1953–61* (New York, 1991), but read first Lloyd C. Gardner, *Approaching Vietnam: From World War II through Dien Bien Phu* (New York, 1988). Specific studies of the Dien Bien Phu crisis include George C. Herring and Richard H. Immerman, "Eisenhower, Dulles, and Dien Bien Phu: The 'Day We Didn't Go to War Revisited'," *The Journal of American History* 71 (September 1984); and Melanie Billings-Yun, *Decision Against War: Eisenhower and Dien Bien Phu* (New York, 1988). On the 1954 Geneva conference, SEATO, and the transfer of responsibility for South Vietnam from France to the United States, see Richard H. Immerman, "The United States and the Geneva Conference of 1954: A New Look," *Diplomatic History* 14 (Winter 1990); Gary R. Hess, "Redefining the American Position in Southeast Asia: The United States and the Geneva and Manila Conferences," in *Dien Bien Phu and the Crisis of Franco-American Relations, 1954–1955*, ed. Lawrence S. Kaplan, Denise Artaud, and Mark R. Rubin (Wilmington, DE, 1990); George C. Herring, Gary R. Hess, and Richard H. Immerman, "Passage of Empire: The United States, France, and South Vietnam, 1954–1955," in ibid.; and George C. Herring, " 'A Good Stout Effort': John Foster Dulles and the Indochina Crisis, 1954–1955," in Richard H. Immerman, ed., *Dulles and the Cold War*.

An informative overview of NATO and allied relations is Lawrence S. Kaplan, *NATO and the United States: The Enduring Alliance* (Boston, 1988). On the battle over the EDC treaty, see Robert McGeehan, *The German Rearmament Question: American Diplomacy and European Defense after World War II* (Urbana, IL, 1971); Edward Fursdon, *The European Defense Community* (London, 1980); and Saki Dockrill, *Britain's Policy for West German Rearmament, 1950–55* (Cambridge, MA, 1991). Dulles receives greater attention in Brian R. Duchin, "The 'Agonizing Reappraisal': Dulles, Eisenhower, and the European Defense Community," *Diplomatic History* 16 (Spring 1992); James G. Hershberg, "Explosion in the Offing: German Rearmament and American Diplomacy, 1953–1955," *Diplomatic History* 16 (Fall 1992); and Rolf Steininger, "John Foster Dulles, The European Defense Community, and the German Question," in Richard H. Immerman, ed., *Dulles and the Cold War*. In the latter volume, Hans-Jürgen Grabbe, "Konrad Adenauer, John Foster Dulles, and West German-American Relations," analyzes this crucial relationship. The best survey, Frank A. Ninkovich, *Germany and the United States: The Transformation of the German Question since 1945* (Boston, 1988), views the relationship through a cultural lens. On the issue of nuclear weapons and West Germany, see Mark Cioc, *Pax Atomica: The Nuclear Defense Debate in West Germany during the Adenauer Era* (New York, 1988). For NATO's nuclear planning, see Robert A. Wampler, "NATO Strategic Planning and Nuclear Weapons: 1950–1957," *Nuclear History Program Occasional Paper* 6 (July 1990).

Two outstanding surveys of U.S. policy toward the People's Republic of China are Gordon H. Chang, *Friends and Enemies: The United States, China, and the Soviet Union, 1948–1972* (Stanford, CA, 1992); and Rosemary Foot, *The Practice of Power: U.S. Relations with China since 1949* (New York, 1995). For relations with Nationalist China, see Nancy Bernkopf Tucker, *Taiwan, Hong Kong, and the United States, 1945–1992: Uncertain Friendships* (New York, 1994); and Robert Accinelli, *Crisis and Commitment: United States Policy toward Taiwan, 1950–1955* (Chapel Hill, NC, 1996). Recent interpretations of the 1954–1955 crisis in the Taiwan Strait can be found in H. W. Brands, Jr., "Testing Massive Retaliation: Credibility and Crisis Management in the Taiwan Strait," *International Security* 12 (Spring 1988); and Gordon H. Chang and He Di, "The Absence of War in the U.S.-Chinese Confrontation over Quemoy and Matsu in

1954–1955: Contingency, Luck, and Deterrence," *American Historical Review* 98 (December 1993). Two provocative examinations of the 1958 crisis that draw on evidence available in the PRC as well as the United States are Shu Guang Zhang, *Deterrence and Strategic Culture: Chinese-American Confrontations, 1949–1958* (Ithaca, NY, 1993); and Thomas J. Christensen, *Useful Adversaries: Grand Strategy, Domestic Mobilization, and Sino-American Conflict, 1947–1958* (Princeton, NJ, 1996). See also He Di, "The Evolution of the People's Republic of China's Policy toward the Offshore Islands," in *The Great Powers in East Asia, 1953–1960,* ed. Warren I. Cohen and Akira Iriye (New York, 1990).

Although dated, Coral Bell, *Negotiation from Strength: A Study in the Politics of Power* (London, 1962) offers insight into Dulles's attitude toward negotiations. On the Austrian State Treaty, see Audrey Kurth Cronin, *Great Power Politics and the Struggle over Austria, 1945–1955* (Ithaca, NY, 1986); Deborah Welch Larson, "Crisis Prevention and the Austrian State Treaty," *International Organization* 41 (Winter 1987); and especially on the treaty's role in the decision to convene the 1955 summit at Geneva, Günter Bischof, "Eisenhower, the Summit, and the Austrian Treaty," in Bischof and Ambrose, eds., *Eisenhower.* On the summit itself, see Walt W. Rostow, *Open Skies: Eisenhower's Proposal of July 21, 1955* (Austin, TX, 1982); and John Van Oudenaren, *Détente in Europe: The Soviet Union and the West since 1953* (Durham, NC, 1991).

Herbert Finer, *Dulles Over Suez: The Theory and Practice of His Diplomacy* (New York, 1964), a scathing indictment of Dulles that was once the standard source on the 1956 crisis, is now mainly of historiographic value. More current but still very critical is Donald Neff, *Warriors at Suez: Eisenhower Takes America into the Middle East* (New York, 1981). The torrent of scholarship that followed the opening of archives in the United States and Britain in the 1980s is more sophisticated. To set the stage, see Peter L. Hahn, *The United States, Great Britain, and Egypt, 1945–1956: Strategy and Diplomacy in the Early Cold War* (Chapel Hill, NC, 1991). Other important works on Nasser's challenge include Geoffrey Aronson, *From Sideshow to Center Stage: U.S. Policy Toward Egypt, 1946–1956* (Boulder, CO, 1986); H. W. Brands, Jr., *The Specter of Neutralism: The United States and the Emergence of the Third World, 1947–1960* (New York, 1989); Steven Z. Freiberger, *Dawn Over Suez: The Rise of American Power in the Middle East, 1953–1957* (Chicago, 1992); and Nigel Ashton, *Eisenhower, Macmillan, and the Problem of Nasser: Ango-American Relations and Arab Nationalism* (New York, 1996).

For studies focused on the Suez imbroglio, see Keith Kyle, *Suez* (New York, 1991); W. Scott Lucas, *Divided We Stand: Britain, the U.S., and the Suez Crisis* (London, 1991); and Cole C. Kingseed, *Eisenhower and the Suez Crisis of 1956* (Baton Rouge, LA, 1995). On the economic aspects of the crisis, see Diane B. Kunz, *The Economic Diplomacy of the Suez Crisis* (Chapel Hill, NC, 1991). William Roger Louis, "Dulles, Suez, and the British," in Robert H. Immerman, ed., *Dulles and the Cold War*, stresses Dulles's anticolonial, Wilsonian convictions. On the concurrent revolt in Hungary, see Gaddis, *We Now Know*; the Soviet archives-based Vladislav M. Zubok and Constantine Pleshakov, *Inside the Kremlin's Cold War: From Stalin to Khrushchev* (Cambridge, MA, 1996); and Khrushchev's surprisingly credible memoir, *Khrushchev Remembers*, translated and edited by Strobe Talbott (Boston, 1970).

Other elements of the administration's policies in the Middle East have received less attention. As a beginning, consult H. W. Brands, Jr., *Into the Labyrinth: The United States and the Middle East, 1945–93* (New York, 1994); and Burton I. Kaufman, *The Arab Middle East and the United States: Inter-Arab Rivalry and Superpower Diplomacy* (Boston, 1996). A superb critique that broadens diplomacy and strategy in the region to encompass South Asia is Robert J. McMahon, *The Cold War on the Periphery: The United States, India, and Pakistan* (New York, 1994). On policy toward Israel, see Isaac Alteras, *Eisenhower and Israel: U.S.-Israeli Relations, 1953–1960* (Gainesville, FL, 1993); and the more critical Douglas Little, "The Making of a Special Relationship: The United States and Israel, 1957–68," *International Journal of Middle East Studies* 25 (November 1993).

The effort to apply the Eisenhower Doctrine to Syria is illuminated in David W. Lesch, *Syria and the United States: Eisenhower's Cold War in the Middle East* (Boulder, CO, 1992). No less important is Douglas Little, "Cold War and Covert Action: The United States and Syria, 1945–1958," *Middle East Journal* 44 (Winter 1990). See also Little, "A Puppet in Search of a Puppeteer? The United States, King Hussein, and Jordan, 1951–1970," *International History Review* 17 (August 1995). Alan Dowty, *Middle East Crisis: U.S. Decision-Making in 1958, 1970, and 1973* (Berkeley, CA, 1984), gives Eisenhower and Dulles high marks for the intervention in Lebanon and its Iraqi prelude. Most of the literature on the Lebanon intervention, however, is more disparaging. In particular see Michael Bishku, "The 1958 Intervention in Lebanon: A Historical Assessment," *American-Arab Affairs* 31 (Winter 1989/1990); Agnes G.

Korbani, *U.S. Intervention in Lebanon, 1958 and 1982: Presidential Decision-making* (New York, 1981); Eika G. Alin, *The United States and the 1958 Lebanon Crisis: American Intervention in the Middle East* (Lanham, MD, 1994); and Irene L. Gendzier, *Notes from the Minefield: United States Intervention in Lebanon and the Middle East, 1945–1958* (New York, 1997). A particularly cogent argument is Douglas Little, "His Finest Hour? Eisenhower, Lebanon, and the 1958 Middle East Crisis," *Diplomatic History* 20 (Winter 1996).

Dulles's unsuccessful challenge to "massive retaliation" and advocacy of the increased conventional forces required to wage limited war is highlighted in Peter J. Roman, *Eisenhower and the Missile Gap* (Ithaca, NY, 1995). The Eisenhower-Dulles dispute over flexible response is traced more systematically in Campbell Craig, *Destroying the Village: Eisenhower and Thermonuclear War* (New York, 1998). On the crisis produced by the Soviet satellites in 1958, see Walter A. McDougall, . . . *The Heavens and the Earth: A Political History of the Space Age* (New York, 1985); and Robert A. Divine, *The Sputnik Challenge: Eisenhower's Response to the Soviet Challenge* (New York, 1993). Divine has also written a thorough study of Eisenhower's efforts to negotiate an arms limitation agreement with the Soviets, which Dulles eventually supported: *Blowing on the Wind: The Nuclear Test Ban Debate, 1954–1960* (New York, 1978). See also Richard G. Hewlett and Jack M. Holl, *Atoms for Peace and War, 1953–1961* (Berkeley, CA, 1989). Of related interest are the memoirs of Eisenhower's science advisors, James R. Killian, Jr., *Sputnik, Scientists, and Eisenhower: A Memoir of the First Special Assistant to the President for Science and Technology* (Cambridge, MA, 1977); George P. Kistiakowsky, *A Scientist at the White House: The Private Diary of President Eisenhower's Special Assistant for Science and Technology* (Cambridge, MA, 1976); and less enlightening, Eisenhower's special assistant for disarmament, Harold Stassen and Marshall Houts, *Eisenhower: Turning the World Toward Peace* (St. Paul, MN, 1990).

An authoritative account of the Berlin crisis remains to be written. Nevertheless, Jack M. Schick, *The Berlin Crisis, 1958–1962* (Philadelphia, 1971), is still valuable, and two recent articles are excellent: Marc Trachtenberg, "The Berlin Crisis," in his collection of essays, *History and Strategy* (Princeton, NJ, 1991); and William Burr, "Avoiding the Slippery Slope: The Eisenhower Administration and the Berlin Crisis, November 1958–January 1959," *Diplomatic History* 18 (Spring 1994). Vladislav M. Zubok, "Khrushchev and the Berlin Crisis (1958–1962)," *Cold War International History Project Working Paper* 6 (May 1993), uses archives in Moscow.

Index